THE LONDON DENNIS TRIDENT

THE LONDON
DENNIS
TRIDENT

PEN & SWORD
TRANSPORT

Matthew Wharmby

Cover: **TNL 1091 (LN51 GMY) was one of a long series of Plaxton President-bodied Tridents for First Capital and is seen at Turnpike Lane on 29 March 2002.** *Author*

Back cover, top: **Between 1999 and 2006 Stagecoach took 998 Tridents, all Alexander ALX400-bodied, with a minority of the shorter 9.9m version like 17449 (Y449 NHK) at Romford on 8 October 2005.** *Author*

Back cover, middle: **London United's superb livery flattered its ALX400-bodied Tridents while it was permitted; this is TA 335 (SN03 DHK) at Kingston on 5 May 2007.** *Author*

Back cover, bottom: **Connex became Travel London and then Abellio during its decade and a half with 128 Alexander ALX400-bodied Tridents. Carrying its second identity at Wandsworth on 14 August 2004 is TA 77 (KU02 YBM).** *Author*

Title page: **Metroline London Northern inherited the 65 Plaxton President-bodied 9.9m Dennis Tridents ordered by MTL London for the 17, 43 and 134 in 1999 and made a fanfare of their low-floor status, adding 'future' to their fleetnames. Holloway's TP 15 (T115 KLD) is seen on 4 July 2002 at North Finchley.** *Author*

First published in Great Britain in 2021 by
Pen and Sword Transport
An imprint of
Pen & Sword Books Ltd.
Yorkshire - Philadelphia

Copyright © Matthew Wharmby 2021

ISBN 978 1 52678 691 3

Designed by Matthew Wharmby

Printed and bound in India by Replika Press Pvt. Ltd

Pen & Sword Books Ltd incorporates the Imprints of Pen & Sword Books Archaeology, Atlas, Aviation, Battleground, Discovery, Family History, History, Maritime, Military, Naval, Politics, Railways, Select, Transport, True Crime, Fiction, Frontline Books, Leo Cooper, Praetorian Press, Seaforth Publishing, Wharncliffe and White Owl.

For a complete list of Pen & Sword titles please contact

PEN & SWORD BOOKS LIMITED
47 Church Street, Barnsley, South Yorkshire, S70 2AS, England
E-mail: enquiries@pen-and-sword.co.uk
Website: www.pen-and-sword.co.uk

or

PEN AND SWORD BOOKS
1950 Lawrence Rd, Havertown, PA 19083, USA
E-mail: Uspen-and-sword@casematepublishers.com
Website: www.penandswordbooks.com

Contents

Foreword

B etween 1999 and 2006, the majority of London operators took over two thousand Dennis Trident low-floor double-deck buses, to two specified lengths (9.9m and 10.5m), with bodies by Alexander (ALX400), Plaxton (President), East Lancs (Lolyne and Millennium Lolyne). Sales were healthy from the outset and were able to recover quickly when the later consolidation of production under TransBus led nearly to disaster. The organisation's new identity again became Alexander Dennis, and Trident production continued until superseded in 2006 by the Enviro400 double-decker.

Reliable and versatile, the Dennis Trident kept level with its immediate competitors, the DAF DB250RS(LF) and Volvo B7TL, though only Volvo was able to match it in numbers purchased in London. Even with today's reduced bus lifespans by comparison with their predecessors, the Trident type managed over twenty years in service in the capital.

Thanks are due as usual to the publishers, to my commissioning editor and to the photographers I have enlisted to fill in pictorial requirements that I couldn't manage myself.

Matthew Wharmby
Walton-on-Thames, September 2020

Antecedents

Below: **The simple but effective Dennis Dominator was a development of the Daimler Fleetline and 1,007 were built for a small number of operators, though the three taken by London Transport didn't spawn further orders. However, Ensignbus, one of LBL's independent competitors and ultimate replacements, took a liking to the Dominator and bought 26 of them in 1990-91. Here at Leyton Station on 9 September 1998 is what by then had become First Capital 264 (H264 KVX).** *Author*

Dennis never expected to become the United Kingdom's major and dominant bus manufacturer. While the twin evils of deregulation and privatisation were felling large company after large company, including MCW and even the mighty, surely unassailable Leyland, Dennis had lain low, continuing to build its commercials and the odd bus on the side for a small number of regular customers. The ageing but likeable Dominator chassis lasted sixteen years in production, continuing to garner small orders that kept the company in business when everybody else went to the wall. In those uncertain early 1990s Dennis also saw where the wind was blowing in the field of full-size single-deckers, producing the Lance successfully against Volvo's and Scania's foreign competition. Eyes were similarly on the ball when the moral shift towards accessibility in the second half of the decade compelled manufacturers to build low-floor buses and make them cost-effective before legislation prohibited the construction of anything else. And then there was the Dart, the bus the industry wanted, and which in its step-entrance and SLF configurations swept everything before it.

Demand remained for double-deckers, however, particularly in London, and while it worked on a low-floor solution Dennis adapted the Lance chassis to carry a double-deck body as the Arrow. Orders proved small, but the way forward to the Trident was

clear. This was originally a three-axle chassis for Hong Kong companies, which required massive capacity and the toughness necessary to carry air-conditioning equipment up and down some particularly treacherous hills.

The three-cornered race to produce the first low-floor double-decker was thus on, Dennis, DAF and Volvo battling it out for the orders that would secure their respective companies' future for the next decade and beyond. DAF may have been first past the post with its DB250RS(LF), but Volvo's early hurdle relating to the specification of a longitudinal engine rather than the British market's preferred transverse one set that company back in its development of what became the B7TL. Dennis thus had a clear run, and in 1999 out came the first Trident 2.

Stagecoach

TA and TAS classes

Stagecoach's association with the Dennis Trident was undoubtedly the most significant in London, even though at one point the group had sold them all, only to buy the lot back for a pittance! In fact Stagecoach was to become intimately involved with the manufacture of the type, and its London companies alone ended up with very nearly a thousand units, which it operated for twenty years.

It was right on the heels of Dennis's launch of the Trident in January 1998 that Stagecoach ordered 100 Alexander-bodied examples straight off, 62 of which were against Stagecoach East London contracts for the 48, 55, 56 and 277. These were about to

be furnished with Volvo Olympians which could then be cascaded to replace Ls and Ts as fit. Now it was a question of waiting for deliveries as Dennis's Guildford works was tooled up for manufacture, and a December 1998 date was tentatively pencilled in.

As 1998 rolled along, tendering brought in or retained routes 5, 15B, 96, 199 and 472 and the Trident order was increased to 98. To enable easy cascade within Stagecoach's provincial companies, they were specified as low-height 10.5m chassis with forward spiral staircases rather than the centrally-mounted straight variant being taken by other London companies at the time. Seating capacity was a healthy 73 (H51/22D).

The first examples of the new TA class did indeed make their December 1998 delivery date, and after chassis modifications at Guildford began gathering at Leyton in January 1999. TA 1 carried Stagecoach corporate livery as a taster of what provincial examples would look like, but was repainted red before going into service.

The TAs' service debut at Leyton on 25 January, in the shape of TA 4 on the 55, was also the first time Tridents had gone into traffic in the UK as a whole. The 55 was concentrated on first, followed by the 48 from 6 February. These displaced VNs and VAs to Plumstead for the 96 and 472 in advance of those routes' own Tridents at some future point.

Seventy-four more TAs were ordered at the start of 1999, as the first examples went into service, with a rethink incorporated to include straight staircases, though still mounted over the offside front wheelarch. However, of the existing batch, one was destined never to enter service at all. This was TA 74, which was completed and undergoing painting at Bus Painters Ltd in Kirkcaldy when it caught

Below: **Long and low, the first 98 Dennis Tridents with Alexander ALX400 bodies occupied that point in time when what became TfL's standard for low-floor buses was not yet fully defined, and other than the red livery and blind boxes, Leyton's TA 9 (S809 BWC), with its spiral staircase and low height, is therefore to full Stagecoach national specification. Seen on a gloomy 29 January 1999 in Hackney, it is fresh into service.** *Author*

Left: **The bonded glazing on the ALX400 body added a futuristic dimension, even if it did encounter expensive difficulties against the worst that north-east London's passengers could offer. Here at Walthamstow Central on 5 March 1999 is Leyton's TA 25 (S825 BWC).** *Author*

Below: **There was one problem with the early low-floor double-deckers; no downstairs rear window. The manufacturers hadn't realised how important these were to Londoners, who in a city of short routes needed to be able to see whether their next bus was pulling up behind. From the other side of the road as the above shot, we see that TA 19 (S819 BWC) has joined TA 25 (S825 BWC).** *Author*

fire and was burned to a crisp. One was thus added to the next order, now increased to 124, as a replacement. These were part of a national order for 172 Tridents and in London were intended to take over routes 30, 69, 96, 147, 194, 241, 294, 330 and 472.

The increased length of the TA class was about to throw up its first problem when tests carried out over the 277 during February indicated that the type would not be able to make it, so those intended for Bow (TA 37-49) were switched to the 26 and entered service commencing on 11 March. The D7 and Sunday 8 quickly saw their first TA appearances. At Leyton, the 56 had still not yet been tried out even as the garage's full complement of TAs (1-36 and 50-62) approached completion, so they took over the 69 instead from 18 March. The 56 was duly cleared for TA operation and was converted on 22 April, allowing the 69 to revert to Titans for the time being.

Barking's 5 was treated next, its Ts being replaced by TA 63-73 and 75-80 between 12 April and 1 May. On the same date the 69 was pulled back from North Woolwich to stand at London City Airport. Barking's TAs also assumed the N15, which worked on and off the 87, and wandered to the 169 and 387. Then, on 28 April Upton Park commenced TA operations with the introduction of TAs 81-98 to the 15B (which was intended to be renumbered 115 later in the year) and associated 15 at evenings and on Sundays. The 330 was also taken over, considerably in advance of plans for that route. Upton Park soon tried out its TAs on the 262 and 473.

Above: **The 69 had to stand in for the 56 when Leyton's batch of TAs entered service; TA 26 (S826 BWC) demonstrates at Walthamstow Central on 5 March 1999.** *Author*

Right: **Once clearance problems along the 56 were sorted out, the route could receive its TAs and here at Dalston Junction on 9 August 1999 is TA 4 (S804 BWC).** *Author*

With the entry of TA 1 into service at Leyton, the first batch was complete, barring the lingering until August of Upton Park's last few. However, they were still subject to sudden moves, as on 19 May Bow switched its TA complement from the 26 to the 25 despite that route's upcoming loss to First Capital. Bow's Saturday-only allocation on the 86 was also treated to TA appearances from 22 May. Upon the 25's departure on 26 June the TAs resumed their place on the 26 and D7 before going onto the 277 on 20 July, now that clearances had been sorted out on this route.

As Stagecoach geared up for the winter intake of TA 99-222, some of its existing TA-operated routes underwent changes associated with the opening of the Jubilee Line Extension. On 18 September the 5 was altered to terminate at Canning Town's new bus station daily, abandoning its Sunday run into town. Upton Park's 15B was duly renumbered 115, though still ceding to the 15 over its full extent during evenings and on Sundays; the increased requirement was taken by removing the 330's TAs for the moment. The D7 was taken over by First Capital, removing the likelihood of TAs.

The next Trident batch commenced delivery early enough for TA 101 to pay a visit to Coach & Bus on 5-7 October. Still to 10.5m length, the new buses were now to full-height (4.4m) spec with straight staircases, wheelchair ramps in the central doorway and individual seats (Lazzerini Pratico), producing a seated capacity of H47/24D, two

Above: **Bow came next in TA allocations, but the 277 had to wait until its own clearance issues were dealt with, so in stepped the 26. The registration system had now been meddled with to produce two letter changes, so S-registrations only got seven months before T-regs came in on 1 March 1999. Even so, the Essex marks continued on Stagecoach East London and Selkent purchases, as we see on TA 46 (T646 KPU) at Bank on 20 August.** *Author*

Left: **The 5 was the first route at Barking to specify TAs. It was being subjected to changes that would position it further away from central London than a route this low-numbered would normally be found, and the Limehouse stand of TA 77 (T677 KPU) on 16 May 1999 would be abandoned.** *Author*

Right: **Upton Park then took a contingent of Tridents for the 15B, but the route's increase upon its renumbering to 115 would need the buses that had started off the 330 at the same time. On 24 June 1999 TA 85 (T685 KPU) is laying over at the new Canning Town bus station.** *Author*

Right: **Quite why Bow decided to shift its new TAs from the 26 to the 25 when the latter had only a month to go with Stagecoach East London is unclear, but perhaps they were saying they could do low-floors better than First (which indeed had to start without most of their order, and in the event lost the contract back to Stagecoach East London after its five-year term). TA 45 (T645 KPU) is coming through Ilford on 6 June 1999, twenty days before the handover.** *Author*

Right: **Otherwise RML-operated, the 15 had been OPO on Sundays since 1987, first with Ts, then Ss and finally VNs before the TAs for the 15B arrived. The service changes of 18 September 1999 curtailed the main route at Blackwall DLR station, where Upton Park's TA 81 (T681 KPU) is heading when espied laying over at Oxford Circus on 28 November.** *Author*

fewer than the originals. Most significantly, there was now a rear window downstairs, albeit very small by comparison with step-entrance designs. They were scheduled to be allocated to Plumstead (routes 96 and 472), Catford (199), Bow (241), Leyton (69), Upton Park (330), Stratford (30), Bromley (194) and North Street (294), though three of those routes would drop out for the same clearance-related reasons as had bedevilled the 277 the previous time around.

After carrying out driver training with two Leyton-based TAs, Plumstead kicked off Stagecoach Selkent's two-decade Trident era on 4 November, albeit on the 122 (won on the basis of existing vehicles but not as yet pencilled in for TAs). As the millennium approached, the 96 and 472 were treated, allowing their VNs to take over the 53, whose 1995-vintage Vs would thereby ease out the company's last Ls. TAs also visited the 53, 99, 177 and P3. Straight away Plumstead took

Right: **The 472 inherited the half-hearted Thamesmead remit of the old 272 and built upon it with a new link to North Greenwich, where the Millennium Dome was now open but rather failing to thrill. It was made a priority to convert all the routes serving this location to low-floor, and in this 2 October 2000 shot of Plumstead's TA 114 (V114 MEV) we can also see East Lancs-bodied Tridents of Metrobus and a DLA from Arriva London North.** *Author*

the opportunity to re-register three of its new intake with Routemaster marks taken from outgoing vehicles (two Ls and one LV).

After Plumstead came the 69 at Leyton (now adding appearances on the 58) and then Bow, but a restriction was discovered on that garage's 241 so the 26 stepped in once again for the new TAs allocated there. Similar problems forced the 147's intended new TAs into Upton Park being diverted to the 330 instead, with the odd one popping up on the 101 (which had by now been retained on the basis of low-floor double-deckers) plus the 104 and 238 (which were due to receive SLDs). Stratford had no trouble phasing in its new TAs on the 30 from 16 November, though three Titans stayed obstinately put and would do so for over a year. Catford's TAs began on the 199 on 5 December, soon wandering to the 136, but the 194 was taken

Right: **Plumstead's TA fleet was for the 96 and 472 but wandered straightaway to the 122, as on 22 July 2000 where TA 104 (V104 MEV) is just drawing up to the Crystal Palace terminus where a new bus station has been built.** *Author*

Left: The 147 was a third route specified blithely with Tridents until it was realised that the roads it served could not handle the lengthy vehicles. There was no physical solution this time, however, so this conversion was postponed until an order for the shorter 9.9m chassis was placed and the intended new TAs used elsewhere instead. One such Upton Park route was the 238, about to undergo a most unwelcome conversion from Scania to Dart SLF, and on 12 August 2000 we see TA 208 (V208 MEV) at Stratford. *Author*

Left: The 30 was the only double-deck route at the otherwise minibus-populated Stratford garage, and accepted its TAs at the beginning of 2000 to replace a like number of Titans. Passing through Hackney Central on 12 August is TA 200 (V363 OWC). *Author*

Left: Catford's 199 was one of the sizeable number of Selkent routes to take new Tridents in 2000, and TA 149 (V149 MEV) was among its first. It is seen swinging into Surrey Quays shopping centre's bus station on 18 May 2000. *Author*

Right: **Another route still not able to take its intended new batch of TAs was the 294 at North Street, so the 86 stood in until this too was added to the list of routes to receive examples of the new, shorter TAS class. The 86, hammering up and down the main Romford Road, was a somewhat better proposition but would have to wait for its own Tridents; until then, TA 213 (V213 MEV) is seen coming through Ilford on 6 April 2000.** *Author*

off the list for the moment and the TAs that were going to go into Bromley were added to Plumstead's complement instead.

As TA numbers crossed 200, Stratford's 30 was completed by the end of 1999 and the batch finished (barring accident-damaged TA 180 and TA 181 away on a national tour prior to delivery) with an allocation to North Street;

although these were meant for the 294, it was the busier 86 that took them beginning on 29 January 2000. With the need for shorter buses in mind, Stagecoach placed its next order at the beginning of the year that would include 38 9.9m Tridents for the so far bypassed 147, 194 and 241, plus 100 more TAs for the 53, 58, 136 and 208. Future possibilities were the 174

Right: **TA 210 (V210 MEV) works a route 15 duty through Charing Cross on 27 August 1999; it was allocated to Upton Park against the 147 but ended up converting the 330.** *Author*

and 175, announced as retained in March but still operating Titans that were now over 20 years old. A new 496 was also awarded, to be carved out of the 296's eastern end.

TA 180, which had hung back for long enough to require re-registration with what would be the only W-mark on a TA, was delivered in July and carried illuminated Stagecoach logos either side of the blind box. Shortly after, the first 9.9m Tridents arrived from the next order, and these inaugurated a new TAS class. The 194 received them first as part of a new Catford allocation introduced on 2 September; TA appearances on the 208 ended for now when Catford came off that route. Catford's new TASs immediately wandered to the 54 and 624, and Bromley's allocation entered service from the 16th. Then followed TAS 237-246 for the 241 at Bow from 25 September and after that, Upton Park's 147 with TAS 253-260. These went into traffic on 23 October, wanderings ensuing to the 8, 26, 86, 262, 277 and 473 (Bow) and 208 (Bromley) with TAs on the 54, 136, 194 and 624 (Catford) and 174, 175, 294, 374, 649 and 652 (North Street). TASs 247-252 were diverted from Upton Park to North Street to start off new route 496 on 14 October pending the receipt of further new TAs. The TASs could soon be found on all of North Street's services.

Existing allocations were now starting to shift, with North Street and Plumstead exchanging several TAs during September to break up their established blocks.

On 7 November 2000 Stagecoach unveiled a new pair of corporate liveries to accompany a group reorganisation carried out earlier in the year. For London, the existing basic red would have a dark blue skirt added and a pair of swirls curving up to the rear of each side, in blue and orange. The logo was similarly refreshed and was immediately dubbed 'beachball' for its cheerful spherical shape. Only on the sides would this be expanded to 'Stagecoach in London'. There was also a new interior pending, with red floors, orange handrails and a blue-based seating, but TAs 261 upward were all in build by the time this was announced so only the livery adornments would be added later. TA 268 was the pattern

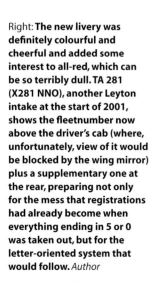

bus, going into service at North Street as its counterparts gathered on the 53 at Plumstead from the second half of November.

The Trident orders grew ever more massive; in December 78 TAs (shortly reduced to 77) and 99 TASs were ordered, the longer chassis for routes 26, 87, 169, 262, 374, 387 and 473 and the shorter for the 47, 67, 106, 160, 174 and 175, and when they arrived they would see off the last Titans in Stagecoach London. As the ink dried on that particular deal, 2001 began with a programme on 20 January that took away the likelihood of TA appearances on the P3 when this route passed to London Central as 343. After a winter break, deliveries from Alexander

Above: **The treatment of TA 180 (W187 CNO) to a pair of Stagecoach logos either side of the blind box was an attractive one-off that had already been superseded by the 'beach ball' carried between the headlights. This bus was to be the only W-registered Stagecoach London Trident, due to having come so late that its previous mark, also non-matching, had to be cancelled. A Leyton motor taken for the 69, it is seen at the Angel on 15 August 2001.** *Author*

Left: **Plumstead's TA 267 (X267 NNO) combines the new Stagecoach logo with the existing all-red livery, on which the swirls would be sprayed later. Seen coming up to Lower Regent Street on 25 September 2001, it was part of a large contingent delivered to convert the 53 from VN and VA operation.** *Author*

Right: **TA 281 (X281 NNO) is in the full new Stagecoach livery as it stands at Walthamstow Central on 18 December 2001, several months after having seen off Titans from the 58.** *Author*

Right: **There are no fleetnames, fleetnumbers or livery adornments at all on this bus, but at least it is in service so a Volvo Olympian can be cascaded out of the Selkent fleet. One of the allocation into Catford for the 136, TA 329 (X329 NNO) instead finds itself put out on the 54 when seen at Lewisham on 9 June 2001.** *Author*

Right: **Bromley's intake of TAs for the 208 were also delivered in all-red and the accoutrements put on later. TA 342 (X342 NNO) is seen setting off from the stand at Lewisham bus station on 5 May 2001, showing the unique windscreen-mounted running number cards that Bromley alone used at the time.** *Author*

Left: **Although the placing of former Routemaster registrations on newer buses had tailed off since the glut at what became London General and South London, Stagecoach inherited a handful and gave them to a total of seven Tridents. TA 99 (VLT 14, ex-V476 KJN), flying into Trafalgar Square on 7 August 2001, was the third carrier of this mark after RM 14 and L 262, and would subsequently bequeath it to Optare Tempo 29001 and finally back to its original host.** *Author*

got going again in earnest, and application of the new skirt and stripes soon followed. TA deliveries to Plumstead were bracketed by examples for Leyton and North Street. Leyton's intake for the 58 and its existing TAs tried out the 230 for the first time, despite not being able to go beyond Whipps Cross. During February and March Catford and Bromley took new TAs for the 136 and 208 respectively, Catford's adding the 47 to their haul and Bromley's wandering to the 269 as

well as the 162, which would not be able to accommodate them after a rerouteing away from Petts Wood on 17 March. TASs 247-252 left North Street for Upton Park, though the TAS class would return to North Street when its new examples came later in 2001.

The two TAs at the end of this build ended up diverted from Stagecoach London to Stagecoach East Kent and a third needed was clipped off the next order, rendering that quantity 76.

Left: **With single-deckers the only vehicles of low-floor capability during the second half of the 1990s, the routes given over to them suffered from overcrowding. The worst such case was the 230, which was tremendously busy and outgrew its nine SLD-class Dart SLFs sufficient to need constant support from whatever Leyton could throw at it. The latest example of such assistance by 2000 was the TA class, exemplified at Wood Green on 2 July 2001 by TA 60 (T660 KPU). During that year Stagecoach East London attempted to solve the 230's problems with more and newer SLDs but it only settled down when converted to TA, which didn't come until 2004.** *Author*

TAs became a possibility on the 54 with the reallocation of part of it from Catford to Plumstead on 17 March. 24 April saw new night routes N55, N58 and N69 begun with the TAs from their daytime equivalents and the reallocation from Bow to Stratford of the 26, N26 and Saturday allocation on the 86, to make room for the 67 ex-First Capital. New TAs were expected for the 26 and TASs for the 67, with existing Bow TAS 238 turning out on the latter on the first day and Stratford's own TAs now appearing on the 26. On Sundays the 241 was reallocated from Stratford to Bow and the whole route became TAS. Tridents left the 8 on evenings and Sundays with the route's reversion to full RML at those times. At North Street the 496 was extended in Romford to the Brewery.

TAs 359-434 commenced delivery on 4 June and Barking's first was in service on the 7th, taking over the 87 and 387 from their very long-established Titans and putting an end to the T class there by 13 August. The 147's Sunday share was not capable of TA operation (Upton Park using TASs on weekdays) and was demoted to SLD on that day of the week. As well as DDA-compliant blinds with via points reduced to two lines, this batch had ZF gearboxes and the new corporate interior. On 25 June the first new TA of Stratford's route 26 batch was noted. One of these was meant to be TA 402, but the bus to have carried this number ended up as Stagecoach East Kent's third Park & Ride Trident and the number was skipped. On 19 July the first of North Street's new TASs

Right: **Barking had operated Titans for 21 years but their time was now at an end, heralded by Tridents from the 2001 issue. These were different and distinctly improved, to the smoother Euro 3 specification and also incorporating the concession made to blinds that otherwise threatened to reduce information to just route number and destination. Pulling up to Barking station on 7 July 2001 is TA 381 (Y381 NHK).** *Author*

Right: **The 26 joined the 30 at Stratford and now merited Tridents of its own. On the afternoon of 14 July 2001 TA 398 (Y398 NHK) is setting off from Stratford.** *Author*

entered service, on the 247 as well as the intended 174, 175 and 496.

Problems encountered with the ZF gearboxes caused a halt to deliveries in July followed by the summer works break, but during August additional TASs arrived. An unusual diversion saw six licensed by Alexander for loan to Connex Bus, whose own new Tridents hadn't all arrived in time for its assumption of the 60 on 1 September. These were TASs 441, 442, 444, 449, 460 and 472, and all that was needed to mask their Stagecoach identity on a fairly similar livery was the application of Connex logos on red vinyls. They lasted till 30 September and

were then sent to Stagecoach. Most of the batch spanned the introduction of the new registration system on 1 September, but Y- and 51-registrations were scattered about all over the place according to date of first registration.

On 1 September the 649 and 652 left North Street for Blue Triangle, on a sub-contract four weeks in advance of their intended transfer. The 7th saw the last three Titans working at North Street and at Stagecoach East London, and by 5 October the T class was eradicated from Selkent and the London operation as a whole when TASs took over the 47, with TAS 470 as the vanguard. On 26 September the 67

Right: **Eight new TAs took over North Street's 374 in October 2001; one was TA 435 (LX51 FKJ), on 13 November seen coming round the back of Romford, where the intrepid photographer stationed at this spot has to balance lining up his shot while holding his nose against the stink of the bins placed at the back of the businesses in pedestrianised South Street!** *Author*

commenced its own conversion to TAS with two into Bow and the rest coming in October.

The 374 at North Street received TA 428-435 during October, though three were loaned to City of Oxford during the month, while TAs 409-427 were the subject of an unusual but ultimately failed experiment whereby Leyton's 55 was converted to crew operation on 13 October, to determine whether this mode was faster even with doored buses, now that the supply of reclaimed Routemasters had run dry. The buses (plus TAs 193-195 already based) had two white-based vinyls applied either side of the blind boxes to distinguish them as crew vehicles, and their input into Leyton allowed

Right: **Despite the reversion of the 55 to crew operation for an unprecedented second time, it had been a generation since Londoners had been used to doored buses carrying conductors and experience showed that the cost of providing them was considered too much to pay for the speeding up of the service. TA 417 (LX51 FJE), with the appropriate posters beckoning passengers to just keep going once they'd boarded, heads south from Shoreditch on 24 November 2001.** *Author*

an equivalent number of earlier TAs to leave, themselves divided between Bow (route 262) and Bromley (route 269). On 13 October the 147's Sunday problem was cleared up with its reallocation into Upton Park on that day.

Coach & Bus 2001 saw TAS 485 displayed in a blue, green and silver livery before its delivery to London in November and placement into service as the last of Catford's route 47 batch.

On 27 October the 106 commenced conversion from PD to TAS with new Tridents into Stratford. The first difficulties were encountered with matching chassis numbers to fleetnumbers where the registration number was no longer an obvious guide, and TAs 425 and 426 had to have their identities transposed, as did TASs 506 and 509. The latter pair enabled the split between the Euro 2 and 3 specifications to be more easily demarcated, not to mention a switch from bonded to gasket glazing (though the new TAS 509 was now out of sequence. It needed new windows anyway when it ploughed into the low bridge at Wick Lane on 20 November!). TAS 522 of the 106's contingent was delivered in New York Sightseeing Tours livery both to advertise Stagecoach-owned

Coach USA and commemorate the tour bus lost in New York on 9/11.

Another round of loans was made to Connex when that company's new TAs were not in sufficient stock to start the 157 on 1 December; TASs 526-531 from Catford's intended batch for the 160 were sent by Alexanders prior to delivery and Catford itself sent TAS 524.

2001 ended with the 86, which had been offered out to tender earlier in the year, retained with the promise of additional new TAs to bolster its newish existing examples. The award back of the 369 from First Capital was also a significant coup, and in January the 54 was announced as retained by Selkent at Catford. All this led to an order for new buses, which was placed over the turn of

Right: **A stroke of luck at Finsbury Park on 29 October 2001 has brought together the two contentious short Tridents just deployed to Stratford before needing their identities exchanged. At left is TAS 505 (LX51 FNH) and on the right is TAS 509 (LX51 FNM).** *Author*

Right: **TAS 522 (LX51 FOC) was given this cheerful livery designed to buck up the spirits of New Yorkers after 9/11, and took it to the 106. On 7 April 2002 it was one of the stars at Showbus and is seen in the bright sun along Brooklands runway.** *Author*

2002 as twenty-six new TAs, followed in March by 31 more TASs and 23 TAs, which together or indirectly would furnish the 54, 75, 86, 160, 262, 369 and 473 in the second half of the year. Otherwise the latest order was now complete, the stragglers at Connex filtering back to the capital between January and April and the Oxford loans lasting a little longer. As 2002 got going, the 48, 55, 56 and

277 were put out to tender from the original batch of TA conquests, followed by the 177.

For the Queen's Golden Jubilee celebrations in 2002, Stagecoach had six of its TAs gilded with the combination of vinyl and paint in combination with a sponsor message. The gold buses ran for approximately six months following their launch in Trafalgar Square on 2 May. Leyton's TA 1 and 50 were sponsored

Above: **Six Stagecoach TAs donned Golden Jubilee livery in 2002, and at Leyton on 21 April TA 1 (S801 BWC) takes on passengers for a run into the City of London on the 48. It has received a numberplate to the post-2001 specifications, which make the numbers and letters look uncomfortably condensed.** *Author*

Left: **Three of the Golden Jubilee TAs were allocated to Leyton, where they could take their sponsor message into Oxford Street if they were turned out on the 55, as TA 409 (Y409 NHK) is doing when seen there on 21 October 2002.** *Author*

Above: **The 86 really needed TAs, but TASs would do for the moment and on 20 September 2002 TAS 554 (LY02 OBF) is at Ilford, halfway through its journey east. Perhaps in reaction to how awkward the new skinny numberplate characters looked, Stagecoach overcompensated with this batch, giving them huge characters!** *Author*

by Mars Celebrations chocolates, with fellow but crew-operated TA 409 carrying an ad for Surf washing powder. Upton Park's TA 96 carried TfL's own advertising and the scheme at the rear of Stratford's TA 111 was for Celebrations. Across the river there was TA 140 out of Plumstead with an ad for Marks & Spencer. Otherwise, routine first repaints were commencing, Stagecoach being rather

more conscientious than most other London operators in keeping their buses in tip-top shape.

May saw TASs 535 onwards commence delivery, and on these the exit door was moved forward by one bay to rest closer to the staircase foot. Capacity was unchanged but there was now an inward-facing seat behind the rear door. Their first deployment

Right: **Stratford's TAS 552 (LY02 OBO) shows that the exit door has been brought forward by one bay, which looks unremarkable on the 9.9m body but really made a difference on the longer one. It is seen on 20 July 2002 at Ilford.** *Author*

was to Stratford, which was to take over the majority of the 86 on 20 July, but until that date, they were stored unlicensed.

At the same time as the N53 was rerouted via Blackheath and diverted to its daytime 53's stand at Plumstead garage rather than Erith (29 June), it was about to sprout an offshoot known as 453, awarded with articulated buses.

On 20 July Stratford duly took up its new majority daily allocation on the 86, putting TASs 535-560 into service. TAS 535 had already tried out the 86 on attachment to North Street. This allowed TAs to leave for Barking to provision the 369 upon its takeover from Capital Citybus and itself make up for the transfer of the 87 to North Street to fill the space made by the 86's move to Stratford. At Barking, an N369 was added at night.

July saw Stagecoach make a clean sweep of the 48, 55, 56 and 277 as well as adding an N277 night route, and an order for 95 new TAs was placed with the appropriate implications of cascading of the incumbent batch. At the same time the 5, 15 and 115 found themselves offered out and in September the 177 was announced as retained.

Stagecoach East London was usually too far away from Notting Hill Carnival's catchment area to participate in the unusual bus happenings to be found, but this year's event saw Barking add nine TAs to the 15 to short-work between Aldwych and Paddington. It was repeated in 2003, 2004 and 2005.

October saw the delivery of TASs 561-591, all but six of which took over Catford's 54, 75 and 160 so that their VNs could cascade Plumstead's VAs out of the fleet. TASs 561-566 went to Stratford so that a handful of TAs could be added to Upton Park and furnish a PVR increase to the 115 on 26 October, even in advance of its tender announcement.

TAS 522 was repainted red in November 2002, losing its New York Sightseeing livery. Regular repaints were now stepping up, being done at Leyton and thus requiring the

Above: **After five years at First Capital, the 369 came back to Barking on 20 July 2002 and this time operated Tridents. TA 71 (T671 KPU) is at Ilford on 1 September.** *Author*

Below: **Leyton's TA 26 (S826 BWC) looks untroubled when caught at the Baker's Arms on 21 April 2002, but it would be withdrawn and disposed of by this time the following year.** *Author*

odd TA loan here and there. Four of the gold TAs lasted into 2003, the last one being TA 96 in April 2003, and by then it was known as 17096.

The next batch of Tridents comprised TAs 592-614, and rather than going directly to Stratford (to cascade TASs from the 86 to Bow's 262 and 473) were sent to Leyton where their routes, particularly the 55 from 4 January 2003, required increases in accordance with their new Stagecoach East London contracts. Inevitably, the 55 lost its conductors on that date and its tethered batch of TAs began to mingle with the rest at Leyton. Twenty more were ordered at this point, theoretically against the 177.

In December the 5, 15 and 115 were announced as retained by Stagecoach, with the important footnote that the 15 was to be converted to OPO, thus implying more Tridents, and indeed 79 more TAs were ordered. However, in a set of tenders based on Croydon, Stagecoach Selkent's 194 was awarded to Arriva London South.

On 6 January 2003 Stagecoach introduced a national numbering system; unfortunately for London this meant discarding class codes.

Both TAs and TASs shared a block in the 17,000s with room for expansion up to 17933 with the existing orders, and to differentiate the former TASs, a little 's' suffix was now carried after the numeric fleetnumber. While fiddlier than it needed to be, this wasn't as complicated as identifying which of five Dart SLF lengths used to be incorporated within one SLD class code!

1 February saw the 48 and 56 set going again and the entry into service of the rest of their new top-up 'TAs', now known as 17592-17614. Stratford's 30 received an increase on 15 February and put into service 17775-17784 (which had come as TA 650-659 and were subsequently renumbered again, to 17740-17749), but that was also the day the 53 was cut down to allow the introduction of new route 453. Falling back from Oxford Circus to Trafalgar Square, the 53 had its PVR reduced from 49 to 30 with the intention that its 'TAs' oust more Olympians, but as it happened, the 453's artics were late coming so the Tridents stood in on the new route for a month. The N53 was similarly curtailed, with new route N453 also 'TA' between 15 February and 15 March.

Left: **With Stagecoach's fleetwide renumbering, its London companies' transition from their London Transport inheritance was complete. Leyton's 17608 (LV52 HHT) heads past Clapton Pond on 22 February 2003; the 55 was OPO again and now fielded these new 52-reg examples.** *Author*

Left: **In 2003 the big thing was artics, and route by route they threatened to take over the whole system. Or at least they did when they were delivered on time, unlike the Citaros intended to separate the central London half of the 53 as 453. Tridents had to fill in for the new 453's first month, as Plumstead's 17221 (V221 MEV) is doing when captured bending the corner into Westminster Bridge Road on 16 February 2003.** *Author*

Left: **Catford's 160 was converted to TAS at the same time as the 54 and 75. The 9.9m variant of the ALX400-bodied Trident at Stagecoach still needed to be distinguished so that longer ones would not be put out by accident, so the former TASs had a little 's' appended to their new fleetnumbers. Seen at Rushey Green on 19 June 2003 is 17524s (LX51 FOF).** *Author*

Right: **Just one 'TAS' received a Routemaster mark, this being Upton Park's 17260s (WLT 575, ex-X374 NNO). Seen at Ilford's revitalising southern quarter on 10 March 2003, it would carry this registration for ten years.** *Author*

There now followed a slew of new 'TAs', the orders for 95, 20 and 79 pouring in between March and August. First up were fourteen for Bow's 277 to fulfil a big increase that accompanied its new contract on 1 March (that included the introduction of new night route N277), followed by twenty-four for the delayed reversion of the 86 from 'TAS' to 'TA' at Stratford. The displaced short Tridents duly moved to the 262 and 473 at Bow, ejecting Volvo Olympians (that were now numbered in the 16000 block), but the surprise was that those new into Leyton pushed out the earliest examples for disposal despite being only four years of age! This astonishingly wasteful practice was at TfL's wish so that buses more in keeping with its defined standard would be phased in and thereby push step-entrance

Right: **Not yet in the new livery or physically renumbered by 21 March 2004, when this photo was taken at Stratford, 17047 (T647 KPU) at least has a post-2001 numberplate to bring it into the modern era. It had been transferred from Bow to Upton Park with the 262 on 30 August 2003.** *Author*

buses closer to extinction. At least at first, the money was available to do so, coming from the introduction of the Congestion Charge.

Quite unexpected amid all these 'TAs' came a lone 'TAS', 17854s, which was added to Bow's contingent transferred from Stratford. Still more Tridents beckoned when the 96, 99, 269, 472 and 653 were announced in February as retained, the 99 representing an upgrade to double-deck. Forty-two more 'TAs' were thus ordered. As deliveries proceeded, 'TAs' into Upton Park for the 115 during April allowed the 104 and 238 to revert to double-deck using older examples staying put. Then the 145 was treated, using new buses, and sixteen more were sent to Plumstead to man the 177's PVR increase upon its new contract applying from 1 May.

Three of the new 'TAs', 17778-17780, were tachograph-fitted for Sunday excursions performed by Stratford, but difficulties navigating past market day traffic caused these duties to be transferred to Leyton in June, with the three buses; Stratford took 17731-17733 in exchange.

June saw allocation of 'TAs' to Barking's 145 and Plumstead's 177 completed, the blocks being more broken up than hitherto, and the lowest-numbered forty had all gone by the summer, save 17001, whose repaint served as an indicator of its continued value within Stagecoach East London.

On 4 August 17879 was named *Dave Gardner 1964-2003* after taking colleagues to his funeral; it would not be the first Bow bus to honour this popular long-serving conductor,

driver and union official. Underscoring its special treatment, it was fitted with a tachograph and then re-registered 527 CLT.

In August the 247 and 294 were announced as retained by Stagecoach East London and the 'TAS' was turned to again with an order for twenty-four which would take numbers from 17976s to 17999s. During the month the balance of the current order arrived and was stored pending introduction to the 15 in crew mode; enough of Upton Park's existing 'TAs' were then put out during the second half of the month to reduce the 15's Routemaster numbers to a mere handful before RML 2760 performed the last rites on the evening of 29 August, setting off the conversions of the final twenty such services between this day and 9 December 2005.

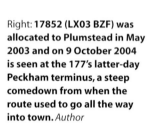

Right: **17852 (LX03 BZF) was allocated to Plumstead in May 2003 and on 9 October 2004 is seen at the 177's latter-day Peckham terminus, a steep comedown from when the route used to go all the way into town.** *Author*

Right: **Converted from T to Darts in 1993, the 247 was just that bit too busy for single-deckers and a decade later thought was put to restoring the route's capacity. New 'TASs' were on order for the beginning of 2004, but North Street's existing examples had visited regularly and on 13 September 2003 17441s (Y441 NHK) is passing its home garage.** *Author*

Left: **The great Routemaster purge of 2003-05 was kicked off by the one-manning of the 15 on 30 August 2003, starring new Tridents from Upton Park like 17914 (LX03 OSK), seen negotiating Pall Mall East on 26 September.** *Author*

30 August was the date of the 5, 15 and 115 renewal and the 15's one-manning, which was accompanied by its reallocation from Upton Park to Bow. The 241 was thus pushed out to Stratford and the 262 and 473 to Upton Park, taking with them the requisite number of 'TASs'. Upton Park also gathered in two Sunday shares that had been at other garages, bringing back the 238 from Barking and 330 from Bow. At night the N50 was taken over from First Capital, using 'TAs' from Upton Park, and part of the N15 was reallocated from Barking to Bow.

At Selkent, the 194 passed to Arriva London South but its 'TASs' stayed put at Catford and Bromley to dislodge some more 'VNs'. On 15 September the 174 was extended south to the new CEME centre at Dagenham.

Left: **The low height by comparison of more usual London-spec vehicles was increasingly seen as a disadvantage, and TfL prevailed upon Stagecoach to dig into its deep pockets for full-height replacements. Converting extremely busy routes like the 104 to Dart SLF operation had been a terrible idea regardless of accessibility, and as soon as 'TAs' were made available, the upper deck came back. 17047 (T647 KPU) at Stratford on 19 October 2004 has had its blind box altered to admit DDA-compliant panels with two lines of vias.** *Author*

Tendering remained positive for Stagecoach's London pair; with the 8 and 30 out by August, the 69, 147, 241, 330 and N69 were all retained during October and at least a proportion of new buses was envisaged.

November 2003 saw the delivery of 17934-17975, which were divided between Plumstead (for the 96, 99 and 472) and Bromley (for the 269) in advance of their 24 January 2004 contract renewal date). Existing Plumstead 'TAs' from the early X-registered batch were transferred to Barking to allow its T-registered examples to leave for Stagecoach South, while Bromley's 'TASs' were gradually divided between North Street and Bow.

The end of 2003 set the clock ticking on Stagecoach East London's remaining Routemasters with the award back of the 8 as an OPO route to be furnished with 34 of 65 new 'TAs' in an order that included enough for the 69 and 330. The 30 was also held on to, but with its existing buses.

As 2004 got going, North Street's new 'TASs' double-decked the 247 and took the last 'VNs' off the 294; both in time to start their new contracts on 27 March.

After the success of the Golden Jubilee buses, TfL went in for all-over ads in a big way, gathering sponsors from far and wide. One such venture was with high-end fashion designers, and in February Plumstead's 17276 was adorned with a scheme by Julien Macdonald. Next came in-house ads for the Oyster card, which would be the game-changer for fare collection and thus worth hustling. Former Golden Jubilee Trident 17140, also at Plumstead and meant for rostering on the 53 past as many central London customers as possible, was a recipient of this livery in two shades of blue.

Right: **Routes turned over to articulated buses were operated on a unique any-door entry system and thus did not allow support by conventional vehicles, so when the bendies were taken off the road to address the fire problems that had destroyed three, their emergency stand-ins no longer carried blinds for the routes affected. This was the case with Plumstead, which had to fashion its own inserts for the 453 and Blu-Tack them into the windscreens of buses like 17158 (V158 MEV), seen at Oxford Circus on 25 March 2004.** *Author*

Right: **The corporate-liveried Tridents borrowed by Stagecoach Selkent for the 453 could display the minimum details on their dot-matrix blinds, a feature TfL disdained (at the same time as dumbing down its own standards of display!). 18125 (YN04 KGK) was intended to go into service at Stagecoach East Midland but in this 26 March 2004 shot at the top end of Oxford Circus is from when it was on attachment to Stagecoach Selkent's Plumstead.**
John Delaney

As the OPO conversion date of the 8 approached (indeed being brought forward to 5 June, ahead of its contract renewal on the 26th), Stagecoach East London carried out celebrations of its Routemaster era on the route and amassed the 'TAs' that would take it over. Also being readied were the Citaro G artics that would assume the 25 on the 26th, but problems encountered with fires to London Central's existing examples prompted TfL to order the removal of all of them currently in service so that emergency inspections could be carried out. This affected the 453 from 24 March, and as well as the return of Plumstead's 'TAs' to the route, plus loans of both lengths from every other East London and Selkent garage, it saw the use of five corporate-liveried Tridents that were otherwise about to go into service in Chesterfield. These lasted until 1 April and the loans until the 5th, with the odd 'TA' coming back later in the month as cover while fire-suppression equipment was fitted to the artics.

8 May saw new contracts on existing Stagecoach East London Trident routes 69, 147, 241 and 330, plus two night changes that saw the renumbering of the N69 and N369 to plain 69 and 369.

Starting on 13 May, the 8 was gradually converted to crew 'TA'; deliveries were sustained despite the wobble in corporate fortunes that forced into receivership what was now TransBus International. Production, particularly at Wigan, which had been assigned a proportion of the latest sixty-five buses, was paused until a sale could be sorted out, but in due course Stagecoach invested in the business which was supplying most of its vehicle needs and on 1 June the organisation was renamed Alexander Dennis.

RML 2760 duly saw out the 8 in the small hours of 5 June and Stagecoach London was now 100% low-floor. Reflecting the reapportionment of production between Belfast (before it closed with the reorganisation) and Falkirk to help out beleaguered Wigan, not all the new 'TAs' had made it in time so loans from other Stagecoach garages had to fill in until they arrived.

Overnight before the major bus changes on the 26th, the N8 was rerouted to Hainault rather than Woodford Wells or Newbury Park; the former terminus was appended to the N55. New route N86 from North Street took over the roads east of Ilford abandoned when the N25 was incorporated into the 25's

Below: **The conversion of the 8 to OPO on 5 June 2004 removed Stagecoach East London's final Routemasters, but no expense was spared to give them a proper sendoff on the 4th. During that day, as much film was otherwise being expended on the outgoing RMLs and myriad guests, crew-operated Bow 18207 (LX04 FWT) sneaks across Bank junction.** *Author*

Above: **Finally, after two generations of Dart SLFs, the 230 was converted back to double-deck on 17 July 2004, and seen opposite Arriva London North's Tottenham garage on 2 September is Leyton's 17411 (LX51 FHW), originally from the crew-operated batch for the 55 but now capable of working any route at that garage.** *Author*

new 24-hour artic contract. Double-deckers did manage to turn out on the 25, however, when the Underground went on strike on 30 June and new 'TAs' were pressed into service.

A particularly welcome double-decking was of the 230 on 17 July; this route had never got to grips with two generations of SLDs. Some of the 'TAs' into Leyton were used to bulk out the 8 at Bow first and then transferred.

Two 'TA'-operated Stagecoach Selkent tenders to be awarded and renewed during the autumn of 2004 were the 672 (4 September) and 199 (18 September), though the planners couldn't decide whether to extend it south to Bromley and ultimately didn't. The 208 would have been pulled back to Catford under this plan and was similarly left alone; this and the 136 were awaiting the results of their own tenders and in August were duly announced as retained with their existing buses. Then the 97 and 158 were won from First London for 2005 implementation, though at the expense of the 58 which was awarded in the other direction. Routes 101, 104 and 238 were all kept hold of and the 101 would be double-decked, its formerly SLW-class Scanias having by now come up to their second decade in service. This took

place by 18 September with new 'TAs' into Upton Park, though the 'SLWs' lingered into 2005. At the end of the summer the 174, 175 and 496 were all offered out to tender again, with plans to incorporate the 374 into the 174. September saw the 58's future needs taken care of with an order placed for twelve more 'TAs'.

Aesthetically, TfL were never what you would call imaginative, and by mid-2004 even 20% non-red was deemed too much for the organisation. The edict went out to restrict any augmentations to a skirt or stripe only (plus a white roof for heat reflection), and Stagecoach thus began deleting the colourful swirls from their buses' rears upon repaint. Oyster-liveried 17140 lost its ad in July and 17276 (ex-Julien Macdonald) followed suit in August. However, in September Bow's 18208 gained a fashion ad for Tata-Naka and in the same month a campaign was launched to win London the 2012 Olympic Games. Styled in blue as 'Back the Bid', this forty-bus scheme had multiple participants and Stagecoach East London's Tridents to take it were Bow's 18209 and Leyton's 18256. In October 18208 exchanged its Tata-Naka livery for Back the Bid colours and was joined by 18210 and 18242 at Bow and Leyton respectively.

Left: **Taking its Tata-Naka dress label ad to Showbus at Duxford on 26 September 2004 is Bow's 18204 (LX04 FWU) from the route 8 batch but dressed for the 277.** *Author*

Left: **The cheerful light blue of the Back the Bid ads was combined with a graphic of a pole vaulter leaping the London Eye. It did the trick and the 2012 games came to the capital. 7 May 2005 is the date of this shot of Leyton's 18256 (LX04 FZA) entering Walthamstow Central bus station on the 97, which had been taken over from First London on 5 March.** *Author*

Left: **The back of the Back the Bid ad! This is Bow's 18209 (LX04 FWV) at Victoria on 20 November 2004.** *Author*

Aside from regular withdrawals, which had tailed off once the first fifty had left the fleet, Barking's 17369 was written off after a fire suffered at Canning Town when coming back from a route 5 journey on 30 July. It was disposed of for scrap in January 2005.

At the beginning of 2005 the 103 was won from Arriva London North and the 257 and 674 from First Capital, portending more new buses still; thirty more 'TAs' were ordered for September delivery. The 174, 175 and 496 were retained with their existing 'TASs' and the former increased to absorb the 374. Still, TA-operated 87, 145, 169 and 387, which represented most of Barking's runout, were offered out in February and joining them were the 62 and 287, which had seen numerous 'TAs' augmenting their Dart SLFs. The 47 was another important route whose

future was up in the air, but in March it was announced as retained by Stagecoach Selkent with new buses to replace its 52-reg 'TASs'.

All five Back the Bid Tridents were concentrated on the 277 at Bow for the duration of the International Olympic Committee's visit between 14-19 February; the two Leyton ones were subbed by two loaned from Bow.

Tridents 18266-18277 were delivered to Stratford in time to take over the 158 on 5 March 2005. The 58 passed to First Capital on the same day but its 'TAs' simply moved over to the 97. At Upton Park the 104 and 238 were renewed, together with the 101, which at least began what would be a long-drawn-out process of replacing its pioneering 'SLWs'.

2005 proceeded in a quieter fashion than some other years; in April an order was

Right: **The 67 spent most of its five years with Stagecoach East London using a different group of 'TASs' than the ones that took over the route; 17552s (LY02 OBD) had started at Stratford on the 86 before coming to Bow but on 24 April 2004 is seen at Stamford Hill.**
Author

Right: **Privatisation and the corporate wranglings thereafter produced a host of goofy fleetnames, but this isn't one of them; someone with a crafty spray can has got at 17580s (LV52 HFN) while it was parked at the side of Catford garage exposed to the main road, and there hasn't been time to clean off the results lest a bus be lost from the schedule. It is seen in Lewisham on 16 July 2004.**
Author

Above: **18266-18277 comprised the new 'TA' batch for the takeover of the 158 from First London on 5 March 2005, and on that first day 18275 (LX05 BWH) is seen at Leyton station.** *Author*

placed for nineteen 'TAs' for the 47, the longer length being permitted since the route's diversion away from the tricky tunnels under the railway lines out of London Bridge. The 136 began a new contract on 28 May, the 208 on 30 July and the 67 was offered to tender, only to be lost straight back to First London from whence it had come. Perhaps solely to free the number, the 87, despite being the major carrier in the area for generations before subsequent downgradings, was selected for withdrawal and absorption by the 5, although the 145, 169 and 387 were held onto with their existing 'TAs', securing Barking's future. At the same time, routes 26, 230 and the 53 were put out to tender.

All the calm of recent months was shattered at ten to nine on Tuesday 7 July when three suicide bombers blew themselves up at key points on London's Underground system. The fourth had been planning the same thing but found his way to Stratford's 17758, which was making its way eastbound along the 30 when it was diverted off line of route to take it away from King's Cross. At Tavistock Square the bomber detonated his rig and blew the bus to pieces, killing fifteen passengers as well as himself.

It didn't stop there, as on 21 July a second quartet made an attempt, though the bus-targeting component this time failed to destroy Stratford's 17762 as it headed up the Hackney Road on the 26. And it wasn't as if the indigenous opposition was any less easy on London buses, as vandals milling around the Noak Hill terminus of the 294 on 20 July took it upon themselves to torch North Street's 17146. Even when not set alight remotely, Tridents were starting to evince an unfortunate propensity to catch fire, due to the incredible strain of such small turbocharged engines having to shift so much dead weight by comparison with previous large-engine/lower-weight combinations, and 17872 was duly immolated while working PD3 on the 122 in Eltham on 1 September. And there couldn't be much worse a place to catch fire and burn to the ground than inside the Limehouse Link tunnel, but that's what 17081 did on 1 October when coming back off an N50.

At least the Olympics bid had proven successful, and, their work done, the Back the Bid buses, including the participating Stagecoach East London 'TAs', all lost their livery during July. Repaints now included the white roof with fleetnumber stencilled thereon for aerial recognition by police, and where possible extra opening windows (protected with new see-through plastic film) were fitted to those Tridents with gasket windows.

During August, 18451-18480, the first in red with just the blue skirt (and white roof) began delivery in advance of the 15 October date on which they would be needed, and North Street's allocation of twelve entered service on the 86 and 87 while Stratford's waited their time out on the 86 before required on the 257. Already, however, the ALX400/Trident combination that was very nearly to breach a thousand examples with Stagecoach in London was at an end; after 18481-18499 for the 47 in 2006 orders from Alexander Dennis would be for the new integral Enviro400 (which was still a Dennis Trident 2 underneath if you looked at the manufacturer's plate, but its distinctiveness has already merited a book on the type in London – see *The London Enviro400*). The inaugural Stagecoach East London example, 18500, was handed over on 3 October with

the name *Spirit of London* to honour the bomb-destroyed 17758 and the Londoners who died aboard it. Along similar lines, 17001 was repainted into its original all-red with TA 1 fleetnumbers restored, as a sort of rolling contemporary heritage vehicle.

15 October was a busy day; to make way for the incoming 103 with its new Tridents, North Street ceded its allocation on the 86 to Stratford, which itself struck up on the 257

with the rest of this thirty-strong 'TA' batch. The 174 duly absorbed the 374 (its rerouteing over the endpiece of this service clearing it for 'TAs') and the 294 was rejigged to follow the rest of it. North Street also took over the 296 from First London but could not field all its new Dart SLFs so used Tridents until they came. The 396 was also a popular posting for double-deckers, as it had been when with First Capital.

Above: **18462-18480 were allocated new to Stratford to take the 257 from First on 15 October 2005, and at Stratford bus station on the first day is 18471 (LX55 ERK).** *Author*

Left: **Without its new Dennis Dart SLFs in place for the contract assumption date of 15 October, the 296 had to fill in with Tridents. Seen at Romford station stand on the first morning is North Street's 17235s (X235 NNO), one of the first repaints to omit the accompanying stripes.** *Author*

At the end of the year the 26, 53 and 230 were announced as retained with their existing vehicles and the 160 was out to tender. 17 December saw some changes to the 69 and 101, the former being withdrawn between Canning Town and London City Airport and the latter diverted to Gallions Reach rather than the time-honoured North Woolwich Free Ferry terminus; the 474 was strengthened to bridge the link with both. A strike timed for New Year's Eve brought double-deckers to the 25 for the day.

On 21 January 2006 Catford's 47 was renewed alongside its night partner N47 and in February Stagecoach London's final Tridents began arriving in the form of 18481-18499. The running total had thus topped out at 998, though not all of them were in service at the same time. The last twelve were taken in March and received 06-registrations, and once all were in place by the 23rd, seven 'TASs' and one 'TA' left for Upton Park to put an end to the former SLW class. Additional examples began a period of cover so that Tridents in the range 17099-17280 could go for refurbishment, a programme split between MCV in Cambridgeshire (30 buses) and Alexander Dennis's new facility at Harlow (150 buses). The first examples treated came from Plumstead, where four former Catford 'TAs' replaced them.

Two advertising campaigns were mounted in early 2006 that had Stagecoach Trident participation; firstly for the NSPCC with white figures on a red background (though, as with all ads now, the front kept in the operators' own livery) and featuring Bromley's 17289, North Street's 17457s,

Right: **Stagecoach London's last Dennis Tridents were the twenty for Catford's 47 at the beginning of 2006. On 3 June 18494 (LX06 AGZ) is performing the awkward leg off the main drag necessary to serve Canada Water station.** *Author*

Right: **The 87 disappeared from the board on 25 March 2006; athough the reasons for its withdrawal were as arbitrary as needing to use the number to renumber the 77A and thus eliminate suffixes, the route had dwindled to just a Romford-Barking shuttle that could be appended to the 5 with its North Street buses. On 1 April Barking's 17391 (Y391 NHK) is in Romford town centre on what was now a long and busy slog westward.** *Author*

Left: **On 22 April 2006 Bromley's 17289 (X289 NNO), carrying NSPCC advert livery, is seen swinging into what was left of the High Street that had not been pedestrianised in 1990.** *Author*

Left: **Another Bromley 'TA' to receive an all-over ad during 2006 was 17356 (X356 NNO), seen on 18 March taking its Oyster message into Lewisham.** *Author*

Catford's 17584s and Upton Park's 18265. Then came another Oyster push (though with the price now advertised as £1.50), applied to North Street's 17456s and 17458s, Catford's 17582s and Bromley's 17356.

In February the announcement was made that the 160 had been lost to Arriva Kent Thameside, though its school partner 660 was retained.

The number 87 bowed out on 25 March with the absorption of its contract into the 5 and consequent extension of that route beyond Becontree Heath to Romford and the introduction of a North Street allocation.

Without the break at Becontree Heath, however, the extended 5 now started to suffer traffic problems. The 145, 169 and 387 were also set going anew with their 'TAs' and the 287 was given one official double-deck journey at school times.

When the 67 passed to First London on 29 April, the 158 was reallocated from Stratford to Bow to take its place; to make sure that the 158 retained 'TAs', a shuffle took Bow's outgoing 02-reg 'TASs' to North Street, which supplied the longer vehicles. The balance of the 'TASs' were put into Upton Park, restarting the process of cascading older 'TAs' out of the

fleet through forcing the withdrawal of early T-registered examples. 17048 and 17049 from this contingent, meanwhile, were transferred to the private hire fleet, converted to single-door and painted white.

Routine contract renewals applied to the 26, 230 and N26 (24 June) and the 53 (29 July), while the 122 was offered out.

And then, on 23 June, Stagecoach sold up! Acknowledging reduced profits within TfL's restrictive framework combined with a need to service existing debt, management sold the London operations to Macquarie Bank Ltd of Australia for £263.5m. This financial services outfit had no experience of bus operations and thus brokered a deal

to retain Stagecoach advice for the next year, but once the sale was formalised on 30 August the first order of business was to rename the acquisition to the East London Bus Group Ltd (ELBG) and reconstitute East London and Selkent as trading names; after a while, the pre-privatisation logos of those two companies returned, combined with the font used by the old East London Coaches operation. Accordingly dropped was the blue skirt and repaints were now to all-red, just as the last bus to have carried it from new was repainted. Application of the 's' appellation to the 9.9m former 'TASs' began to fall away as well, though the lengths of buses were still kept apart in most cases.

Above: **Another 'TA' with no visible indicator of ownership pending the ELBG's taking out of mothballs of the old Selkent identity is 17133 (V133 MEV) of Plumstead, caught passing Charlton station on 19 August 2006.** *Author*

Left: **Invariably the future was all-red; unimaginative, sure, but helped by what was now East London's general good care lavished on its buses. An unusual 'TAS' for Barking, 17527 (LX51 FOK), now without the 's' suffix that once denoted its shorter chassis, serves a 169 through Ilford on 27 January 2007.** *Author*

Above: **Selkent's logo was also familiar, bringing back the sprig of hops that London Transport had designed to denote its old Selkent District. It was applied to repaints and existing colour schemes alike, Plumstead's 17100 (WLT 491, ex-V474 KJN) carrying the second of three post-LBL liveries. This route 53 journey photographed on 12 November 2006 may be going to County Hall, as shown on the unusual black-on-yellow ultimate panel, but with the demolition of the building and removal of the roundabout there would no longer be a turning point here and future short workings would have to fall back to Lambeth North.** *Author*

Having sprouted a new 636 and 637 on 15 April, the 638 found itself and its new offshoots tendered in May. That month saw the retention of the 624 with its own new offspring numbered 658, plus the winning of the 625 from London Central, but on 22 July the 653 was withdrawn. The other school services resumed on 2 September and on the 16th the 160 passed to Arriva Kent Thameside, releasing its 'TASs' from Catford to Barking to make possible the conversion to double-deck of the 287 on 30 September. Two more were loaned to Arriva Kent Thameside so that its shortage of buses for its new route wouldn't prove quite so embarrassing, and more still roved around the fleet as refurbishment cover, incidentally bringing 'TASs' to Plumstead for the first time.

The takeover of the 61 by what was now plain Selkent on 2 December was accomplished with ELBG's first Enviro400s, but only three of them were available to Bromley for the start date so existing and loaned 'TAs' and 'TASs' appeared from the outset. On 3 January 2007 school routes 624 and 658 at Catford began new terms and were joined by the 625, taken over from London Central and operated by Plumstead. Another dedicated school route was introduced on the 27th as Barking-operated 687, replacing the school double-decker on the 287. Then came the 678 into Stratford as a win from First London on 31 March, the same day that North Street's 647 began a new term.

The Oyster card adverts in place since January 2006 had now run their year and were removed at the start of 2007. As repaints rocketed along, a new dark blue moquette with 'ELBG' accents was devised and began to appear on refurbished Tridents, though as this took place they were all downseated by one to remove the contentious tip-up in the lower saloon. An attempt to address overheating involved the fitting of two air-recirculation pods either side of the upper-deck rear windows.

East London Coaches closed on 2 February and the two Tridents operated, 17048 and 17049, were sold to Ensign with the rest of the fleet.

From 9 July Catford mounted two peak-hour journeys on the 53. Between 16 July and 9 September the closure of the bridge over the District Line at Dagenham Heathway forced the diversion away of routes crossing it and the manning of a single-bus 574 from North Street to fill the gap. On 21 July the 630 was withdrawn with the closure of one of its catchment schools, but 29 September saw the 472 given a night service and a daily frequency increase. There was a running day on the Heritage Routes that day and to tie in, 17001 (or TA 1) was loaned to Bow and ran on the 8. On the regular 15 was 17774, a Stratford bus that had been given an advert for Venezuela tourism in August, just as the last NSPCC ads were removed. In October Bow's 18212 received an ad for a Tutenkhamun

exhibition being held at the O2; it lasted a year.

On 13 October 2007 the 15 and N15 were extended from Paddington to a new stand at Paddington Basin. Bow had run the 15's Notting Hill Carnival augmentation for 2006 and again in 2007 (alongside Barking), but the Paddington Basin extension took a long time to clear and was repeatedly postponed.

2007 had proven quiet; other than repaints, comparatively few route alterations had affected the East London Bus Group, though the 106 and 177, tendered in February, were announced as retained in October on the basis of new buses (and in a break from Stagecoach practice, ELBG plumped for Polish Scanias for each). The 96 and 472, plus the 262 and 473, were Selkent and East

Right: **Bow's 17784 (LX03 BVM) is at Tower Hill in the company of preserved RM 2059 (ALM 59B), a Routemaster brought out to work the Heritage Route 15H on 30 September 2007.** *Author*

London pairs offered out again at the end of the year. The N50 was also retained though split into two with the resulting N550 and N551 being divided between East London and Docklands Buses respectively.

The need to start clearing the site chosen for the Olympic Park forced the closure of every London bus garage already occupying that expanse of land between Stratford and Hackney Wick; first went First London's Hackney garage, then East London's Waterden Road artic garage and then Stratford itself after 23 February 2008. An extensive new site at West Ham, inheriting its illustrious predecessor's WH code, opened on the 24th and took over the 26, 30, 86, 106, 251, 257, 276 and 678 plus N26 and N106. 119 Tridents made the transfer, though 17532 was not one of them, having been destroyed by fire the previous 21 November when returning off an 86 duty last thing at night.

Between February and March Bow's 17915 carried an all-over ad for the DVD box set of *101 Dalmatians*, followed in March by 17885

Right: **Stratford garage was closed on 23 February 2008 and its site engulfed by Olympic Park construction. In its place came a second West Ham garage, which inherited buses like 17401 (Y401 NHK) and the 30 route which it was seen serving on 24 May at Marble Arch.** *Author*

from the same garage plugging London's museums with a pink livery. 18210 was given an ad for *Prince Caspian* in June and in August 18206 and 18232 received ads for Visa. These latter three lasted until October.

On 26 April the 106 was renewed, though the N106 was withdrawn. This and the 177 at Plumstead (its own contract renewed on 31 May) were awaiting new Scanias, but deliveries slipped to the autumn; two routes won in the interim, the 51 from London Central and the 248 from Blue Triangle, also had Scanias ordered for them (as did the 96) but would have to start off with existing Tridents. The 472 was retained with its incumbent Plumstead 'TAs' and would be supplemented by school routes 601 and 602 ex-London Central.

31 May saw the N26 and sundry workings on and off the 26 transferred from West Ham to Leyton and on 30 August the new N550 replaced the N50. Tendering during the summer put out the 8, 48, 54, 55, 56, 75, 86, 277 and 672, retained the 262 and 473 with their existing Tridents and cost East London the 369, which would be revamped under the East London Line brand with Blue Triangle. ELBG was not quite as adept at tendering as Stagecoach had been, and the announcement in September that both the 54 and 75 had been lost to Metrobus was a bitter blow to Selkent and Catford.

The 248's commencement on 27 September saw it put into Rainham, which had hosted the 25's artics for a spell and otherwise served as an overspill and storage facility. A 30-bus O-Licence was secured for operations under the name of East London Bus Ltd. Nine 'TAs' and seven 'TASs' were scraped together from all over East London and Selkent to provide Rainham with the 248's initial runout, having to sub them with Darts, which proved inadequate, particularly on Bromley's busy routes.

2008's major contribution to London bus history was iBus, the advanced GPS-powered control system with all sorts of potential spinoffs. A schedule was planned whereby companies would send their vehicles to the two conversion sites, garage by garage, and while they were away a roving band of buses spare from other operators would stand in for them. Selkent started the ball rolling with eleven Metroline Tridents of TA class, putting them into action at Plumstead on 9 October. On the 10th Rainham's loaned Tridents were released back to their home garages through the hire from Wealden PSV of eleven East Lancs-bodied Tridents that had been made redundant by Metrobus. Six had most recently served with Metroline as ET 765-770. Unusually, the hires received Stagecoach fleetnumbers for the duration, the East Lancs-bodied Tridents assuming numbers 18875-

Below: **Upon seeing their blue skirts, casual passengers and observers would almost mistake these Metroline TAs for Selkent's own vehicles until they boarded to find a different interior. 18888 (T69 KLD) and 18892 (T75 KLD), seen in Woolwich on 13 December 2008, were TAs 69 and 75 respectively and came to Plumstead to fill in for some of that garage's own Tridents away for iBus fitment.** *Author*

18885 and the TAs becoming 18886-18896. Four TPs turned up at Rainham in November and were known there as 18897-18900. Finally, however, the first Scanias arrived and entered service from the 12th. Their completion of the 248 allowed five of the East Lancs Tridents to move to West Ham, where their appearance on the 86 and 241 from the 27th, plus the conversion of the 106 to Scania,

allowed eleven 'TAs' to leave for Plumstead in time to start the 51 on 6 December, joined there by two of the Metroline TPs. At the same time, Plumstead's fleet completed iBus fitment and the Metroline TAs moved on, first to Bromley and then to Catford.

The year ended with good news where tendering was concerned; the 8 was held on to (albeit withdrawn between Tottenham

Court Road and Victoria) and the win of the 205 from Metroline would give Tridents a chance alongside an order for Scanias; the 86 and 672 were also retained with their existing buses and the 97 offered out.

Between 4-15 January 2009 extras were mounted on the 86 to cover for the rail line being out. On 24 January the 96, 99 and 472 began new contracts at their incumbent Plumstead garage at Selkent, as part of which the 99 was extended from Erith to Bexleyheath and school routes 601 and 602 were assumed. The first four of the 51's new Scanias entered service on 13 January but there would still be a long wait for the rest, requiring the retention of the Metroline-liveried loans that had found their way from Catford back to Plumstead.

iBus fitment now commenced at East London, tackling Bow first, followed by Leyton and then Upton Park by mid-February. Rainham's contingent was done by Siemens' mobile team. A dedicated pool of eleven West Ham 'TAs' and one 'TAS' was gathered, and when at Leyton they stuck to the 69 due to already having that route on their blinds. More Scanias arrived from Poland in March and completed the conversion of the 51, letting the East Lancs-bodied Tridents move over to West Ham, the last East London garage to have its buses fitted with iBus, following Barking and North Street. This was finished on 28 April and marked the end of the programme as a whole. When the balance of Plumstead's allocation arrived in April and took over the 96, all the loaned Tridents were returned.

On 28 March the 262 and 473 commenced their new contracts, but the 75 left for Metrobus on 25 April and the 54 followed it on 2 May. However, Metrobus's East Lancs-bodied Scania fleet was not all in place so Catford loaned twenty-eight Tridents, all of which were the routes' existing 'TASs'. The Scanias were so late that the loans lasted over five months at Metrobus. All this meant withdrawals were looming again, and the rest of the T-registered examples at Upton Park (including fire-damaged 17098, which was repaired to make it fit for sale) were replaced first.

In May, Rainham's operations and buses received a new name, Thameside, and a River Thames-shaped logo to go above the fleetname. June saw 17915 gain a second advert, this time for TOUS jewellery.

The summer of 2009 was characterised by multiple reallocations to go with contract renewals; when the 8 was set going again on 27 June the 26 and 30 were put into Bow from West Ham, which took the 15 in exchange. The 8 and N8 both fell back from Victoria to Oxford Circus so that the C2 could take over most of the Mayfair section. Then on 18 July the 86 commenced a new contract and with it was reallocated from West Ham to North Street, which ceded the 174 to Rainham and its third-share of the 5 to Barking; two Enviro200-operated routes (300 and 325) were thus put into Upton Park and the 115 left that garage for West Ham, bringing things full circle and, most importantly for diesel-wasting dead mileage in what was now a full-blown recession, bringing East London's routes closer to their bases. By now it no longer particularly mattered whether 'TAs' or 'TASs' operated together, as the extensive transfers of 18 July in particular mixed lengths and batches indiscriminately, though an effort was made to concentrate newer Tridents on routes operating under new contracts. Some of the routes earlier restricted to the shorter chassis, like the 47 and 174, had since been cleared for the 10.5m examples and only the 147 was truly incapable of fielding 'TAs', though they often popped up in error before substitution.

Of the examples withdrawn at this point, Upton Park's T-reg 'TAs' were sold to Ensignbus and another eighteen (thirteen from the earliest V-reg batch plus 17395-17399 with ABS braking) were converted to trainers to replace the former DA and SLW classes on this work. 17099-17101 had all lost their ex-Routemaster registrations by the time this happened, and the last but one such holder, 17879, bequeathed both its 527 CLT mark and dedication to Scania 15100.

Right: **On 27 June 2009 the 26 was reallocated from West Ham to Bow, which was a little closer to line of route. 18226 (LX04 FXR), an April repaint, was already based at Bow and on 14 August has arrived at Waterloo.** *Author*

Above: **The new Thameside logo for routes operating out of Rainham is shown on 17449 (Y449 NHK) on 22 October 2010 at Romford station. The actual bit of the river closest to its routes, however, is somewhat further east than the extent of the river diagram!** *Author*

Finally came the 205's takeover on 29 August, which was meant for new Scanias from the outset but saw 'TAs' from the first day; it was allocated to Bow, which pushed out the 277 to West Ham. The 672 started another school year at Plumstead on 5 September.

The rest of 2009 was quiet, and it had to be after that level of upheaval! A tube strike on 10 June brought Selkent Tridents out to help on the 15 and 25, and this year West Ham operated the ten Carnival extras on the 15. In September 17885 and 17915 lost their adverts but the latter donned a third scheme, this time a loud red-and-white diamond-patterned affair for Burlington. Other than 'heritage' 17001, the last 'TA' in service from the first batch of 98 was Upton Park's 17086 on the 473 on 10 October, and withdrawals were now cutting into the next batch as well.

'TAs' would stay on the 55 and 277 with their retention when announced in July, but new buses (Scanias again) would replace them from the 48 and 56. October saw the

Left: **West Ham's 17887 (LX03 OPV) is seen on the 277's Highbury & Islington stand on 20 July 2010, by which time a new contract had commenced on this route. Tucked in behind is 17933 (LX03 OTJ).** *Author*

97 retained with its existing buses and the 215 scooped with new ones. The 174 and 496 went out that month, followed in November by the 47, 145, 169, 247, 287, 387 and 687 and the big concern was the 5, 15 and 115, all of which were kept with their incumbent 'TAs'.

On 28 November a small round of reallocations transferred the 158 from Bow to Leyton and the daytime 69 from Leyton to West Ham; at night the Bow allocation on the N15 passed to West Ham. In advance of the new contracts on the 48 and 56 from 27 February 2010, these routes were converted to Scania operation during December and January, but an age jump in withdrawal terms saw the 52-reg 'TAs' from the leased 17592-17611/17731-17733 batch targeted, followed by three fire victims of 2009.

At the end of the year 17915 had taken on advert number four, for M&G, a scheme shared with 17926, while 18234 donned one for TOUS. The former two's ads lasted until the following September.

2010 began with the long-standing plan to withdraw the 369 put into effect on 20 February; its replacement comprised two Blue Triangle routes numbered EL1 and EL2. On the 27th the 55 began new terms with its incumbent 'TAs', which continued to wander to now Scania-operated 48 and 56, as did Bow's 'TAs' away from the 277 to the 205. Then on 6 March the 97 and 238 started

their own new contracts and the 215 was taken on; though commenced with four new Scanias, it soon saw Leyton's own 'TAs'. The 238 was intended to be extended over the 5 to Becontree Heath and thereby allow the latter's PVR to reduce, but this was deferred repeatedly and finally cancelled. Withdrawals now spread to the 51-reg members spanning 17409-17424.

In April the 174 and 496 were announced as retained but with new buses to replace their 'TASs'; the 674 was lost to Blue Triangle. May heralded the retention of the 47 with its existing Catford 'TAs', the most recent members of the class. That spring and summer's set of tranches offered out the 69, 147, 241 and 330, followed by the 26 and 30 and finally the 53. Announcements made in June were of the retention of the 99 and 269 with their existing buses, and jubilation was in the air for Barking in July as its entire complement of Trident-operated routes was announced as retained, with the 62 getting a proportion of double-deckers. Even so, their Tridents would be replaced.

On 28 August the 5, 15, 115 and N15 began new terms with East London; the 5 was not reduced as planned but the 15 ceded the Paddington Basin leg to the 159, falling back even further to terminate at Regent Street. The 115 was reallocated from West Ham to Upton Park, the 147 going the other way in exchange (and by habit retaining 'TASs', even though this route had now also been passed for 10.5m buses). At Bromley seven buses were taken off the 208 to reflect the 320's extension northwards to replace the nominally independent southern section; nine 'TAs' released were shared between six garages. A little later a small shuffle took place to transfer to North Street 'TASs' that had been working at Barking, replacing them with 'TAs' ex-West Ham.

The ELBG's woes had become increasingly apparent, having suffered multiple strikes and eventually its book value dropped so substantially that Macquarie Bank resolved to sell it, and who should come swooping back into the picture on 14 October but Stagecoach, which paid a knock-down £59m for East London, Selkent and Thameside and their vehicles and garages. Despite Stagecoach's well-publicised dissatisfaction with the inflexibility of the tendering regime in London, it was too good an offer to pass up, and before long it was as if Stagecoach had never been away, with vinyls reapplied at a furious pace and the familiar 'beach ball' seating moquette returning on refurbished buses.

Left: **Leyton's 17001 (S801 BWC) was kept on long after the withdrawal of its age peers to serve as a special purposes vehicle and it eventually found its way into preservation, though the numberplate and blinds are of later standards than when the bus was new. On 30 April 2011 it is seen at Hackney Central.** *Author*

Left: **Upon the return of Stagecoach another interregnum followed where buses went around bare of logos until the new (old) parent had enough printed. On 13 February 2011 Plumstead's 17957 (LX53 JYY) is off route at Waterloo, but there is one of the increasingly large number of demonstrations going on along the 53's normal route down Whitehall and around Parliament Square.** *Author*

17260 was the last Stagecoach Trident to carry a registration once belonging to a Routemaster, but lost it in November.

On 22 January 2011 the 47 was renewed with its Tridents and on 26 March new deals began for the 'TA'-operated 247 at North Street and the 145, 169, 387 and 687 at Barking, with one double-deck journey added to the 62. The 287 was also set going anew but reallocated with three 'TAs' and four 'TASs' from Barking to Rainham, which had now dropped the Thameside appellation with the return of Stagecoach. Barking's 'TAs' were going through refurbishment at this time and isolated examples from around the fleet came in to free them. In February Bow's 18223 received an ad for G-Star Raw, exchanging it in May for one for Capital One's Click Card.

With the Trident fleet now between five and eleven years old, route awards to Stagecoach were increasingly being made on the basis of new buses, and such were the awards of the 199 and 660 in February 2011. The new buses themselves were once again Alexander Dennis products, this time the Enviro400, and examples were delivered in February that began to take Plumstead 'TAs' off the 99 starting on 4 March. In this case five 52-reg 'TASs' left for Upton Park to displace five of the X-registered examples. Withdrawals were now well along in the V-MEV batch and beginning to bite into X-NNO numbers. During March and April the 99's Enviro400 conversion was completed (allowing more

Above: **Bromley occasionally put out the 'TAs' from its 269 on the 61, a route regained from Metrobus at the end of 2006 but otherwise operated by Enviro400s. In the town centre on 30 July 2011 is 17967 (LX53 JZK).** *Author*

16 October saw the 174 and 496 start new terms with Thameside (Rainham) and East London (North Street) respectively, and the 674 departed for Blue Triangle. Although the 69, 147, 241 and 330 were retained, a bad blow cost both the 26 and 30 when Tranche 352 was announced in October, these important routes being lost to First, but the 53 was retained when the results of Tranche 356 were revealed. The winter offers put out at this time included the 101, 104, 158 and 238 and the last result of 2010 was a loss, of the 608 to First from the following September.

Right: **CapitalOne bank sponsored a single Bow Trident to carry an advert for its Click credit card, and on 30 July 2011 the result, 18223 (LX04 FXL), is seen at Tottenham Court Road, which would soon become the 8's western terminus.** *Author*

'TASs' to pass to Upton Park, this time to see off longer but older precedessors) and the 174 at Rainham followed suit by May.

The 69 began a new contract with its existing 'TAs' on 30 April. On 2 May a temporary route 541 was introduced with West Ham Tridents to fill in while Victoria Dock Road was isolated from the Kier Hardie Estate normally served by the 147 and 241. It was intended to last six months but the works overan into 2012. The 147 and 241 themselves plus the 330 in the same area began new terms with their existing Tridents on the 7th.

Forty-two new Enviro400s were expected by Barking, and their takeover of the 145, 169, 287 and 387 during April and May resulted in extensive Trident withdrawals. The 496 at North Street lost its 'TASs' for Enviro400s between 17-20 May.

25 June saw the 26 and 30 depart for First London. To fill the gap at West Ham as best as could be done with so much work lost, the 158 was put in from Leyton with a number of 04-reg 'TAs' made spare from Bow to allow V- and X-registered 'TASs' and 'TAs' to leave, but Stagecoach took a deep breath and announced that Upton Park garage would be closed.

Following on from the announcement in March of the loss of school routes 624, 625 and 658 to London Central, July's awards kept the 101, 104, 158 and 238 and won the 275 from Arriva London North; of these the 101 and 158 would be keeping a proportion

of their current Tridents. The 647 and 678 were both lost to Arriva London North. In August the 136 at Catford was announced as retained but with new buses and in October the 621 was picked up from London Central.

As Enviro400 deliveries resumed, the heavily-provisioned 53 at Plumstead was tackled, commencing on 13 July. Amid this conversion a second batch went into Rainham to convert the 287; four of the

Above: **On 3 July 2011 West Ham's 17517 (LX51 FNV) has reached Ilford town centre on the 147, transferred from Upton Park the previous year and now safe with East London for the next five years at least.** *Author*

Left: **On 17 September 2011 Upton Park closed and its routes were reallocated, for the most part, to West Ham. 17941 (LX53 JYD) went with it and when seen at London City Airport on the 24th hasn't yet had its new 'WH' codes applied.** *Author*

Above: **Leyton's 17409 (Y409 NHK) is laying over at the 97's Chingford terminus on 3 July 2011. Olympics expansion would see the 97 projected beyond the Leyton, Downsell Road turning circle to the new Stratford City site.** *Author*

Below: **On 25 March 2012 West Ham's 17932 (LX03 OTH) is pulling into the relocated and much expanded East Beckton bus station.** *Author*

Maps and 18235 for G-Star Raw). First London's takeover of the 608 took place on 3 September. Refurbishments continued into the 2004 batch of 'TAs', now adding a filled white roundel with 'BUSES' across the crossbar, and by year's end the 53-reg 'TASs' at North Street were being treated.

When the Westfield shopping centre at Stratford City opened on 10 September, the 97 and 241 found themselves extended to the new bus station to be found there. But it was on the 17th that Upton Park's long and distinguished career of 104 years ended, although it would have had to have closed in due course anyway once West Ham FC moved from the adjacent Boleyn Ground to the Olympic Stadium after 2012. The 104, 115, 238, 262, 330, 473 and N550 were reallocated to West Ham (in turn bouncing the 15 and daytime 277 out to Bow) and the 101 was put into Barking. At the close of play it fielded ninety-four Tridents (42 'TA' and 52 'TAS'). South of the river Catford's 199 and its school partner 660 began a new term, with the expectation of more Enviro400s.

Out to tender during the last quarter of 2011 were the 103, 175 and 257, though the 208 was retained by Selkent with new buses and the 636, 637 and 638 plus 664 with those they already had. In October 18223 lost its Click Card livery and November saw 18234 and 18235 regain all-red. 17915's fifth advert, applied in December, was one for Calabria tourism.

'TASs' withdrawn from frontline service at this time regained swirls to serve as a special reserve. A further group of withdrawn 'TAs' released by Bow was earmarked as a roving rail replacement fleet, but even so, departures to Stagecoach provincial fleets ramped up during July.

Plumstead concentrated on withdrawing its V- and X-registered 'TAs' as the 53's conversion progressed during August. Miscellaneous happenings that summer and into autumn were the treatment of two Bow buses to all-over ads (18234 for Google

From 3 December Rainham's 372 was treated to Christmas augmentations; until the appearance of 17424 on this day it had never seen a Trident. 2011's final contract announcements saw the 103 and 175 stay put at Stagecoach East London with a third of their PVR converted to new double-deckers, but the 257 was lost to Blue Triangle.

With effect from the 31st the 624, 625 and 658 left for London Central. 2011 had been rough for the Stagecoach Trident, with 150 disposals, but 2012 was to see more withdrawals and straight away, as the 15 commenced its conversion to E40H hybrids on 21 December 2011, gradually displacing 'TAs' in the 17900s to upgrade the 147 and 241 from the last of the X-reg 'TASs'. In January Catford's 199 took twelve new Enviro400s to put an end to some more X-reg 'TAs' occupying the 17300s block and then followed it with fifteen more for the 136 during March. Trident refurbishments were still proceeding, these 'TAs' being earmarked for Olympics support.

Below: **On 5 June 2012 Bromley's 17347 (X347 NNO) calls at Bromley North in driving rain. This would be its last year and it was withdrawn in December.** *Author*

3 March was the date of the renewal of the 101, 104, 158 and 238, and to make space at Leyton for the input of the 275 (which started off with 'TAs') part of the 97 was reallocated to West Ham. West Ham's share of the night element of the 15 was transferred to Bow alongside the day service. On 31 March the 647 and 678 left for Arriva London North and on 2 April the 541 came off, its work done (at least at this point in time; it was required again from 1 October).

As the spring progressed, Barking's 101 was converted to E40D, followed by the 136 at Catford from 24 March. Then came two batches for West Ham (a proportion of the 104 and 158 from 24 April and then the 238) and eleven for the 275 at Leyton from 11 May. Withdrawals had now crossed into the Y-reg batch 2001, West Ham's holdings of that age being replaced by 03-reg 'TAs' ex-Leyton and also made redundant from Bromley when the 208 received E40Ds beginning on 30 June.

Despite the Olympics support buses (supervised by Stagecoach and using the defunct Upton Park as one of their bases) not being allowed to carry anything that could be construed as a brand in competition with those sponsoring the event, there was no hang-up against local buses being plastered with advertising and run past the maximum number of punters, and in June Samsung bought space on fifteen 'TAs' to plug its new Galaxy S3 phone. These were 17742, 17767, 17772, 17773, 17775, 17776, 17796, 17875, 17892, 18226, 18266-18268, 18270 and 18271. Visa then chipped in with its own campaign, which included 17741, 17788, 17877, 17908, 18202 and 18220, and not to be outdone, Vodafone sponsored 17748, 17759, 17880, 17898, 17951, 17961 and 17964.

The Olympics were held between 27 July and 12 August, and to free space at Plumstead for buses coming in and out on attachment to the support operations, the 122

was reallocated to Catford on 21 July, using 51-reg 'TAs' made spare from Bromley, and operated there until 18 August, after which these were withdrawn. There were also augmentations to existing routes passing the Olympic Park and other event locations, which in Stagecoach terms added buses to the 8, 15, 53, 69 and 177. These were from the reserve fleet of Tridents.

After the Olympics died down, Trident disposals restarted (beginning with the higher-numbered 'TASs' of Y- and 51-registration that started at North Street in 2001 but finished their careers at West Ham) and the business of tendering could be resumed, but the 230 was announced as lost to Arriva London North. The 636, 637, 638 and 664 at Bromley began their new terms on 1 September and on 13 October the 103 and 175 were renewed, each putting into service new E40Ds before the contract renewals. Upon the simultaneous exit of the 257 to what was now London General, 18465-18480 were transferred to North Street to ease out Y-reg 'TAs'; all the X-NNO variety had now left service.

During September and October all the Visas, Samsungs and Calabria 17915 lost their ads but in October 18230 was given one for Stagecoach's Megabus services and November saw Apple mount a campaign for its iPod, the Stagecoach Trident participants

in which were 17767, 17772, 17773, 17775, 17845, 17875, 17892, 17945, 17962, 18202, 18222, 18226, 18266-18268, 18270 and 18271. On a longer-term basis, refurbishments continued and had now reached the end of the Trident build with the treatment of the 47's 06-reg batch.

2012 ended with the loss of the N550 to First and the offering out of the 122, 262, 472 and 473. 18202, 18222 and 18226 lost their Apple ads and 18230 its Megabus ad in December; 17845, 17875, 17892, 17945 and 17962 followed suit in January. However 18202 now gained an ad for Thailand, 18203 for Cancer UK and 18235 for the Lord Mayor's Appeal.

On 5 January 2013 the 372 at Rainham gained a second double-decker and this time it was a 'TAS', 17467 restored from withdrawn stock. Due to the ongoing recession having put a hold on most innovations, the first half of the year was quiet; the second 541 came off on 1 April and a similar temporary 572 in Thamesmead was operated by Plumstead 'TAs' between 4-9 March, although the withdrawal of the 473 between London City Airport and North Woolwich for Crossrail construction on 6 April was filled in by a Blue Triangle-operated Dart route numbered 573 until 6 October. Having already sold Northumberland Park's runout to Go-Ahead and lost four Dagenham routes to Stagecoach East London (the 165, 179, 252, 256 and 365, all

of which would become Trident possibilities when taken up on 28 September), First decided to abandon London altogether.

Two departing routes took with them the possibility of Trident appearances, the 106 to Arriva London North on 27 April and the 230 on 22 June; the 'TAs' made spare from the latter loss remained at Leyton to cover the 275 while that route's E40Ds served on the Silverstone service Stagecoach put on every year.

In July 17759 and 17964 lost their Vodafone adverts. Between 5 July and 9 September the diversion of the 122 away from Ladywell Road spawned a temporary 522 with one Catford 'TAS', 17485 transferred from Leyton. Then on the 13th came the 588, a three-'TA' (18459-18462 with one spare) West Ham operation linking Stratford City and Hackney Wick via the Olympic Park. On 31 August this new part of town gained a more permanent service with the diversion of the 97 on its way

Above: **There were a variety of iPod ads in the 'collect 'em all' mode that matched consumer aspirations for the product itself. Despite this being a device very much on the decline with the incorporation of all of its functions into increasingly powerful iPhones, Apple drove this campaign hard and saturated the streets of London during the autumn of 2012. Here at Hackney on 9 December is Leyton's 17875 (LX03 NFZ).** *Terry Wong Min*

Left: **From time to time construction would sever routes from their established termini, and when this was in the longer term the resulting replacement routes would merit fixed numbers of their own. Just such was the 522, operated by Catford to cover the diversion of the 122 during the summer of 2013. Seen at Brockley Rise on 10 July is 17485 (LX51 FMD).** *Terry Wong Min*

to and from Stratford City, and that night saw the N550 lost as planned, only the recipient had now been handed over to the new Tower Transit company that inherited half of First London. The night element on the 277 thus transferred from West Ham to Bow.

Two pairs of wins announced in August were most significant for Stagecoach even if one bore ill tidings for Tridents (the 262 and 473, which would be taking Scanias displaced from the 96); the other announcement brought the 54 and 75 back to Selkent after five years with Metrobus. The 372 was held on to with the promise of new buses, and in the same group of tranches the 261 was taken back (having spent 26 years with Metrobus) and the 8 and 672 were offered out again. Plumstead's own routes 96, 122, 472, 601 and 602 were all kept on the basis of new buses.

It seemed that London was beset constantly by roadworks, with the appropriate negative effects on buses. On 24 August the 8 (and N8) was forced to fall back at either end (Holborn Circus and Bow Church), with no direct replacement.

All the Vodafone ads had been restored to red by the second week of August, though 18230 now had one for Lycamobile.

On 14 September the 147 and 241 were cut back to Prince Regent again, but this time the third incarnation of the 541 filling the gap to Canning Town was given to Docklands Buses. With refurbishments still accruing to the 'TAs' in the 17700s, 17800s and 17900s,

no withdrawals from that large batch had occurred until 17747 caught fire and burnt out on 6 October on its way back to Leyton off an N55. West Ham's 18251 was the first to go from its own age group when a rear-end fire suffered on 16 December when returning from a route 158 journey damaged it beyond economic repair.

First's remnant at Dagenham gave up the ghost on 28 September and Rainham took on the 165, 252 and 365; though specified for a mix of Scanias and new E40Ds, all three (plus the single-deck 256) were capable of visits by Rainham's existing Tridents of both lengths. On 26 October the 387's last remaining journeys beyond the revitalising Barking Reach to the studiously ignored Creekmouth were withdrawn.

The input of the 261 into Bromley on 30 November was done with new E40Ds, but Tridents appeared within four days. 14 December saw the withdrawal of West Ham's temporary 388; the N8 had already been restored to Oxford Circus but the daytime 8 had to wait until the New Year.

It was the era of the Borismaster, Wrights' three-doorway, two-staircase nod to the RM, and in December the 8 was announced as retained by Stagecoach East London on the basis of conversion to this type. As 2014 got under way, it was decided what would be replacing the Tridents on the Plumstead routes being renewed (the 96 and 472 on 25 January and the 122 on 8 February) and then

Right: **After over a quarter of a century with Metrobus, the 261 came home to Bromley on 30 November 2013. It had its own batch of new 63-reg E40Ds, but the 269's existing 'TAs' soon wandered across and here at Lewisham as night falls on 21 January 2014 is 17842 (LX03 BYU).** *Author*

Left: **Another refurbishment with the bumper-mounted daytime running lights was West Ham's 18275 (LX03 BWH), seen coming round the southern side of Canning Town bus station on 7 September 2013.** *Author*

minds were changed again when prestige considerations diverted the new Volvo B5LHs to the 53. When these began arriving at Plumstead their first task was to displace E40Ds to Rainham and double-deck the 372 in its entirety rather than with just one or two 'TAs'. As well as the 53, the 122 was the new B5LHs' next major posting at Plumstead and seven 'TASs' left for Catford to top up

the 136, projected on 10 May from Peckham to the Elephant pending the delivery of eight new E40Ds for this purpose. The complete batch into Plumstead, followed by additional E40Hs, then pushed Scanias out to West Ham to convert the 262 and 473 from 'TA' in accordance with their contract renewal since 29 March. West Ham received enough Scanias to convert the 277 from 'TA' as well.

Left: **The 262 and 473 were converted to Scania operation during the spring of 2014, but Tridents were still capable of appearing as long as they were based at West Ham. Seen at Stratford on 7 July 2013 is Bow's 17909 (LX03 OSC).** *Author*

Right: **17563 (LV52 HDU) was withdrawn in 2014 anyway but never made it to its next owner, due to catching fire on the M11 at Saffron Walden on 12 June. In happier days it is seen with the O2 in the background as it carries out a route 472 duty from Plumstead on 4 February.** *Author*

On 28 June Bow's 8 was converted to LT operation in concert with its contract renewal, though the Borismasters themselves had been creeping out since the 19th. These conversions made spare up to eighty Tridents, which were readied to be sent to Glasgow to serve at the Commonwealth Games. 17563 disgraced itself on the way there by burning to a crisp in what was becoming a regular and embarrassing occurrence for the Trident type. Former Stagecoach 'TAs' and 'TASs' also saw out their London days on attachment to the Festival of Speed at Goodwood (26-29 June)

and the Grand Prix (4-6 July) at Silverstone. After the Games 18201-18220 returned to London, being doled out in small numbers to five garages which had older Tridents to cascade (two to Barking, three to North Street and Bromley, four to West Ham and eight to Leyton), but withdrawals were now menacing the large 2003 batch. Not that it was all over for some of the 04-reg 'TAs' lost off lease; the risk was that a competitor would take them up instead, and so it proved with nine that went to Tower Transit as its TAL class.

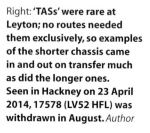

Right: **'TASs' were rare at Leyton; no routes needed them exclusively, so examples of the shorter chassis came in and out on transfer much as did the longer ones. Seen in Hackney on 23 April 2014, 17578 (LV52 HFL) was withdrawn in August.** *Author*

Left: Bow was the first Stagecoach garage to dispense with the services of Dennis Tridents; 17818 (LX03 BXN) is seen at Tottenham Court Road on 22 June 2013 but Borismasters subsequently took over the 8 and this bus was transferred to West Ham in September 2014. *Author*

July saw two more tender awards that would prove detrimental to Tridents; the 55 and 56, both retained by Leyton but the former with conversion to LT and the latter receiving hybrids. Leyton, meanwhile, stood down 17001, putting it into service one last time on 22 August as strike day cover on the 158; it was intended to donate it to the London Bus Museum. The last Trident to operate at Bow was 17818 on 3 September, but unlike Rainham, which had also ceased to operate them during 2014, Bow did not subsequently regain members of the type.

During the summer and autumn additional E40Hs flowed into Plumstead to finish off the 472 (and associated 672, renewed on 6 September) and then see to the rest of the 122, though a mix of types prevailed with the remaining 'TAs' remaining very much present. The 53-reg 'TAs' released edged out older examples from West Ham and Barking. Summer advert happenings restored 18202, 18203 and 18230 to red and gave 17828 an ad for the Gap which itself lasted until December. 18235 took its ad with it to Tower Transit!

Left: The Children with Cancer UK fund sponsored 18203 (LX04 FWN) for eighteen months. On 31 May 2014 it is in New Oxford Street. *Author*

Above: **The Peckham-Elephant section of the 343 was identified as a corridor needing enhancement, and on 10 May 2014 the 136 was projected from Peckham to join it. As well as the route's existing E40Ds and eight more taken to fulfil the 136's increased PVR, Catford's Tridents joined in, as 17851 (LX03 BZE) is doing when seen at the revamped Elephant & Castle road layout on 12 May 2015.** *Author*

November saw E40Ds 10198-10205 replace Catford's oldest Tridents on the 136. On the 29th the 97's Leyton allocation was swallowed up by an increase at West Ham, carrying with it six 'TAs'.

2014 ended with the re-tender of the 47 plus Barking's usual cohort, of which the 387 and 687 were still officially 'TA'-operated and the rest saw the type regularly. A switch

during December saw Plumstead exchange a sizeable quantity of its remaining 53-reg 'TAs' for some slightly older ones from Barking.

12 January 2015 saw ten buses added to the 47 to cover problems being encountered at London Bridge during its comprehensive refurbishment. These comprised spare Tridents added to West Ham and supported by four more former London examples

Right: **The 160 had long been lost to Arriva, but its school offshoot 660 stayed put with Catford and on 13 March 2014 was in the hands of 18489 (LX06 AFZ) at Rushey Green.** *Author*

loaned from Manchester in the shape of 17002, 17010, 17011 and 17567. The whole route was cut back to Liverpool Street anyway for the duration of the roadworks, and the 53 was similarly cut back to County Hall.

Beginning on 17 January, the 55 at Leyton began converting to LT in advance of its 28 February contract renewal date. This particular conversion, however, pushed out

Scanias rather than Tridents, and a handful of Leyton 'TAs' were sent to West Ham to add a partial allocation to the 15 on 17 January, even before that route (but not the N15) began receiving its own Borismasters on 2 March. Bow thus sent the displaced E40Hs to Leyton to take over the 56 and the 15's supplementary West Ham allocation (now reduced from five to three buses) was

Above: **Another route whose Tridents had officially departed some time ago was the 101, the lone route put into Barking when Upton Park closed. On 17 March 2015 at East Beckton, its E40Ds were being backed up by 18216 (LX04 FXD).** *Author*

Left: **Itself converted from 'TA' to Scania some time back, the 48 could still field the likes of 17752 (LX03 BTU), seen on 27 February 2015 in Hoe Street south of Walthamstow Central. The thick-legged side advert was a new wheeze, albeit one that obscured most of the view out from the lower deck.** *Author*

Above: **Leyton's 17813 (LX03 BXH) is seen at the Barbican on 4 May 2015, shortly after the 56 had otherwise been converted to Scania. This bus was spared, withdrawals taking out the earliest of the 03-reg batch at this time.** *Author*

transferred to the 277 on 28 March. With enough Scanias now returned off lease, the 56's conversion threatened Tridents once again and twelve 03-reg 'TAs' were disposed of in March. Four promptly bounced straight back with Tower Transit!

The Manchester Tridents went home on 15 February and the supplementary schedule

on the 47 was reduced to five buses on 21 March before coming off on the 27th.

With the 53, 69, 86 and 147 out to tender by May, Stagecoach was heartened with the re-award of the 47, though on the basis of new Enviro400-bodied Volvo B5LH hybrids. A quantity was already on order for the 177 in tune with its 30 May contract renewal date,

Right: **A rare long Trident on a route more used to the shorter examples, 18203 (LX04 FWN) out of North Street is coming into Romford town centre on 18 June 2015.** *Author*

Left: **North Street commenced operations for Stagecoach East London on the 498 on 27 June 2015, using existing Tridents until the E40D MMCs on order arrived. Seen in Romford on the 29th is 18470 (LX55 ERJ).**
Mark McWalter

and in both cases Tridents would not be the beneficiaries. Still, when these began entering service at Plumstead on 15 June, the 177's outgoing Scanias were put into West Ham to release Tridents to North Street, which took over the 498 from Blue Triangle on 27 June but didn't yet have its new buses in stock. Nor were the MMC E20Ds for the 499, so older examples were taken from the 296 and replaced by Tridents, effectively double-decking that route and on aggregate adding thirteen 'TAs' to North Street's contingent. 27 June was also when the 277's extras ceased.

The 296 and 498 received their rightful buses in July and the 'TA' loans drifted back to West Ham with a couple into Leyton. However, two 'TASs' and a 'TA' restored Tridents to Rainham in August and they managed to stick, visiting the 103, 248, 252 and 365.

Still capable of using 'TAs,' the 53 was awarded once more to Stagecoach Selkent in September and new buses would again be specified, with the inevitable cascades, this time of the 14-reg Volvo B5LHs. On the 12th the 47 was restored through to Shoreditch. Barking retained the 62, 287 and 387 and lost

Left: **The 296 had been obliged to take on single-deckers when split in half in 2000, but loaned them to the 498 upon that route's acquisition, substituting Tridents instead. Making its way round Gants Hill on 31 July 2015 is North Street's 17869 (LX03 NFP).**
Author

the 687 when the tenders of those tranches were awarded in the autumn, and the simultaneous retention of the 86 portended the replacement of its North Street's 'TAs' with newer, though not outright new, double-deckers. There were uncharacteristic losses for Stagecoach, however, with the loss of the 69 to Tower Transit and the 147 to Docklands Buses.

A one-off visit was of West Ham 'TAs' to the D3 on 3 and 4 November while the DLR was on strike. At the same garage, the 147 and 241 were restored to their rightful Canning Town terminus on 31 October, after a diversion lasting for over two years.

In the twilight of their years, Stagecoach's Tridents were now no longer first choice for refurbishments or all-over ads, but 17759 carried an ad for Homesense between April 2015 and July 2016.

When the 47 received its new B5LHs at the end of January and into February, the incumbent batch of 06-reg 'TAs' shifted, twelve going to Bromley and eight crossing the river to Barking and in each case ousting older examples for return off lease, with only two or three that had been transferred elsewhere remaining from the 269's original batch of 53-reg 'TAs'.

On 6 February 2016 the 69 departed for Tower Transit, but there was a twist as the new contractor could not field any of its intended new buses. Therefore Stagecoach loaned them 18237-18250 and 18252-18256, which ran around without fleetnames for a couple of months.

On 30 April the 687 left for Docklands Buses and the 147 was taken over by the same company on 7 May, dooming another sixteen West Ham 'TAs', but the garage could still field over eighty Tridents. In May the 5 and 115 were tendered, these being two 'TA' routes to have operated the type for over a decade and a half now at Barking and West Ham respectively. The 103 and 175, both with Trident capability, were out to tender by the autumn.

On 16 July the 86 at North Street began a new contract together with its N86 night partner, and as Plumstead restocked the 53 with new MMC E40Hs, the existing Volvo B5LHs stayed put to take over the 122 and 472, thus releasing those routes' E40Ds across the river to oust most, but not all, of North Street's 'TAs', plus start breaking up the 53-reg 'TAS' contingent through transfers to West Ham and Barking. Similarly, the Trident was not finished off at Plumstead either;

Below: **Newly transferred from Catford to Bromley, 18489 (LX06 AFZ) makes a visit to the 208 on a sunny 5 May 2016; the route had otherwise been E40D-operated for four years.**
Author

Left: **18498 (LX06 AHE) was one of the 'TAs' transferred from Catford to Barking when the 47 received its Volvo B5LHs at the beginning of 2016. On 10 April it is visiting the 62, still single-deck with Enviro200s and a number of Optare Versas in backup.** *Author*

Left: **On 7 May 2016 the 147 was taken over by Blue Triangle and 17825 (LX03 BXY) was one of the Tridents to be withdrawn at West Ham. Two days before the handover it is coming round the back of Ilford.** *Author*

Left: **In August 2016 a number of 03-reg 'TAs' were withdrawn by West Ham and replaced by an equivalent number of slightly younger 'TASs' leaving North Street. 17996 (LX53 KGF) was one of them and on 10 May 2017 it is seen at Stratford.** *Author*

Right: **The career of 17854 (LX03 BZH) came to an end when most of the 86 at North Street was upgraded to Enviro400. On 5 June it is seen at Ilford and it would depart the fleet in August.** *Author*

though no routes there were now scheduled for the type, the dozen holdouts visited the 51, 96, 99, 122, 177 and 472 as fit, plus the school routes. 17807 and 17810 donned a blue livery to serve as classrooms for engineering apprentices.

The 256's two double-deck journeys were transferred from North Street to Rainham on 16 July, remaining 'TA' possibilities. 20 August saw a night service added to the 158

on Friday and Saturday nights, and a sizeable service increase to the 158 implemented on 3 September was what used up the 'TASs' put into West Ham. The 104 was similarly increased on 15 October. During that month the ten training 'TAs' were moved from Rainham to West Ham.

2017 saw Trident stocks reduced to barely more than two hundred, with only a handful of routes still 100% thus operated. The

Right: **Scanias had been the standard type on Plumstead's 96 for some years, but the garage's Tridents continued to turn out; here at Bexleyheath on 19 July 2016 is 17843 (LX03 BYV).** *Author*

Above: **West Ham's 18220 (LX04 FXH) pilots a 104 through East Ham on 6 August 2016.** *Author*

lengths had been mixed up for years and each garage operated quantities of each. Two Barking routes ceased to be possibilities as the year got going, the 387 on 18 February (taken over by Blue Triangle as EL3) and the 101 on 4 March (also lost to Blue Triangle). Leyton also lost the chance to put its small number of supporting 'TAs' out on the 48 when that route left for Arriva London North on 25 February.

Stagecoach was now starting to falter noticeably with its tender bids; in February 2017 it lost the 103 and 175 to Arriva London North and there would be worse later in the year. Time was about up for the Bromley 'TAs' still holding out on the 636, 637 and 638 trio with their retention under just the 638 identity and newer buses. The 664 was also kept hold of but merited 2012-vintage vehicles. At the same time North Street's

Left: **Barking had operated the 5 more or less continuously since its second OPO conversion on 2 November 1985, but the route was put out to tender and lost to Blue Triangle; even if it had been retained by Stagecoach East London, Tridents like 17904 (LX03 ORW), seen in Barking on 5 May 2016, would have been replaced.** *Author*

100%-'TAS'-operated 247 and Barking's 169 and 287, which were both perfectly capable of fielding Tridents, were put out to tender, followed by Plumstead's 99 (partially-Trident) and Bromley's 269 (100%). Two of the last three routes with majority Trident operation were West Ham's 241 and 330, and they were tendered in April with the 104.

On 4 March two routes received temporary allocations to free single-deckers for routes that had been let down by the manufacturers' failure to deliver their new buses on time. They were unusual deployments too, the 165 at Rainham and the 178 at Catford receiving three and four 'TAs' respectively.

March saw the award of the 5 and 115 to Blue Triangle together with Borismaster-operated 15, in a terrible blow for West Ham and Barking and certainly for a large number of Tridents that would be departing. This month saw the 277 converted to E40H MMC and the Scanias displaced used to convert the 97 from 'TA' at West Ham (a reallocation to Leyton having been cancelled).

In spite of the likelihood of their withdrawal sooner rather than later, eight of the 247's 'TASs' found themselves included in a branding exercise based on buses running through Barkingside. In April 17978-17985 had a large yellow '247' added on each side with frequency and via point details underneath. Stablemates 17976, 17977 and 17995 were spared so that some measure of flexibility could be ensured while making sure branded buses couldn't wander unless absolutely necessary.

The 165 and 178 had their new buses by May and on the 24th the Trident stand-ins ceased; Catford's were withdrawn and Rainham's were redistributed.

Right: **The 178 had long since been single-deck, with just a brief flourish of VNs when it returned to Stagecoach Selkent in 1999, but on 4 March 2017 Catford needed to lend its Enviro200s to Barking to start off the 167 and 549 and thus Tridents stepped in. The height restriction that would have prohibited them from the 178 had since been eliminated with the diversion of the route via a different part of the former Ferrier Estate in Kidbrooke, so buses like 17824 (LX03 BXW), seen coming into Lewisham on 24 April, were safe to allocate.** *Author*

Right: **When TfL devised the Barkingside branding exercise, it hedged its bets against the likelihood of branded buses turning out on wrong routes by treating only a proportion of vehicles allocated to a particular service and making sure that these were pet allocations. The 247 was just such a route, and on 6 December 2017 North Street's 17981 (LX53 KAO) serves Romford station on its way to Barkingside.** *Author*

Left: **The loss of the 5, 15 and 115 to Blue Triangle on 26 August 2017 was a hammer blow for Stagecoach and saw the withdrawal of over fifty Tridents. West Ham's 18263 (LX04 FZH), seen at Canning Town on the evening of 5 May 2016, sidestepped withdrawal at this stage, but 17878 (LX03 NGJ), behind it on the 5, didn't even last that long, being sold in June after an E40D MMC replaced it at Barking.** *Author*

Left: **Stagecoach was hit hard south of the river too when the similarly lower bids of Arriva carried the 99 and 269. On 19 July 2016 Bromley's 17845 (LX03 BYY) is setting off from Bexleyheath, carrying a set of the revived white-on-black blinds, but would be stood down the following February after the routes left for Dartford. However, it was put back into service by West Ham and lasted until September 2018.** *Author*

Further calamity for Stagecoach came in July when the 99 and 269 were awarded to a resurgent Arriva London North, today's incarnation of the former and latterly moribund Kentish Bus. And it looked like the end for the Trident at Stagecoach East London when the 241, 247 and 330 were announced in August as retained but on the basis of new buses. It just remained to see whether the type would make its 20th birthday, and if so, at which garage was still operating the type, as none of the remainder showed any particular inclination to give up all of their stragglers.

26 August was the date the 5 and 115 departed Barking and West Ham for new Blue Triangle berths at River Road. Over fifty Tridents were withdrawn and more than a few of them went for scrap despite their comparatively low age. Next fell the 103 and 175 on 14 October, departing for Arriva London North (the descendant of Grey-Green in this part of town). Four of the 18467-18480 batch leaving North Street were retained.

On 20 January 2017 the 99 and 269 were taken over by Arriva's Dartford. Other than the school routes 638 and 664, the 269 was Bromley's last Trident route. A very late development came out of the withdrawal of these 06-reg 'TAs' from here and North Street, with nine selected to be the mainstay of a new London tour operation called

megasightseeing.com. 18474, 18475, 18477 and 18482 were converted to full open-top by Alexander Dennis at Harlow and named *Queen Victoria*, *King Henry III*, *Lord Nelson* and *Sir Winston Churchill*, while South Yorkshire at Anston converted 18467, 18471, 18473, 18496 and 18497 to partial open-top and gave them the names *King George V*, *Queen Elizabeth II*, *King Charles II*, *Sir Christopher Wren* and *King William I*. Operations commenced on 7 May.

The 241 and 330 began new contracts on 5 June and the clock was set ticking on their Tridents, although 17845, 18215 and 18485-18493 were reactivated to free enough Enviro400s to man the 474, taken over from Blue Triangle on the same day but without

any of its expected new E40D smart hybrids. These were also meant for Barking's 169 and thus cascade E40Ds to the 247 at North Street, but plans changed repeatedly when emissions considerations were factored in and North Street's 'TASs' kept going a little longer. West Ham even introduced some of its still sizeable fleet of Tridents to the 474.

Stagecoach continued to ship route after route, losing three of the remaining West Ham Trident possibilities in quick succession; the loss of the 104 to Blue Triangle was followed by Tower Transit's scoop of the 262 and 473. Tridents were not even in the picture now where tendering was concerned, so although Stagecoach Selkent retained the

Above: **One of the features of the 2010s has been to remove cumbersome one-way systems and gyratories and restore two-way traffic. By the summer of 2018 Stratford town centre was accordingly being pulled apart, and on 4 August we see West Ham's 18267 (LX05 BVZ) on the 241, a route whose conversion to new E40D MMC smart hybrids was under way.** Author

Left: **The conversion of the 330 to E40D smart hybrids was undertaken at the same time as that of the 241. On 11 August 18490 (LX06 AGO) is pulling into Canning Town bus station, but this would be its last full month and it last operated on 16 September.** Author

Above: **A decade had now passed since the Stagecoach swirls had started to disappear, but they stayed put on trainers, as if Londoners couldn't tell the difference. On 3 April 2017 17363 (Y363 NHK) is proceeding gingerly through the revamped Warren Street junction, although since the loss of the 30 to Tower Transit no Stagecoach East London routes served those roads any more.** *Author*

472, 601 and 602, their presence was tolerated at best, especially when the need to make some truly drastic cuts loomed inescapably over TfL. Meanwhile, a corridor identified as excessively polluted had one pre-hybrid route still going, and the 136 was thus chosen to host the 169's intended smart hybrids, plus

those that the 179 was expecting later in 2018. Catford would thus send some of its existing 12-reg E40Ds to see off the 247's 'TASs'.

The 474 was first in line to receive West Ham's new E40D smart hybrids and the 330 and 241 followed; the resulting withdrawal of Tridents put 'TA' and 'TAS' numbers below

Right: **By the late summer of 2018 North Street's 17791 (LX03 BWE) was the oldest Stagecoach Trident still in service; it was one of seven 'TAs' there that had managed to dodge various purges and continued to turn out on the 86, as this one was doing when seen in the construction zone that central Stratford had become by 4 August.** *Author*

one hundred. Plumstead's 17840 was one of them, living up to the Trident's old tricks by burning to the ground while on the 472 on 1 September.

During August and September 2018 Catford's 136 gave up its E40Ds to North Street, which withdrew every 'TAS' on the 247 except 17979, which remained doggedly in service, in the spirit of long-time holdout TA 40247 at London United and the five 05-reg TAs at Metroline. By October North Street could field just nine Tridents, and Catford's change didn't finish off its final four 'TAs' either. Bromley could still put three into

Right: **Still going strong on 1 November 2018 is North Street's 18203 (LX04 FWN), seen in Ilford. This was another one with white-on-black blinds, indicating at least a medium-term future for the bus when they were ordered in what would otherwise be prohibitively small volume.** *Author*

Right: **The 241 and 330's conversion to E40D left the 158 as West Ham's last predominantly Trident-operated route, and indeed the majority of the 'TAs' and 'TASs' remaining clustered on it by the autumn. Having arrived at Stratford at 4.30pm on 1 November 2018, 18469 (LX55 EPZ) has found a spot to lay over in the subtly redesigned bus station.** *Author*

Right: **The withdrawal of the 247's 'TASs' in October 2017 reduced numbers of the 9.9m Trident to single figures. 17989 (LX53 KBP) is visiting a Scania-operated route at Stratford on 1 November 2018, and one which would be passing to Tower Transit the following March.** *Author*

action, Plumstead fourteen and across the river Leyton had four, Barking seven and West Ham forty. Just the 158 remained as an official Trident allocation, despite it having just as officially been converted partially to Enviro400s several years earlier. Rainham's last three, 17981 (escaped from North Street), 18465 and 18466 were stood down in October, only for 17981 to slip the noose again and

pitch up at Plumstead, where it was joined by 18465.

The race was now on as to which would be the last and where. The 104's departure for Blue Triangle on 8 December 2018 stood down a dozen Tridents at West Ham, including four of the five 'TASs' remaining, and by the turn of the years there were just 51 Tridents left in service throughout Stagecoach East London

Right: **Plumstead finished 2018 with fourteen Tridents, these numbers dwindling only slowly as the very utmost was wrung out of what were now veterans. The 51 was removed as a possibility for appearances with its loss to Metrobus, so the 'TAs' and single 'TAS' tended to gather on the 472. On 14 December 18208 (LX04 FWU) serves Woolwich.** *Author*

Below: **The 158 was the last route with a majority Dennis Trident allocation across any London bus company. On 28 February 2019, its penultimate day with Stagecoach East London, West Ham's 18461 (LX55 EPK) gets going from Chingford Mount in a downpour. 18461 itself survived for nearly three more months to become West Ham's last Trident on 21 May.** *Author*

and Selkent. Bromley's trio became a duo upon the entry into service of E40Ds on the 261, but even the commencement of a new contract on Plumstead's 53 on 26 January 2019 didn't touch its ten surviving Tridents. Still, there were developments; on 24 January Leyton's five 'TAs' were removed from the 56 due to its inclusion in the forthcoming ULEZ and instead switched to the 215 and 275.

25 January marked twenty years in service for the Trident family; from the 998 Stagecoach had received, just 49 were left in service to mark the type's birthday. Only Metroline on the other side of town could still field Tridents.

1 March was the last day of the 158 with Stagecoach East London, and West Ham fielded twelve of its 'TAs' (including its last

'TAS', 17989) on the eighteen workings before the route passed to Arriva London North on the 2nd. 18462 as WH416 was the last into the garage. West Ham's Trident tally was now reduced to seven.

Barking proved the first to crack; 18483 finished on 27 February and 'TAS' 17999 on the 28th, leaving just 18498, whose last day on the 169 was 15 March. However, one West Ham evictee popped up again this week, 18457 making it four at Catford. Then, on the 30th, West Ham's 262 and 473 passed to Tower Transit, but 18211, 18212, 18220, 18454, 18458 and 18461 remained based, their work being increasingly on the 97 with visits to the 238 and, less often, the 241 and 330.

As the service buses were undergoing their protracted decline, the Megasightseeing 'TAs' came off at the same time, their place being taken during April by 56-reg Enviro400s recently displaced from the 61 at Bromley (despite there being two 'TAs' still based there). Due to the introduction of a Low Emission Bus Zone along the Bromley Road, Catford's small allocation was now compelled to withdraw, 18455 last working on 12 March, 17876 on 6 April, 18463 on the 11th and 18457 bowing out at 14:41 on the 12th, all on the 199. The simultaneous application of an LEBZ to the Romford Road drove North Street's 'TA' holdouts off the 86 but failed to kill the buses' sheer will to survive, so from 25

Above: **Leyton's small band of holdouts abandoned the 56 at the beginning of 2019 and gathered on the 215, out-county enough not to traumatise the emissions-obsessed. Coming through a rainy Chingford Mount on 28 February is 18218 (LX04 FXF).** *Author*

Left: **On 5 April 2019 North Street's 17858 (LX03 NFC) comes into Stratford on the 86. It was one of four Tridents still based there, the others being 17791, 18478 and branded route 247 bus 17979.** *Author*

April the 247 became their host, with the 296 also featuring and the even more improbable 256 seeing a peak-hour visit from 18478 that day. At the end of April 'TASs' 17979 and 17981, both reactivated after a fortnight off each, and twenty 'TAs' remained in traffic.

During May West Ham's 'TAs' were put to weekend use on rail replacement-related augmentations of the 238, known internally as 238U, and working just far enough off the main drag not to arouse TfL opprobrium. Former Catford 18457 and 18463 found themselves reactivated by West Ham on 11 May also to serve as rail replacement buses, though in this case on a DLR service identifying as 'UL46'. But for West Ham, the end came before that of the stragglers, 18212 finishing on 16 May and 18461, the last of what until recently was the biggest allocation by far, on the 21st, both on the 97.

Right: **With such a huge allocation, you would have thought that West Ham would retain the Trident all the way to the end, but the fleet was gradually whittled down until just 18461 (LX55 EPK) was left. On 10 May it is setting off from Stratford City bus station on a diversion of the 97 that had come in from the opposite direction, with just eleven days to go.** *Author*

Above: **Plumstead's sizeable contingent gradually dwindled to single figures as 2019 progressed, but 17843 (LX03 BYV) remained on the front line, sticking to the 472 with only occasional outings to the 96 and 601 and just once visiting the 177. On the afternoon of 30 June it is seen powering past new development alongside Woolwich's putative Crossrail station.** *Author*

Left: **Plumstead's 18208 (LX04 FWU) is bending the corner at Woolwich Arsenal on 18 April 2019; it was the last Stagecoach Trident in the 'eighteen thousands' in service and came off after 2 August.** *Author*

Above: **Just two 'TAs' made it into 2019 at Bromley, nominally retained for school routes 638 and 664 but continuing to earn their keep on the 61 until the loss of the 208 to Metrobus on 27 July removed their justification for remaining. On 12 January we see 18495 (LX06 AHA) at Bromley South.** *Author*

Amazingly, 17791 was loaned from North Street to Rainham at six o'clock on Sunday 9 June and spent the next three hours covering the 174. This was the first Trident appearance at Rainham in eight months. 18478 last worked at North Street on 14 May and Plumstead stood down 17862 after 22 May, reducing its complement to four.

The loaning out of two Enviro400s to CT Plus to cover that company's shortfall on the 20 came to an end when the 388 was cut back on 15 June, meaning 18209 could now be stood down at Leyton; its last operation on the 18th was on the 275. With just three left here, there were only a dozen Tridents in operation across Stagecoach East London and Selkent. Plumstead's 18465 made a rare foray to the 177 on 20 June, but was withdrawn after 25 July.

Bromley was next to crack, when the loss of the 208 to Metrobus on 27 July made Enviro400s available to see off 17864 and 18495; the latter operated until 13:00 on Thursday 25th and 17864 finished at 20:03 on Friday 26th, both on the 61. With the final standing down of North Street's stalwart 17979 after a journey on the 247 finishing at ten to ten on the same day, following the withdrawal of 17858 five days earlier and Leyton's 18484 on the 22nd, Stagecoach

thus went into August with just six Tridents operational; 17791 at North Street, 17811 and 17836 at Leyton and 17843, 18208 and the last 'TAS', 17981, at Plumstead. Of these, 18208 fell out after the 2nd, reducing totals to five.

At last came the inevitable final push; after the morning peak on 5 August North Street stood down 17791 after service on the 247, sparking a fight to the finish between Plumstead and Leyton, with two Tridents each. Plumstead's 17843 and 17981 both found themselves rostered on the 472 on Thursday 7 August, but 17981 (as PD28) was taken out of service at 14:00, finishing the career of the 9.9m 'TAS', and 17843 (as PD23) followed it at 20:50. That was the end for Plumstead, and Leyton now began preparations to see off 17811 and 17836. Having worked all weekend, 17836 managed just the morning peak as T1 on the 215 on Monday 12 August before being subbed by Enviro400 19870 – and then there was one. 17811 continued on alone as T5 (Monday 12th), T203 on the 275 (Tuesday 13th) and T4 (Wednesday 13th) before taking Thursday off to be spruced up.

17811 almost didn't make it out on Friday 16 August, but some judicious manoeuvring got it placed on T5, the 215's latest-starting duty and it worked all day. Thoughts of

Left: **17979 would have hung around longer but for difficulties with its exhaust, so Plumstead's 17981 (LX53 KAO) took the honours as Stagecoach London's last 9.9m 'TAS'. On its last day, 8 August 2019, it is in West Parkside, North Greenwich, as PD28 on the 472.** *Ian Jordan*

Below: **New to Upton Park, 17836 (LX03 BYM) subsequently served at Plumstead, North Street and finally Leyton. On 8 August 2019 it is negotiating the much-simplified turning arrangements from Hoe Street into Selborne Road and Walthamstow Central Station; prior to this an awkward roundabout over the hump of the bridge had to be circumnavigated. It worked as T1 on 12 August 2019 and came off at 9.44 am, leaving 17811 the distinction of being the last in service of a fleet of Tridents that once numbered 998.** *Ian Jordan*

Above: **For the last ten days of 'TA' operation, the 215 couldn't make it further north than its old Yardley Lane Estate terminus due to waterworks in Sewardstone Road. On its official last day, Friday 16 August 2019, Leyton's 17811 (LX03 BXF) poses on the stand with a board in the background explaining the reasons for the curtailment.** *Author*

subbing it when it came into Walthamstow Central for a driver change at 14:19 fell away when a spare Enviro400 could not be found (Leyton having 10160 out of action at the time), so 17811 kept going. Upon arrival at Yardley Lane at 21:47 (the customary Lee Valley Campsite terminus having been cut off by waterworks since 5 August), 17811 returned to Leyton out of service, as was customary for duty T5 to do for an hour. It wasn't replaced at this point either and came back to finish, coming off at 00:47. So ended

twenty years, six months and 22 days of Stagecoach 'TA' operation – or so it looked, because as morning broke on Saturday 17 August, 17811 was put back into service as T5! There it spent the whole day, and on Sunday 18th it came out again to assume T4, the 215's late-appearing fourth working. Monday 19th saw it back once again as T5, but only until the driver change at 21:26, when 10155 replaced it. That really was the end; it didn't come back and on the following morning it was driven to West Ham.

Right: **Having reached Walthamstow Central at four o'clock on 16 August, 17811 (LX03 BXF) goes out again and would stay in service until the end of traffic on that Friday, and over the ensuing weekend too! As well as the roundabout in Hoe Street, improvements had been made to the turning arrangements into the bus station itself, removing the awkward bottleneck and, for the photographer, permitting unobstructed nearsides (and rear offsides).** *Author*

Above: **The finish of Leyton's 17811 (LX03 BXF), seen leaving Walthamstow Central on 16 August 2019, proved protracted, as the non-availability of the full complement of Enviro400s at the garage obliged the last Trident to hold out over the weekend following its official last day and finally into Monday 19 August, after which it finally bowed out. By the following June, 17811 had found its way into private preservation.** *Author*

Registrations

TA 1-73, 75-98	S801-839 BWC, T640-665 KPU, T699 KVX, T667-673, 675-698 KPU
TA 99-222	V473-475 KJN, V102-109 MEV, V476, 477 KJN, V112-120 MEV, V478 KJN, V122 MEV, V479 KJN, V124-179 MEV, W187 CNO, V181-186 MEV, V362 OWC, V188-199 MEV, V363 OWC, V201-221 MEV, V364 OWC
TAS 223-260	X361-366, 229, 367, 231-239, 368, 241-243, 369, 371, 246-249, 372, 251-254, 373, 256-259, 374 NNO
TA 261-358	X261-269, 376, 271-274, 377, 276-279, 378, 281-289, 379, 291-299, 381, 301-304, 382, 383, 307-309, 384, 311-315, 385, 317, 386, 319, 387, 388, 322, 389, 324, 391, 326, 327, 392, 329, 393, 331, 332, 394, 334-339, 395, 341-344, 396, 346-349, 397, 351-354, 398, 356-358 NNO
TA 359-401	Y359, 508, 361-369, 509, 371-374, 511, 376-379, 512, 381, 382 NHK, LX51 FPF, Y384-386 NHK, LX51 FPC, Y388, 389 NHK, LX51 FPD, Y391-393 NHK, LX51 FHN, Y395 NHK, LX51 FHO, Y397, 398 NHK, LX51 FHP, Y514, 401 NHK
TA 403-435	LX51 FHS, Y404 NHK, LX51 FHT, Y517, 407 NHK, LX51 FHU, Y409 NHK, LX51 FHV/W/Y/Z, FJA/C-F/J/K/N-P/V/Y/Z, FKA/B, Y429 NHK, LX51 FKD-G, Y434 NHK, LX51 FKJ
TAS 436-534	Y436-438 NHK, LX51 FKL, Y522, 441-443 NHK, Y523 NHK, Y445-449, 524 NHK, LX51 FKR, Y452-454, 526, 527 NHK, LX51 FKT, Y458 NHK, LX51 FKU, Y529 NHK, LX51 FKW, Y462 NHK, LX51 FKZ, Y464 NHK, LX51 FLB-F, Y531 NHK, LX51 FLG, Y472 NHK, LX51 FLJ-N/P/R/V/W/Z, FMA/C-G/J-M/O/P/U/V/Y/Z, FNA/C-G/M/J-L/H/N-P/R-W/Y/Z, FOA/C/D/F/H/J/K/M/N/P/T-V, FPA
TAS 535-591	LY02 OAA-E/G/N-P/S/U-X/Z, OBB-H/J-M, LV52 USF, HDO/U/X-Z, HEJ/U, HFA-F/J-P/R-U/W-Z, HGA
TA 592-614	LV52 HHA-G/J-P/R-U/W-Z, HJA
17740-17853	LY52 ZDX/Z, ZFA/F, LX03 BTE/F/U/V/Y/Z, BUA/E/F/H/U/J/P/U-W, BVA-H/J-N/P/R-W/Y/Z, BWA-H/J-N/P/U-W/Y/Z, BXA-H/J-N/P/R/S/U-W/Z, BYA-D/F-H/J/L-N/P/R-W/Y/Z, BZA-G
17854s	LX03 BZH

Registrations

17855-17933	LX03 NEU/Y, NFA/C-H/J-N/P/R/T/V/Y/Z, NGE/F/J/N/U/V/Y/Z, NHA, OPT/U-W/Y/Z, ORA/C/F-H/J/K/N/P/S-W/Y/Z, OSA-E/G/J-N/P/R/U/V/W/Y/Z, OTA/H/J
17934-17975	LX53 JXU-W/Y, JYA-H/J-L/N-P/R/T-W/Y/Z, JZA/C-H/J-P/R/T/U
17976s-17999s	LX53 JZV/W, KAE/J/K/O/U, KBE/F/J/K/N-P/V/W/Z, KCA/C/E-G/J, LX04 GCU
18201-18265	LX04 FWL-N/P/R-W/Y/Z, FXA-H/J-M/P/R-W/Y/Z, FYA-H/K-N/P/R-W/Y/Z, FZA-H/J/K
18266-18277	LX05 BVY/Z, BWA-H/J/K
18451-18499	LX05 LLM/P, LX55 EPA/C-F/J-L/N-P/U/V/Y/Z, ERJ/K/O/U/V/Y/Z, ESF/G/N/O, BDY/Z, BEO/Y, BFA/E/F, BEJ, LX06 AFZ, AGO/U/V/Y, AGZ, AHA/C-F

Date	Deliveries	Licensed for Service
01.99	TA 1-10	TA 2-10 (**T**)
02.99	TA 11-36	TA 11-36 (**T**)
03.99	TA 37-46, 48-57	TA 37-46, 48, 49 (**BW**), TA 50, 53-57 (**T**)
04.99	TA 47, 58-73, 75-89, 91, 93-95	TA 1, 51, 52, 58-62 (**T**), TA 47 (**BW**), TA 63-73, 75-80 (**BK**), TA 81-89, 91, 93-95 (**U**)
05.99	TA 97	
06.99	TA 96, 98	TA 96-98 (**U**)
07.99	TA 90	TA 90 (**U**)
08.99	TA 92	TA 92 (**U**)
10.99	TA 100, 107	
11.99	TA 99, 101-103, 105, 106, 108-131, 133, 134, 136-141, 145, 146	TA 99-102, 105, 107-115, 117-124, 126-131, 133, 134, 137, 138, 140, 141, 145, 146 (**PD**)
12.99	TA 104, 132, 135, 142-144, 147-177, 179, 182-199	TA 103, 104, 106, 116, 125, 132, 135, 136, 139, 142-144, 147 (**PD**), TA 148-158 (**TL**), TA 159-167 (**BW**), TA 168-177 (**SD**), TA 182-195 (**T**)
01.00	TA 178, 200-216	TA 178, 179, 196-202 (**SD**), TA 203-210 (**U**), TA 211-216 (**NS**)
02.00	TA 217-222	TA 217-221 (**NS**), TA 222 (**U**)
05.00	TA 181	TA 181 (**T**)
07.00	TA 180	TA 180 (**NS**)
08.00	TAS 223-229	
09.00	TAS 230-246	TAS 223-229 (**TL**), TAS 230-236 (**TB**), TAS 237-239 (**BW**)
10.00	TAS 247-260	TAS 240-246 (**BW**), TAS 247-252 (**NS**), TAS 253-260 (**U**)
11.00	TA 264-272, 274, 276	TA 264-267, 269-272, 274, 276 (**PD**), TA 268 (**NS**)
12.00	TA 261-263, 273, 275, 277-284	TA 261-263, 273, 275, 277, 278 (**PD**), TA 279-284 (**T**)
01.01	TA 285-303, 305, 307-309, 311-315	TA 285-291 (**T**), TA 292-301 (**NS**), TA 302, 303, 305, 307-309, 311-315 (**PD**)
02.01	TA 304, 306, 310, 316-358	TA 304, 306, 310, 316 (**PD**), TA 317-333 (**TL**), TA 334-358 (**TB**)
06.01	TA 359-368, 370-376, 378, 380, 382, 386, 389, 392, 393, 397, 398, 400	TA 359-368, 370-376, 378, 380, 382, 386, 389 (**BK**), TA 392, 393, 397, 398, 400 (**SD**)
07.01	TA 377, 379, 381, 384, 385, 388, 401, 404, 406, 407, TAS 436, 441	TA 377, 379, 381, 384, 385, 388 (**BK**), TA 401, 404, 406, 407 (**SD**),TAS 436, 441 (**NS**)
08.01	TA 391, 395, 409	TA 391, 395 (**SD**), TA 409 (**T**)
	TAS 437, 438, 440, 443, 445-448, 450, 452-456, 458, 462, 464, 470	TAS 437, 438, 440, 443, 445-448, 450, 452-456, 458, 462, 464 (**NS**), TAS 470 (**TL**)
09.01	TA 369, 383, 387, 390, 394, 396, 399, 403, 405, 408, 410-417, 423-435	TA 369, 383, 387, 390 (**BK**), TA 394, 396, 399, 403, 405, 408 (**SD**)
	TAS 439, 451, 457, 459, 466	TA 410-417, 423-427 (**T**), TA 428-435 (**NS**), TAS 439, 451, 457, 459, 466 (**NS**)

Date	Deliveries	Licensed for Service
10.01	TA 418-422	TA 418-422 (**T**)
	TAS 441, 442, 444, 449, 460, 463,	TAS 441, 442, 444, 449, 460, 463, 465 (**NS**),
	465, 467, 469, 473-482, 484, 486-503,	TAS 467, 469, 471-482, 484 , 500 (**TL**),
	505, 506, 508-518	TAS 486-499, 501 (**BW**),
		TAS 503, 505, 506, 508-518 (**SD**)
11.01	TAS 468, 483, 485, 504, 507, 519-525	TAS 468, 483, 485 (**TL**),
		TAS 504, 507, 519-522 (**SD**)
12.01	TAS 461, 532-534	TAS 523, 525 (**TL**)
01.02	TAS 526, 527, 529	TAS 461 (**NS**), TAS 485, 533, 534 (**TL**)
02.02	TAS 528	TAS 526, 527, 529, 532 (**TL**)
03.02	TAS 530, 531	TAS 528, 531 (**TL**)
05.02	TAS 535, 536, 538	TAS 530 (**TL**)
06.02	TAS 537, 539-551	
07.02	TAS 552-560	TAS 535 (**NS**), TAS 536-560 (**SD**)
10.02	TAS 561-591	TAS 561-566 (**SD**), TAS 567-584 (**TL**)
12.02	TA 592-614, 650-659	TAS 585-591 (**TL**),
		TA 592-597, 599, 600, 601, 607 (**T**)
01.03		17598, 17602-17606, 17608-17611,
		17731-17733 (**T**)
02.03	17750-17768	17750-17757 (**BW**), 17758-17768 (**SD**)
03.03	17769-17791, 17793-17800, 17854s	17769-17781 (**SD**), 17782-17787 (**BW**),
		17788-17791, 17793-17800 (**T**), 17854s (**BW**)
04.03	17792, 17801-17819, 17826, 17827,	17792, 17801-17819, 17826, 17827 (**T**),
	17834-17847	17834-17847 (**U**)
05.03	17820-17825, 17828-17832,	17820-17825, 17828-17832 (**T**),
	17848-17853, 17855-17859,	17848-17850, 17889, 17890 (**U**),
	17889-17895	17851-17853 (**PD**), 17855-17859 (**BK**)
06.03	17833, 17860-17878, 17896-17908	17833 (**T**), 17860-17863 (**BK**),
		17864, 17865, 17891, 17903, 17904 (**U**),
		17866-17878, 17892-17902, 17905-17908 (**PD**),
07.03	17879-17888, 17909-17933	17885, 17912, 17921, 17923, 17927, 17928 (**BW**)
08.03		17879-17884, 17886-17888, 17909-17911,
		17913-17920, 17922, 17924-17926,
		17929-17933 (**BW**)
12.03	17934-17947, 17949, 17950,	17934-17942, 17949, 17952 (**PD**)
	17952, 17953, 17957, 17961,	
	17965-17968, 17961	
01.04	17948, 17951, 17954-17956,	17943-17948, 17950, 17951, 17953-17964 (**PD**),
	17958-17960, 17962-17964,	17965-17975 (**TB**), 17976s-17984s (**NS**)
	17969, 17970, 17972-17975	
	17976s-17984s	
02.04	17985s-17999s	17985s-17997s (**NS**)
03.04		17998s (**NS**)
04.04	18201-18205	
05.04	18206-18227, 18246, 18247	17999s (**NS**), 18201-18218 (**BW**)
06.04	18228-18234, 18236-18239,	18219-18228, 18233, 18236-18238, 18248,
	18248-18252, 18254-18259	18251, 18254, 18255 (**BW**),
		18229-18232, 18234, 18239, 18246, 18247,
		18252 (**T**)
07.04	18235, 18240-18245, 18253	18235 (BW), 18240-18245, 18253, 18256 (**T**),
		18257-18259 (**U**)
09.04	18260-18265	18260-18265 (**U**)
02.05	18266-18277	18266-18277 (**SD**)
08.05	18451-18454	18451-18454 (**NS**)
09.05	18455-18469	18455-18462 (**NS**), 18463-18469 (**SD**)
10.05	18470-18480	18470-18480 (**SD**)
02.06	18481-18488	18481-18488 (**TL**)
03.06	18489-18499	18489-18499 (**TL**)

Re-registrations

11.99   TA 100 from V474 KJN to WLT 491
01.00   TA 99 from V473 KJN to VLT 14
03.00   TA 101 from V475 KJN to WLT 461
12.00   TAS 260 from X374 NNO to WLT 575
10.01   TAS 444 from Y523 NHK to LX51 FKO
12.03   17879 from LX03 NGN to 527 CLT
08.06   17890 from LX03 OPZ to WLT 890
11.07   17100 from WLT 491 to V474 KJN
11.07   17890 from WLT 890 to LX03 OPZ
02.09   17099 from VLT 14 to V473 KJN
07.09   17101 from WLT 461 to V475 KJN
08.09   17879 from 527 CLT to LX03 NGN
11.10   17260 from WLT 575 to X374 NNO

Renumbered, 06.01.03

TA 1-73, 75-222 to 17001-17073, 17075-17222
TAS 223-260 to 17223s-17260s
TA 261-401, 403-435 to 17261-17401, 17403-17435
TAS 436-591 to 17436s-17591s
TA 592-611 to 17592-17611
TA 612-614 to 17731-17733
TA 650-659 to 17775-17784 and then to 17740-17749

Loaned from Stagecoach East Midland, 24.03.04-03.04.04
18121, 18122, 18124-18126 (YN04 KGE/F/G/K/P)

Loaned from Wealden PSV, 09.10.08-30.04.09
18875-18885 (T402, 411 SMV, LV51 YCN/O/C/E/F/G/J/K, T403 SMV)

Loaned from Metroline, 10.10.08-24.04.09
18886-18896 (T67-69, 37, 43, 74-76, 87, 78, 61 KLD)
18897-18900 (LR52 KVS/T, KXB/N)

Loaned from Stagecoach Manchester, 12.01.15-15.02.15
17002, 17010, 17011, 17567 (S802, 810, 811 BWC, LV52 HEJ)

Disposals

03.03	17002-17004, 17007-17010
04.03	17005, 17006, 17011-17013, 17015, 17016, 17020-17022, 17025
05.03	17014, 17017-17019, 17026-17029, 17031-17035
06.03	17023, 17024, 17030, 17036-17038, 17050-17052, 17055
07.03	17054, 17056-17059
09.03	17076, 17078, 17079
10.03	17053
01.04	17067-17069
02.04	17066, 17070, 17071
03.04	17072, 17073, 17075, 17077
01.05	17369
04.05	17060, 17061
07.05	17758
11.05	17081, 17146, 17872
05.06	17039-17047, 17062, 17063
02.07	17048, 17049
11.07	17532
07.09	17088, 17089, 17091, 17093, 17095, 17096, 17098
08.09	17064, 17065, 17080, 17082, 17085, 17087, 17090, 17092, 17094, 17097
09.09	17083, 17110, 17121-17123, 17135, 17137, 17147
10.09	17108, 17110, 17115, 17125
11.09	17084, 17086
02.10	17592-17596, 17598, 17599, 17601, 17603-17609
03.10	17189, 17250, 17542, 17597, 17600, 17602, 17610, 17611, 17731-17733
04.10	17139, 17410, 17411
	Reinstated: 17108, 17135, 17137
06.10	17108, 17118, 17124, 17131, 17132, 17135, 17137, 17191
07.10	17116, 17117, 17119, 17133, 17139, 17142, 17365
12.10	17492
02.11	17138, 17155
03.11	17148, 17150, 17156, 17158, 17173, 17176, 17179, 17201, 17204, 17269, 17271-17276, 17283, 17287, 17325
04.11	17099, 17106, 17107, 17264-17266, 17329-17333, 17388
05.11	17114, 17145, 17154, 17160, 17163, 17168, 17169, 17187, 17188, 17210, 17213, 17223, 17235-17237, 17284, 17320, 17327, 17334, 17335, 17337
06.11	17126, 17128, 17194, 17212, 17267, 17281, 17290, 17301, 17328, 17332, 17336
	Reinstated: 17333
07.11	17100, 17102, 17127, 17129, 17130, 17166, 17167, 17170, 17175, 17180, 17192, 17196, 17221, 17241, 17261-17263, 17277, 17299, 17333
08.11	17134, 17136, 17149, 17151, 17157, 17159, 17161, 17162, 17171, 17172, 17174, 17177, 17178, 17193, 17195, 17197-17200, 17202, 17211, 17214, 17216, 17218, 17225, 17239, 17240, 17242, 17244, 17245, 17251, 17253, 17255, 17268, 17296, 17298-17300, 17303-17306, 17309-17311, 17312, 17315, 17316, 17318, 17321, 17338
10.11	17140, 17144, 17152, 17153, 17222, 17212, 17286, 17293, 17297, 17313, 17324
11.11	17294, 17295
12.11	17185, 17289
02.12	17548
03.12	17101, 17103, 17141, 17143, 17164, 17165, 17181-17184, 17190, 17203, 17205-17209, 17215, 17219, 17220, 17226-17229, 17234, 17238, 17246-17249, 17252, 17256, 17257, 17270, 17278-17280, 17282, 17291, 17292, 17302, 17326, 17412, 17417
04.12	17285, 17308, 17314, 17317, 17319, 17323, 17339, 17341, 17343, 17345, 17350, 17366
05.12	17371, 17375, 17376, 17384, 17385, 17389-17391
06.12	17112, 17224, 17232, 17233, 17254, 17258-17260, 17307, 17340, 17349, 17352-17355, 17357-17361, 17420, 17433
08.12	17231, 17243, 17344, 17346, 17356, 17367, 17373, 17377, 17382, 17386, 17400
09.12	17405, 17406, 17413-17416, 17418, 17421, 17422, 17428, 17429, 17436-17439, 17442, 17456-17459, 17461-17464, 17468, 17471-17475, 17477
10.12	17403, 17465, 17476, 17480, 17481, 17483, 17513, 17514, 17533, 17534, 17544

Disposals

11.12	17383, 17387, 17392-17394, 17539, 17558
12.12	17105, 17347, 17348, 17351, 17370, 17372, 17374, 17378-17381, 17424, 17430, 17435, 17455, 17470
02.13	17111, 17113, 17446, 17479, 17502
03.13	17496
04.13	17469, 17579, 17584
05.13	17109, 17491
06.13	17104
08.13	17230, 17342, 17401, 17407, 17423, 17432, 17445, 17447, 17450, 17482, 17510
09.13	17408, 17431, 17433, 17440, 17444, 17453, 17467, 17488, 17512, 17515, 17517, 17518, 17747
10.13	17531
12.13	17541
02.14	18251
03.14	17485, 17543, 17546
06.14	17563, 17568
08.14	17425, 17448, 17449, 17452, 17484, 17486, 17493, 17494, 17497, 17499-17501, 17504, 17507, 17511, 17516, 17519-17522, 17524, 17527, 17535, 17549, 17561, 17567, 17575, 17578, 17591, 17740-17744, 17785-17787
09.14	17525, 17571, 18221-18231, 18234, 18235
10.14	17523, 17540, 17552, 17562, 17569
11.14	17451, 17454, 17460, 17498, 17508, 17547, 17550, 17554, 17555, 17560, 17565, 17571, 17576, 17577, 17582, 17586
12.14	17489, 17490, 17495, 17528, 17529, 17536, 17538, 17553, 17566, 17582, 17585, 17587, 17590, 17790

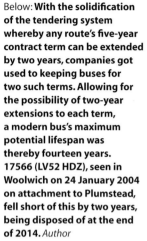

Below: **With the solidification of the tendering system whereby any route's five-year contract term can be extended by two years, companies got used to keeping buses for two such terms. Allowing for the possibility of two-year extensions to each term, a modern bus's maximum potential lifespan was thereby fourteen years. 17566 (LV52 HDZ), seen in Woolwich on 24 January 2004 on attachment to Plumstead, fell short of this by two years, being disposed of at the end of 2014.** *Author*

Disposals

01.15	17487, 17509, 17526, 17586
02.15	17580
03.15	17478, 17503, 17545, 17551, 17570, 17588, 17589, 17751-17757, 17781-17784, 17805
04.15	17441, 17466, 17505, 17506, 17573, 17794, 17801
05.15	17559, 17572, 17574, 17803, 17804, 17806
06.15	17895
07.15	17556, 17557, 17812
09.15	17530, 17581, 17583, 17745, 17746, 17802, 17839
12.15	17819
02.16	17789, 17798, 17922, 17945-17949, 17954, 17957, 17964-17975
04.16	17362, 17950, 17986, 17987
05.16	17419, 18232, 18233, 18239, 18242, 18243, 18245-18250, 18254, 18255
06.16	17910, 17911, 17916, 17918, 17920, 17943, 18241, 18244, 18252
07.16	17398, 17404, 17792, 17793, 17829, 17830, 17835, 17846, 17867-17869, 17874, 17909, 17912-17915, 17917, 17919, 17921, 17925, 17926, 18236-18238, 18240, 18253, 18256
09.16	17759-17778, 17808, 17854
10.16	17809, 17870
11.16	17409, 17748, 17797, 17942
03.17	17750
04.17	17816, 17817, 17821, 17828, 17866, 17893, 17907
05.17	17815, 17816, 17818, 17820-17828, 17871, 17879, 17896, 17908
06.17	17564, 17841, 17878
07.17	17795, 17873
09.17	17779, 17780, 17813, 17814, 17831, 17832, 17847-17850, 17852, 17853, 17865, 17880-17891, 17897, 17901-17905, 17934, 17935-17941, 17944, 17951-17953, 17955, 17956, 17958-17963, 17998
12.17	17898, 17899, 18201, 18213
01.18	18207, 18219
02.18	18202, 18210
03.18	17788, 17988, 17993, 18216, 18452, 18476, 18480
06.18	17837, 18275, 18464, 18481
08.18	17923, 17924, 17927-17933, 18257-18265
09.18	17807
10.18	17749, 17840, 17845, 17900, 17976, 17992, 17995, 18215, 18485, 18491-18493
11.18	17877
12.18	17844, 17855, 17856, 17875, 17906, 17977, 17990, 17991, 17996, 17997, 18204, 18206, 18214, 18217, 18269, 18453, 18460, 18466, 18468, 18469, 18486, 18487, 18494
02.19	17859, 17994, 18203, 18277
03.19	18218, 18273, 18274
04.19	17857, 18266, 18271, 18467, 18471, 18473-18475, 18482, 18496, 18497
05.19	17861, 17989, 18205, 18268, 18451
06.19	17363, 17368, 17399, 17427, 17434, 18267, 18459, 18462
07.19	17426, 17860, 17861, 18220, 18272, 18454, 18455, 18461, 18472, 18488
08.19	17834, 17851, 17858, 18276, 18458, 18478, 18484
09.19	17001, 17791, 17864, 17979, 18211, 18212, 18457, 18463, 18465, 18495
10.19	17364, 18208, 18270
11.19	17395-17397, 17810, 17811, 17833, 17862, 17863
12.19	17836, 17843, 17876, 17981
04.20	17838, 17842

First

TN, TAL, TNL and TNA classes

Within eighteen months of its acquisition of Centrewest from its management, FirstGroup added Capital Citybus to its London holdings on 3 July 1998, and operations soon began to converge. Centrewest had already been awarded back its existing route 18 on tender, and this was chosen to be the host for 30 new Plaxton President-bodied Dennis Tridents, an order being placed in July 1998 for 1999 delivery. These would also encompass the 23 at evenings and weekends and the N18, N23 and N139 at night, all of which were M-operated from Westbourne Park.

First Capital was already intending to take an East Lancs-bodied Trident for evaluation when one became available, but for the moment it had the 1 and W8, won from neighbours during 1998, to provision and 22 more Tridents with President bodies were added to the order, with deliveries to run concurrently and in a common numbering sequence. Shortly after that, First Capital won the 25, which would need thirty new double-deckers.

In December Centrewest hired a Trident demonstrator and tested it out over the 18 and 207 roads; the 207 was out to tender by now and would be a strong possibility if retained.

As 1999 got going, the Tridents' number series was firmed up, combining Centrewest's London Transport-derived class codes with First Capital's numerics to produce TN 801-822. In March thirty-four more TNs were ordered for the 25 and the East Lancs-bodied demonstrator was no longer needed.

With the takeover of the 25 set for 26 June it would be a race against time to get as many TNs delivered and into service as possible,

Right: **The rush to get TNs into service and thereby displace buses needed for the 25 was such that the vinyl parts of their livery were applied later, producing an all-red look that would become all too familiar within a few years. For now, TfL indulged First Capital's brightly lit-up front panels and comprehensive blinds of a standard of excellence not seen since the RT family. After a brief flowering and then cruelly sudden decline, the 1 had regained a sense of stability by 1999 and was ready to expand again, with an extension from the Surrey Quays terminus, where Dagenham's TN 805 (T805 LLC) is pulling in on 25 August, to the new Canada Water station as a complement to the Jubilee Line Extension.** *Author*

Right: **Northumberland Park's W8 had spent nine months under Metrobuses since its takeover by what was now First Capital, but after a couple of temporary deployments while several batches of new Tridents were delivered concurrently, settled with a reasonably stable batch of ten TNs. TN 811 (T811 LLC) is seen at Edmonton Green on 28 June 1999, but this bus would move on to Dagenham within the year.** *Author*

but if that wasn't the case, the stalwart band of second-hand Metrobuses currently occupying the W8 and 1 would play their part. A new livery was introduced with the TNs, where First's willow-leaf device was carried as part of a bodyside stripe in white and yellow; it was tested on Arrow 417 and further refined on TN 802, which had an extra white stripe at the front that was not subsequently adopted.

With weeks to spare, the first TNs started arriving in June and were deployed to Dagenham's 1 from the 11th, but the need to release Ms to furnish a two-week emergency contract on the 23 was perceived as greater and the TNs available entered service in all-red and with KM/NN blinds fitted in the wider blind boxes. Then, the 25's start on the 26th saw as many TNs as possible commence First Capital's contract out of Dagenham. To

Left: **It will be seen that the yellow front band on TN 802 (T802 LLC) is carried slightly higher, as a white band of similar height was worn underneath until removed to standardise with the livery decided on for the rest of the TNs. It is seen in Oxford Street on 30 September 1999, by which time Dagenham's extremely busy 25 had its full complement of Tridents.** *Author*

Right: **Illustrating the opposite circumstance from page 103, TN 819 (T819 LLC) is seen at Tottenham Court Road on 31 August 1999 but would settle as a Northumberland Park bus. The 25 operated via Bank on Mondays to Fridays but diverted past the Tower at weekends, so part of the blind displays on this route showed a specific via point encased in a dedicated shape (that for the Tower was indeed sort of tower-shaped, with a little battlement!).** *Author*

release Ms to back them up, the 1 was turned over to ten ex-Stagecoach Selkent Leyland Olympians (Ls) hired from Ensignbus. On the 24th Northumberland Park's W8 (and night N1) began operating TNs.

Westbourne Park's intake was now revised to thirty-one, comprising TNs 823-853, and TN 819 was loaned between 15-

25 June to train the 18's drivers. This batch commenced delivery in July and was put into service beginning on the 9th, releasing Ms to Dagenham and see off the Ls while TNs 854-887 were awaited.

There would be more Tridents coming, as the 207 was indeed won from June. This time the buses, to be shared between

Right: **Otherwise identical to their First Capital siblings, Centrewest's TNs for the 18 at Westbourne Park could be distinguished by the continued use of standard-sized white fleetnumbers. TN 830 (T830 LLC) is seen at Warren Street on 5 August 1999.** *Author*

Above: **The offside view of a Westbourne Park TN on its regular Sunday deployment; the 23 was otherwise RML-operated and would remain so until 2004. The Gold Arrow appellation that had been superseded by First as an identity is vestigial on buses like TN 823 (T823 LLC), in Oxford Street on 25 July 1999, and would wither away before long.** *Author*

Uxbridge and Acton Tram Depot, would be longer versions coded TNL. And further to that, the Walthamstow-area tenders to be implemented at the start of 2000 came out well for First Capital, with the 97 and 357 (97A) scheduled for conversion to low-floor double-deckers.

The 18's conversion was complete by August, allowing debut Notting Hill Carnival appearances on the 7, 28, 31 and 328, though a handful of Ms stayed put at Westbourne Park. Then followed the 25's batch, which not only allowed the balance of TN 801-810 to gather as planned at Northumberland

Left: **After the 1, W8 and 18 were completed it was time to finish off the 25, resulting in the entry into service of all 87 of the first order for TNs by the autumn. Coming through Ilford town centre on its way west on 2 September 1999 is TN 873 (T873 KLF).** *Author*

Above: **With such a large and extremely diverse fleet, First Capital's Dagenham was in the habit of putting out whatever was available rather than let a route go without a bus, and soon enough its new intake of TNs began to drift away from the 1 and 25. The 123 was an early conquest, otherwise run by fast all-Leyland Olympians but on 8 September 1999 at Wood Green host to TN 878 (T878 KLF).** *Author*

Park but released Ms to ease ex-Mainline examples out of the company. TNs 854-887 straddled the T/V registration-letter change now applying from 1 September, resulting in an unholy mess as vehicles were delivered out of order due to the need to fit them with ticket machines. Some already T-registered TNs thus found themselves re-registered with V-marks and even vice-versa! TN 887 was the last, after making an appearance at Coach & Bus in Birmingham on 5-7 October. Dagenham's now extensive fleet was soon seen on the 123, 179 and 369 plus school route 645, while Northumberland Park's would visit the equivalent journey on the 20.

The TNs may have ticked boxes through being both new and low-floor, but their capacity on the busy N25 was quickly found to be patently inadequate and Arrows were substituted from 13 August; to that end, the 22 Tridents ordered against the 97 and 357 were, like the 207's forthcoming batch of 43, also 10.6m examples but this time with Alexander ALX400 bodywork.

The 1 was extended from Surrey Quays to Canada Water on 18 September, tying in with the new Jubilee Line Extension, but the extra PVR on this route was furnished by a quickly changing succession of additional operators, beginning with Blue Triangle.

The new contracts for the 207 and night counterpart N207 applied from 13 November, with the new TNLs expected the following April. To make available their expected stock numbers following on from the existing TNs, Volvo Olympians VN 888-907 were renumbered VN 88-107.

After a New Year's Eve in which a TN worked an N253 extra, 2000 got going with the extension of the N1 from Plumstead to Thamesmead on 8 January; it was also reallocated from Northumberland Park to Dagenham.

The Walthamstow network was introduced on 26 February, but the 97 and 357 were set going with existing vehicles due to the new TALs not being delivered. In any case they were now ordered redeployed to

the 25 for a capacity increase, which would displace an equivalent number of TNs to Northumberland Park.

The 207's long-wheelbase Tridents comprised TNLs 888-930 and Uxbridge's allocation was phased in first, beginning on 17 February. This garage soon spread its new acquisitions to the N207 (as planned) and 222, 607 and school route 697 (which weren't), while lending them to Acton Tram Depot to train that garage's own drivers. Acton Tram Depot's allocation followed in April, service running commencing on the 22nd, and the whole 207 was completed by June.

On 27 April TALs 931-952 began entering service at Dagenham and that batch was all in place by June, allowing TNs to take over the 97 and 357 out of Northumberland Park. At the latter, TN wanderings commenced, the 215 being the first non-scheduled route to see the new type.

On 29 April the N1 was rerouted to terminate at the daytime 1's stand at Tottenham Court Road rather than Trafalgar Square. Similarly the N25 was withdrawn between Oxford Circus and Trafalgar Square and its Barkingside leg projected to Hainault. Similar standardisations affected Centrewest's N98 and N207, both of which were rerouted to Holborn, Red Lion Square.

In May Centrewest won the 27 from London United. Shortly after came another boost with the announcement of the retention of the 258 but with a conversion to double-deck and thus more Tridents, though ordered weren't placed until later in the year. Of the N18, N98 and N139, tendered in April, the latter pair were lost to Metroline.

After trouble finding an operator who could stick with them, the extras on the 1 were taken over by Dagenham on 5 June.

This year's Notting Hill Carnival extras now included TNLs from both Uxbridge and Acton Tram Depot as guests on the 31 and 328 alongside Westbourne Park's own TNs visiting for the two days.

Right: **At 10.5m length the Dennis Trident took on new elegance, being better proportioned and, more importantly for the people who would be travelling on them, carrying more seats. The TAL class, ordered against the 97 and 357 but in the event set going on the 25, seated 68. Seen coming out of Stratford's busy bus station on 7 July 2001 is TAL 947 (W947 ULL).** *Author*

Right: **Those TNs displaced from Dagenham by the entry into service of the TALs found their way to Northumberland Park, where they replaced Metrobuses from the 97 and 357. TN 862 (V862 HBY) is caught leaving Chingford bus station on 23 July 2000.** *Author*

Left: **TN 816 (T816 LLC)**
was already based at
Northumberland Park for the
W8 but from the spring of
2000 added the 97 and 357 to
its remit. On 9 May it is coming
round the second incarnation
of Walthamstow Central bus
station. *Author*

11 September saw the takeover of the 27 as planned, but no new-vehicle order had yet been revealed so Ms and LLWs had to step in. An unlikely side-effect saw the reallocation of the 7 on Sundays from Westbourne Park to Acton Tram Depot and conversion on that day from DW to TNL.

In November the 105 was announced as retained and would be gaining new low-floor double-deckers. This was when the order for this route and the 27 and 258 was formally announced as 47 TNs. Existing Westbourne Park TNs were seen trying out the 27 during December, though without blinds.

In December came an order for 36 more TNLs; ten would displace the 25's minority TNs to the 191 in fulfilment of that route's concurrent contract award and the rest would take over the 123 in accordance with the 'Bus Plus' initiative.

Left: **From 22-seat Dart SLFs to**
full-size double-deckers was
a sea change for passengers
of the 7 on Sundays, but
Westbourne Park didn't have
the capacity and Acton Tram
Depot did. On 29 October 2000
TNL 897 (V897 HLH) is calling
at East Acton. *Author*

Right: **First had started off its Westbourne Park-based contract on the 27 with the reliable but by now very elderly Metrobuses, waiting until TNs were delivered. These duly arrived in February 2001 and are represented in Turnham Green on the 25th of that month by TN 963 (X963 HLT).** *Author*

Right: **Then came the batch of TNs for the 258 at Alperton, personified at Harrow & Wealdstone on 5 March 2002 by TN 978 (X978 HLT). Despite the addition of a second TN-operated route (79) by the end of 2001, Trident operation would be relatively shortlived at this garage, which subsequently standardised on Volvo B7TLs.** *Author*

Right: **The third batch of TNs for Centrewest in 2001 consisted of seventeen, which restored the upper deck to the 105 in place of its London Buslines-liveried Dart SLFs. On 28 July Greenford's TN 999 (Y933 NLP) is in the midst of making the right turn into Greenford Broadway.** *Author*

2000 ended with the appearance of TAL 951 on the 510's last day, 30 December. On 27 January 2001 the 258's new contract from Alperton commenced and 3 February saw the N98 and N139 leave for Metroline. Between 13-27 February the 27 (and just-introduced N27) at Westbourne Park was converted to Trident operation with TNs 954-973 and Alperton's 258 was supplied between 1-14 March with TNs 974-983. Wanderings to the 83 and 92 soon ensued.

February 2001 saw more options for new low-floor double-deckers with the award to and retention by First Capital of the 165, 252 and 365, and the retention of the 179 in April foresaw more still. Then in May the 79 was won from Metroline London Northern and specified for low-floor double-deckers.

The 105 was duly set going again on 30 June with TN 984-1000 operating from Greenford in lieu of the previous London Buslines 'DMLs'. An N105 at night was introduced at the same time and visits to the E1 were now possible, if rare in practice. This batch, unfortunately, had DDA-width blinds with only two lines of via points, and worse standards were to come. By this point

the operation was collectively known as First London, though the appropriate fleetnames took longer to remove or change and the company identities remained the same. First Capital East and First Capital North were now the official names behind Dagenham and Northumberland Park garages respectively. New blind inserts produced for the latter by July permitted TN appearances on the 76, 97, 191, 259, 263 and 341 and occurrences were soon regular.

On 15 October six articulated buses were added to the 207's regular TNL runout as an experiment that would foreshadow the future direction of this route. The same month saw another TN order placed for seventeen against the 91, announced as retained in July.

The autumn of 2001 saw a slew of Trident deliveries into First Capital, tying in with the contract renewal dates of the 252 and 365 on 29 September and the 179 on 20 October. First, however, the 25's conversion to 10.6m TAL/TNL was completed with the input of TNLs 1001-1012 into Dagenham between 28 September and early October, which allowed TNs to leave for Northumberland Park and the 191. After that it was time to rectify the

Below: **The 25 was one of those routes that would absorb any service increase you cared to throw at it and still beg for more. Having already partially upgraded to long-wheelbase TAL, it still needed more higher-capacity buses and accordingly ten TNLs were added in October 2001. The wider blinds pioneered by Capital Citybus had now been forcibly replaced by the inferior DDA-satisfying compromise (which on this bus should have had a lower-case destination blind), whilst the new registration system, which permitted the use of the letter Z for the first time, is shown on TNL 1007 (LK51 UZE), calling at Holborn on 15 October 2001.** *Author*

Above: **The impetus towards accessibility didn't quite coincide with the availability of new buses with capacity enough to handle both wheelchair users and regular passengers, so early conversions were carried out with Dart SLF-sized single-deckers and suffered accordingly. One such was the 257, until moves were made to replace its DMLs quickly, and one of the new Tridents delivered to Hackney in the autumn of 2001 to do this was TNL 1020 (LK51 UYX), seen at Walthamstow Central on 21 November. Although the post-September 2001 registrations mandated a thinner, 51mm-wide character set, a die has been used for this batch with the previous (and much more readable) 57mm width.** *Author*

mistake made by converting the extremely busy 257 to DML operation earlier in the year; three Ms had already been added as extras but from 10-17 November the whole route was double-decked, with TNLs 1013-1032. Before going to Hackney as intended, these too wandered to the gamut of Northumberland Park routes, though without blinds at first. Then, TNLs 1033-1036 were deployed to Dagenham to start off the 123.

The input of TNs and TNLs into the east was broken on 24 November with the takeover of the 79, which commenced from Alperton with TNs 1037-1047.

On 1 December the 1 (and N1) was reallocated from Dagenham to Hackney, taking with it TNs 801-812. Another irregular shoppers' route to come off at this time was the 511, which saw TNL 1016 out on its last day (7 December). During December

Right: **The 79 was taken over on 24 November 2001 and also gained back its upper deck. TN 1046 (LN51 DVL) is seen at Wembley Central on the first day of Alperton operation; its batch would subsequently move multiple times.** *Author*

TNs 1048-1071 arrived for the 179 and 365, followed by TNLs 1072-1099 for the 123 and 252, though mixing was inevitable, as well as visits to the 165, 296 and 369.

More TNs were in the offing with the award to and retention by First of the E1 and E3 in December, the latter representing a conversion to double-deck operation. Meanwhile, the 91 and N91 started their new contracts on 2 February 2002, expecting TNs 1113-1129.

On 23 March 2002 Dagenham closed for rebuilding and its routes were transferred to a new site at Rainham (R); for the purposes of this book the Trident-operated routes that made the move were the 25, 123, 179, 252, 365 and N25. On 27 April Westbourne Park gained back part of the 7 on Sundays, using DMLs. This was the day of a hefty increase to the 207, for now using eleven of the 91's intended TNs until eleven more TNLs could be delivered to furnish it. The

Left: **The long-wheelbase TNLs looked good in First's livery; a batch replaced the 123's all-Leyland Olympians over the cusp of 2001/02 and on 6 May 2002 TNL 1072 (LN51 GOC), still with part of its fleetnumber to be applied even after transfer from Dagenham to Rainham, is setting off from Wood Green.** *Author*

Left: **There were also TNs in First Capital's autumn 2001 intake, intended for the 179 and 365 but in reality mixing freely with the TNLs coming at the same time for the 123 and 252. At Chingford station on 29 March 2002 we see TN 1065 (LN51 GKZ).** *Author*

Right: **On 9 March 2002 Dagenham's TNL 1005 (LK51 UZC) from the 25's batch is seen at Romford on the 252.** *Author*

Right: **The 207 was also due ten TNLs for a big boost to its frequency, but until they arrived the TNs intended for the 91 had to step in. Here at Ealing Broadway on 20 May 2002 is TN 1120 (LT02 NWC).** *Author*

artic accompaniment was withdrawn. TNs 1113-1118 nonetheless started off the 91 at Northumberland Park.

In April Dagenham's TAL 951 was chosen as one of the fifty buses to go into gold livery in celebration of the Queen's Golden Jubilee. The group's additional Trident participation consisted of TN 832 (Westbourne Park for the 18), TN 963 (likewise but for the 27) and TN 1113 (Northumberland Park for the 91). The contract was until the end of 2002, TAL 951 being the last back into red in May 2003.

New route RV1 introduced on 27 April 2002 was operated by EC-class Mercedes-Benz Citaros, but Hackney's own TNLs soon turned out in strength.

TNLs 1130-1140 duly arrived in May and were added to Uxbridge's fleet, releasing TNs 1119-1129, but the latter lingered within 'Centrewest' through a temporary deployment to Greenford to start off the E1 and E3 from their contract commencement date on the 25th, until enough of those route's intended buses from the TN 1141-1177 batch had arrived. The interim TNs carried lazy blinds and lasted until mid-June, but even after that they had work to do before they could join their fellows on the 91. Seven were transferred to Hackney for the double-decking of the D7 from 20 July and four went to Rainham, although the boost to the 25 for which these ones were intended was cancelled. Hackney's D6 thus began to see the odd TN.

Above: **New route RV1 was meant to meander serenely between tourist attractions for the benefit of international visitors, but it became an unlikely conduit into the West End for commuters spilling out of Waterloo. Its inaugural Citaros were immediately backed up by Hackney's TNLs already in residence for the 257, and on 27 May 2002 TNL 1020 (LK51 UYX) is seen at Waterloo. The need to replace a skirt panel has unwittingly clipped off the ends of First's leaf-shaped pair of side stripes.**
Author

Right: **Finally the 91 got its TNs, but a photo like this one of Northumberland Park's TN 1117 (LT02 NVZ), early in the morning of 27 May 2002, was only possible for a few more months, as on 1 September 2002 the north side of Trafalgar Square was pedestrianised.** *Author*

Left: **At the same time as a handful of the 91's TNs were bedding on the Uxbridge-operated extra duties on the 207, still more from that batch got the E1 and E3 started; the latter represented a welcome upgrade to double-deck and is seen in the person of TN 1125 (LT02 NVN) at Greenford Broadway on 25 May 2002. The ultimate blind is most interesting and is of a type since outlawed.** *Author*

Left: **The 105's batch of TNs could also be counted on to assist on the E1 and E3 when they started assuming the type and soon became intermixed. This short but busy route E1 journey has just come to an end on 25 May 2002 and TN 997 (Y997 NLP) is about to proceed to stand at Greenford Broadway.** *Author*

Left: **TN 988 (Y988 NLP) from the same batch hasn't managed to muster a blind when seen at Acton Town Station on 24 June 2002.** *Author*

The E1 and E3 were wholly TN by July and were followed from August by TNs 1178-1199, the 295's intended batch. The first four went into service immediately at Westbourne Park, covering a PVR increase to the 18 from 14 September, and eight more were sent to Alperton, where an increase to the 83 applied from the same day. The extra TNs into Westbourne Park allowed the Sunday allocation on the 7 to convert from DML. At night, the N23 was reallocated to Alperton but the rest of the N18 was taken back in exchange.

In August the 282 was announced as retained with the promise of new low-floor double-deck buses, and in October one of the Uxbridge-area routes announced as won, the U4, was specified for the same.

First had now discovered the Volvo B7TL and increasingly orders were for this type rather than for the Trident; a batch of VTLs into Alperton for the 83 during October released the interim TNs; not only did the 295's batch pass to Westbourne Park as intended, but the well-travelled remainder finally took up their place on the

Right: **Also DML-operated, the 295 was far too busy for single-deckers (as it had been for DRLs in 1993) and TNs were ordered the next time its contract was awarded. Seen laying over at Clapham Junction on 21 September 2002 is Westbourne Park-allocated TN 1195 (LT52 XAF).** *Author*

Right: **After a batch each of VTL- and VFL-class Volvo B7TLs, the TN class resumed with those taken for the 414, a new route altogether. Despite shadowing the 14 all the way from Putney Bridge Station to Hyde Park Corner, it then skated off up Park Lane and the Edgware Road without actually taking passengers into the West End where they really needed to go. On 5 April 2003, TN 1232 (LT52 WXK), another Westbourne Park motor, is seen at Hyde Park Corner.** *Author*

91 at Northumberland Park in replacement of Volvo Olympians 224-238 (minus 225, destroyed by fire earlier). Alperton also converted the 79 to VTL, sending TNs 1037-1047 to Rainham for another big hike to the 25 from 23 November and passing the 258's X-registered examples to Westbourne Park to help start off new route 414. This was one of the routes drawn up in connection with the forthcoming introduction of the Congestion Charge and in this case awarded to First London. Commencing on 23 November, its intended batch comprised new TNs 1229-

1248 from Westbourne Park. These had gasket-glazed windows, after unhappy experience replacing bonded versions that had been ruined by etching.

2003 began with the standardisation of the evening and Sunday service on the 7 as Westbourne Park TNs, the Acton Tram Depot TNL allocation coming off. This change, on 1 February, was accompanied by the takeover by Westbourne Park of the 10 as an OPO route, whose scheduled VFL-class Volvo B7TLs were immediately bulked out by existing TNs. Another new route was the 476

and Northumberland Park TNs could soon be found alongside its own batch of new Volvos (in this case VTLs).

On 8 March the 282 at Greenford began its new contract and its buses would follow in April as TN 1277-1293. The final batch of TNs for First London were TNs 1328-1342, delivered in May for Uxbridge's U4, whose contract applied from the 3rd of the month.

Something quite different was in the offing for the 18; to accompany its contract renewal (extended from 23 August to 15 November), it would be converted to artic operation out of a new garage. This would accompany the OPO conversion of the 23, which had 44 more TALs ordered for it. There was also a comparatively rare tendering defeat when the W8 was lost to Metroline during April.

This route departed on 26 July, its TNs being divided between Westbourne Park (four) and Hackney (three, to serve a long-postponed PVR boost to the D7). At the advanced age of four years, TN 822 found itself converted to a trainer!

On 30 August the N23 was altered to resemble its daytime counterpart, giving up its Northolt section to new Alperton VTL-operated N7.

With the 18's Citaro G artics not yet delivered, the 207 was now specified for them with its 26 September award to and retention by First London. It was on 15 November that the 23 was converted to OPO, using not only new ALX400-bodied long Tridents from the TAL 1343-1386 batch but TNs made spare from the 18's simultaneous turning over to ECAs (later EAs) and reallocation to Willesden Junction. Once the TALs were all in place, the TNs were intended to double-deck the 92 and upgrade the 341 from Volvo Olympians, as well as topping up the 1, 25 and 91 where necessary. The N18 remained TN-operated, using buses drawn from the 295 and 414 batches.

From 1 November 2003 First's group-wide renumbering programme was extended to London, but with so many buses to keep track of, management insisted on a compromise that would retain the traditional class codes, albeit with some alterations. Where Volvo B7TLs needed some renumbering to get them into their own chassis-differentiated blocks rather than just continue sequentially as had been the habit since TNs first arrived, Tridents retained their numbers but with the addition of 32,000. The TAL class of two batches, however, was reclassified to TNA. Fleetnumber transfers were uniformly white, seeing off the larger yellow versions familiar on the earliest 'First Capital' Tridents.

Where the award of the 25 to First Capital heralded a period of great expansion, its loss upon retender at the end of 2003 heralded disaster, not just for its Trident fleet but for the poor passengers who would now be expected to cram themselves into artics operated by Stagecoach East London from June 2004. From 19 January three fuel cell Citaros were put into service alongside the existing TNLs and TALs on the 25.

Below: **The final Tridents for First London were 44 ALX400-bodied 10.5m TALs for the OPO conversion of the 23 on 15 November 2003. The order to specify DDA-compliant blinds has left the blind box with an uncomfortably short-finishing yellow light-up panel as well as less information for the passenger. Westbourne Park's TAL 1376 (LK53 EYV) is seen in Regent Street on 9 April 2004, by which time it had officially been renumbered TNA 33376 but not yet physically altered.**
Author

Right: **After the 23 was one-manned, the 7 couldn't be far behind and indeed its last Routemasters went out in a gala finish on 2 July 2004. On that day TNA 33380 (LK53 EYZ), still labelled as TAL 1380, was also out but carrying a conductor. It is seen at lunchtime at Marble Arch.** *Author*

Right: **The conversion of the 18 to Citaro artics on 15 November 2003 freed TNs for Northumberland Park's 341, which had Volvo Olympians to replace. TN 32853 (T853 LLC) demonstrates at Waterloo on 29 May 2004. By now all appellation other than the basic 'First' had been stripped, but it now obliged the entire operation to be on its best behaviour, lest the public tarnish all of it with the failings of one subsidiary!** *Author*

Right: **The Gold Arrow routes had endured fifteen years with minibuses and only the increased frequency made up for the terminal lack of seats. However, in 2004 new contracts were struck that specified double-deckers and a large fleet of Volvo B7TLs took over. They were assisted on occasion by Tridents, one of which on 27 December 2004 at Golders Green is TN 33248 (LT52 WVA).** *Author*

Left: **After a spate of engine fires to London Central Citaros, TfL got spooked and ordered all of them off the road for emergency fitment with fire-suppression equipment under warranty. That included the EA class on the 18, which was supplanted for a little bit with whatever Westbourne Park could spare, and on 25 March 2004 this included TNA 33377 (LK53 EYW), seen at Euston. Blinds were already carried for when double-deck augmentation was needed during Carnival.** *Author*

The entry into service of the last TALs proved slow, but once they were all in service at Westbourne Park by the end of January 2004 (not only on their normal 23 but the 7, 10, 27, 295 and 414 as well), TNs were released for transfer, principally to Northumberland Park for the 341 and the remaining step-entrance component of the 91. Hackney took the rest, seeing to the 1 and indirectly cascading the last Metrobuses and Arrows out of the fleet.

Application of the new fleetnumbers was similarly slow, taking place gradually from February 2004 onwards. Repaints to TNs also commenced at this point, though whether through full repaints or just to the lower deck, the buses lost their side striping.

Well-publicised problems affecting the Citaro G bendy buses of several London operators' fleets obliged TfL to suspend them from 24 March, and in First London's case the 18 saw TALs and TNs substituted, alongside assistance by Metroline using TPLs. All returned to normal on 3 April. The fitting of fire-suppressant equipment to what was now the EA class obliged the odd double-decker to return until 1 May.

Left: **Seen with its new fleetnumber but without its willow-leaf stripes on 31 May 2004 at Mile End is TN 32817 (T817 LLC); the D7 had regained its upper deck and was much the better for it, especially when it came to the splendid blinds carried for this route.** *Author*

On 20 March the N27 was renumbered plain 27, followed on 17 April by the removal of the N-prefixes from First London's N23, N105 and N341. TNs were already familiar as strange visitors to the 28, 31 and 328, but these routes' new contracts from 1 May included formal double-decking when their new VNW-class Volvo B7TLs appeared; Tridents continued to turn out when needed. As well as DMs moving to Alperton, TN 32963 headed there as well, reintroducing the Trident chassis to that Volvo B7TL-dominated garage briefly.

The solution to the expected redundancy of forty Tridents with the loss of the 25 was realised at the expense of RML-operated route 7, the current contract on which had always had the option to convert to OPO. The 25 duly passed to Stagecoach East London on 26 June and the 7's one-manning was advanced to 3 July, allowing the TALs to make their way across to Westbourne Park

for preparation. Six of the 51-reg TNLs new to the 25 left Rainham for Hackney, where they took over the 158, while seven more were allocated to a long-term rail replacement based on Manningtree and TNs 33037-33045 were transferred to Westbourne Park to help out the incoming VNWs on the 28, 31 and 328.

In anticipation of a November contract date, 27 more Citaro artics were ordered for the 207 in June, but the difficulty finding a base which could fit them caused the prolongation of the existing contracts into 2005. Tendering over the summer of 2004 saw the 357 and D7 retained with their existing Tridents (the D7 with an 18 September start date), but the 97 and 158 were lost to Stagecoach East London and the 123 to Arriva London North. It was envisaged that the 97's TNs would migrate across to the 215 and replace its Olympians. At the same time the 58 was scooped from Stagecoach East London.

Below: **The loss of the 25 to Stagecoach East London on 26 June 2004 freed its TALs for redeployment to the 7 a week later, and that was the end of Centrewest's Routemasters. On 28 August 2005 at the junction of Elgin Avenue with the Harrow Road, TNA 32952 (W952 ULL) is powering through that year's incarnation of the Notting Hill Carnival.** *Author*

Relative quiet ensued thereafter, though a new wheeze was the creation of intricate and entertaining all-over adverts to squeeze out that bit more revenue. During June TN 32959 received an advert for the ill-fated live-action *Thunderbirds* movie and in September replaced it with a fashion-themed ad by Robert Cary-Williams. Its third scheme by the end of the year was into blue to 'Back the Bid' for the 2012 Olympic Games, and was joined by TNs 32808, 32818, 32838 and 32851.

TN 33055 sustained upper-deck fire damage at the hands of arsonists at Hornchurch on 2 September, but was repaired. Similar mistreatment accrued to TN 33064 on 11 December and in this case the evening service on the 252 had to be entrusted to Darts. TN 33064's repair took nearly two years.

At the end of an indifferent 2004 for tendering, the 27, 257 and 295 were out and only one of those would be held on to, the announcement being made in January that Stagecoach East London would be taking the 257. The award of the 150 from East Thames Buses saw an order for more VNWs, but existing Tridents would be a possibility.

Between 14-19 February the five Back the Bid-liveried TNs were concentrated at Hackney and used on the D7 during the visit of the International Olympic Committee.

5 March 2005 saw the implementation of the major programme which shuffled a number of existing First London routes; the loss of the 158 was made good by the transfer of its TNLs to the 58, but the loss of the 97 released several Northumberland Park TNs to Rainham to serve as a reserve fleet for rail replacements. Similarly, TNLs displaced from the 123 either stayed put for the same purpose or were distributed here and there, three going into Northumberland Park, three to Westbourne Park, one to Uxbridge and one to Greenford.

Left: **All-over ads came back with a vengeance in the first half of the first decade of the 21st century, and became an art form in themselves, even if the subject itself wasn't particularly inspiring; the live-action *Thunderbirds* movie being touted by TN 32959 (X959 HLT) at Notting Hill Gate on 29 July 2004 was a box-office bomb.** *Author*

Left: **London lobbied hard to win the 2012 Olympic Games and was ultimately successful; one of the planks of the bid was the treatment of several buses across multiple contractors to this cheerful 'Back the Bid' scheme in sky blue. On 15 January 2005 in High Holborn we see TN 32808 (T808 LLC), now based at Hackney with the 1.** *Author*

The announcement of the retention of the 295 was tempered shortly after by bad news for the 1, which was going to be detached from First after its existing contract expiry and despatched to East Thames Buses to fill in for that company's loss of the 128, 129 and 150. Then, in April, the 27 was awarded to London United and the 105 was offered out to tender. Two pairs of school routes were awarded to either end of First during the spring, the existing 616 and ex-Arriva 699 in April and the 649 and 651, both ex-Blue Triangle in June.

The 207's new EAs had been in store pending the search for a new base, and after being knocked back at North Acton,

First secured premises at Hayes and on 9 April the changes were made that put the articulated vehicles into service. The route was withdrawn between Hayes By-Pass and Uxbridge and the overlapping Uxbridge-Acton section, retaining Acton Tram Depot's TNLs, was renumbered 427. The rest of the TNLs remaining at Uxbridge took over the 607 from its Vs, and finally school routes 697 and 698 were transferred from Uxbridge to Acton Tram Depot and converted to TNL.

On 25 June a new route commenced; numbered 435, it was operated by Greenford and ran between Heathrow Cargo Centre and Southall with three TNLs repainted for the occasion into all-over red.

Disposals of surplus TNs commenced in May and June, even though the buses in question were barely six years old; First Glasgow was the beneficiary of seventeen of them. A new role, however, was secured when the 67 was won back in June after five years with Stagecoach East London.

The terrorist bombings of 7 July 2005 saw th scrambling into action of First Tridents on emergency bus services and then on augmentations to the 27 and 205. The Olympics having now been won, the Back the Bid buses lost their blue adverts.

On 15 October the 1 and N1 left for East Thames Buses and the 257 was taken over by Stagecoach East London. The latter's TNLs were transferred to Hackney to take over the D7 from TNs, which, together with those displaced from the 1, were put in store at Hayes. Of these, the X-reg variety new to the 258 were intended for the 67 in 2006, while others were kept around for repaint cover. The assumption of the 150 on the same day immediately led to TN and TNL appearances alongside the scheduled new VNWs.

The 295 started a new contract on the 29th with existing Westbourne Park TNs. On 12 November the 27 passed to London United, prompting the storage of more TNs at Hayes; six of those already there found themselves loaned to Metroline from the 19th. In December ten more were added, their role being to replace the last step-entrance buses in London, in this case Volvo Olympians (AVs) working Holloway's route 4. Even so, further sales at the end of 2005 brought former TNs to First Devon & Cornwall at Plymouth.

Left: **Stripped of their stripes and illuminated front panels, the TNLs refurbished and repainted for new route 435 looked terribly bare, but that was the modern TfL aesthetic and it soon spread. Seen at Hatton Cross on 1 September 2006 is TNL 32894 (V894 HLH).** *Author*

Left: **Still smart, on the other hand, is TN 33054 (LN51 GKL), coming into Romford town centre on 15 October 2005. The 365 was in its last weeks of operation out of First Capital's Rainham depot, which stood in for Dagenham between 23 March 2002 and 17 November 2005.** *Author*

Right: **The 476 had been designed as an adjunct to the 73 which would also clip the top end off the 76. From the outset it was operated with Volvo B7TLs, but Northumberland Park TNs were known to turn out rather than there be no bus, and accordingly at the Angel on 26 October 2005 is TN 32878 (T878 KLF).** *Author*

Below: **Having operated the 67 between 1996 and 2001, First won it back in 2006 and this time specified refurbished TNs like TN 32976 (Y223 NLF), seen at Stoke Newington on 13 May. The use of blinds with just two via points was a terrible waste of the resources offered by the wider apertures.** *Author*

On 17 December the new premises at Dagenham opened and Rainham's allocation moved in wholesale.

2006 hardly started auspiciously when a teenage arsonist set fire to the overspill parking area adjacent to Westbourne Park on Sunday 22 January; destroyed were TNAs 32932, 32933, 32938 and 32943-32945, TNs 33038, 33241 and 33243 and TNL 33130. As well as calling in isolated spare TNs from around the system to cover for them, plus damaged TNs 33245 and 33246, First borrowed six Volvo B7TLs (VPs) from East Thames Buses. They lasted until August.

In March 2006 Uxbridge's TNs 33333 and 33342 received an all-over advert for the Oyster card; Dagenham's TNL 33072 soon joined them.

The TNs loaned to Metroline returned between mid-February and March and went back into store before heading out to Alexander Dennis's premises at Ware for refurbishment. That done, they took up the 67 on 29 April out of Northumberland Park. The fleet comprised TNs 32967-32983 and was immediately assisted by TNLs.

The 7 found itself put out to tender in June, and on 1 July the 105 began another

term with its Greenford TNs (which began receiving all-red repaints shortly after), but 2 September saw the 697 and 698 leave Acton for London United, allowing their six TNLs to replace the East Thames Buses VPs at Westbourne Park. The last of the TNs loaned to Metroline were also returned by this time. The large number of school routes in the Romford area were subject to tender every year, and by the autumn term of 2006 Dagenham had amassed the 649, 650, 652, 656, 679 and 686 plus the appropriate part of the 370, with Northumberland Park in charge of the 616 and 699.

Tendering had rather stabilised by now, but at the same time as the E1 and E3 received two-year extensions, the important 7 and its night partner N7 were awarded to Metroline.

As 2007 got going, repaints were well along, and a new feature was the remasking of the blind boxes in black to remove the illuminated 'f' logos. Blinds themselves were being severely curtailed to show just two via points, leading to some remarkably unhelpful displays that were particularly wasted on the wider blinds developed specially by First Capital to help passengers. Fear of litigation if the same passengers were stupid enough to get themselves caught in the tip-up seats in the wheelchair area forced a move by TfL to remove them entirely, thus reducing seated capacity on TNs to just 59. The three Oyster-liveried Tridents lost their adverts in January, and by the spring the TN batches for the 105 and 295 had all been refurbished.

On 17 February TNA 32931 was loaned to Uxbridge to become the first of its type there; it worked on the 607. Otherwise, type mixing was comparatively fluid by now when broadly similar classes were held in stock and no specific length restrictions prohibited one or the other at any particular time. Even so, we could see TNs at Acton Tram Depot. Following on from regular TN augmentations of the D6, sister route D7 at Hackney received two TNLs for the introduction of peak-hour extras on 17 March.

Above: **The dumbed-down blind panel for the 191 is just as unattractive, but even if the route's passengers have less of an idea where the route actually goes, they have a nicer place to wait than hitherto, in the form of the new bus station at Edmonton Green. This is TN 32852 (T852 LLC), seen on 27 January 2007.** *Author*

Left: **TNA 32939 (W939 ULL) managed to dodge the disastrous arson fire at Westbourne Park that torched six of its batchmates, and on 31 March 2007 is seen on the 23 at Charing Cross, showing the benefits of the full blind panel on the wider display as compared to the later batch of ALX400s for this route. However, this would be the X-reg TNAs' last year.** *Author*

An isolated tender victory as other routes, like the 282, received two-year extensions, awarded route 498 in April with a mix of single- and double-deckers. May saw the 165, 179, 252 and 365 put out to tender in the same area. Then First picked up the ELW, one of the three replacement routes planned to cover the East London Line's transformation into the London Overground from December.

On 23 June the 7 departed First London for Metroline and the surviving sixteen X-reg TNAs were stood down; Glasgow was their intended destination, but prior to that twelve of them, plus six TNLs, were lent to Metroline for refurbishment cover. The N18 was transferred to Alperton and in exchange Westbourne Park took on the N7, converting it from VNW/VNX to TN operation.

There was refurbishment as a catalyst for unusual Trident movements, and in 2007 another one manifested itself in the form of iBus, the GPS-powered bus control system with accompanying on-board 'next stop' indicators. A float of nine First Tridents from the TN 32958-32966 batch was detached and sent wandering for the next year, first serving at London United when that firm's buses were fitted with iBus by the contractor allocated to companies serving the northern half of London.

As the TNAs gradually came back from Metroline in August and September to be moved out to First's disposal pool or directly to Glasgow, TNLs 32900-32905 remained on loan and worked the 297 until December. TNA 32939 was the last in service in London, working the 23 on 9 November, and all had gone by the end of the year.

On 15 September the 295 added a night element and in October the clock was set ticking on the 191's TNs with its award on the basis of new buses. These would be the inaugural DN-class Enviro400s and were also expected for the 498 and ELW. The 91 was also re-tendered.

To make room for the construction of the Olympic Park, Hackney garage was obliged to close and did so on 15 December, passing Trident-operated route 58 and D7 (with two TNs and 29 TNLs) to new premises named Lea Interchange (LI) but formerly known as Leyton (L or later TM) when with Kentish Bus. TN visits resumed on the D6, but now with Dagenham buses.

Right: **For the second time in a decade, the East London Line needed comprehensive reconstruction but this time it was in the interest of creating a whole new line. While this was being done, three bus replacements were commissioned and the ELW was allotted Tridents at first. One of the four Dagenham TNs fitted with dedicated advertising is class code-less TN 33245 (LT52 WUW), laying over at Wapping on a foggy 23 December 2007, the ELW's first day.** *Ty Campbell*

Northumberland Park's TNL 33005 suffered an engine fire while on the 215 on 19 November and was declared unsalvageable, passing for scrap the following February.

The ELW was set going on 23 December with four Dagenham TNs (33245-33248) plus the two DNs that had actually arrived and were meant for the 498 before that route's assumption was put back to June 2008.

Another First garage closed, making three following Hackney and Orpington (whose minibuses had all been transferred with their contracts to Metrobus); this was Acton Tram Depot on 15 March 2008 and the 427 passed with its TNL fleet to Hayes, which also gained an allocation on the N207. On the 22nd of that month the 435 was withdrawn, its replacement 482 operated by London

United. Three TNLs passed to Hayes and two to Northumberland Park.

March saw a clean sweep of the 179, 252 and 365 but their Tridents would all be replaced by new buses, which were invariably Enviro400s now First had got used to this type. The order for DNs included enough to partially convert the 23 from TNA.

First's TN cover was returned from London United by 20 February (one lingering until 6 March) and now formed the company's own iBus float, rotating through Greenford, Hayes and Uxbridge during April while their own buses were sent to Arriva at Clapton to go through the iBus process.

The 23 was partially converted to DN starting on 19 May but no TNs departed for the moment. The iBus TNs moved on to Westbourne Park where they had begun and finished off 'Centrewest'. Late delivery of further new DNs forced the company to collect the same roving Tridents to partially convert Dagenham's D6 and Northumberland Park's 212 to double-deck operation (TNLs and TNs respectively) so as to release DMLs to Alperton for the assumption of the 245 from Metroline on 28 June. Having lost its TNs for the intended DNs on the same day, the ELW was reallocated from Dagenham to

Lea Interchange on 19 July and demoted to single-deck, reflecting poor customer takeup.

Of course TNs would turn up on the 231, the latest route won by Northumberland Park and assumed at much the same time as the 191. A further conduit of TN operation, when rail replacement work required Dart- or more recently Enviro200-sized single-deckers, was the 165. And even before the 212/D6 situation had been resolved, First's iBus went wandering again, this time to London General.

In June the 91 was lost to Metroline, from whom First Capital (then known as Capital Citybus) had won it in the first place. The 414 was put out to tender in August, and 27 September saw the 252 and 365 start new deals pending the manufacture of DNs to serve them; the 365 sprouted a night service at the same time. After a long wait, the E1 and E3 tenders were announced in October as good for First, which retained both, but bad for their TNs, which would be replaced by new Enviro400s.

The 191 was converted from TN to DN from 13 October and three days later saw the first DNs appear on the 179, 252 and 365. Hefty TN withdrawals followed, with 51-reg examples displaced by DNs moving to release surviving examples of the original 87 for conversion to single-door format and repaint into FirstGroup's national livery for cascade to Devon & Cornwall (Plymouth again) and Eastern Counties (Norwich); TN 32884 was the prototype conversion for the latter.

iBus now spread to the 'First Capital' end of the company and the usual band of TNs, their work done at London General's Stockwell, came over to Dagenham, following on to Lea Interchange in November and finally Northumberland Park.

First hadn't had it all its own way in tendering by any means this year, and the end of 2008 saw all of the 58, 97, 212, 215 and 282 up for grabs once again, followed shortly after by the offering out of the 427 and U4.

By January 2009 Northumberland Park's Trident fleet on the 97, 215, 341 and 357 consisted of 51-reg TNs and TNLs rotated in. On 7 February the 91 and N91 departed for Metroline, freeing enough 02-reg TNs to ease out some more T- and V-registered examples, but withdrawals now extended to that batch as well as the oft-travelled TNLs 32900-32903, which joined First Berkshire's fleet at Bracknell. The 14th saw the despatch of iBus cover TNs 32958-32961 to East Thames Buses, which operated them until April.

May saw the announcement of the loss of the 414 to Travel London; the simultaneous loss to London United of the 10 would stop TNs and TNAs from visiting that route too. On the 3rd the E1 and E3 began their new terms and from the 22nd DNs began to eject their TNs, which joined First's disposal pool despite being only seven years of age. There was no more iBus cover work to be done now, so TNs 32958-32962 were disposed of.

The 341 was offered to tender in June and in September results from the next set of announcements proved mixed; with First keeping the 58, 282, 427 and U4 but losing the 212 and 215. All but the 282 and U4 would be gaining new buses, reducing the still hardly vintage TN and TNL fleet still further. The 23 and 295 were put out to tender again at the end of 2009 or the cusp of 2010. On 21 November the 414 departed for Abellio (formerly known as Travel London) but the brunt of withdrawals fell on the VN class of ex-Orpington Volvo B7TLs which had gravitated to Westbourne Park; seven TNs were transferred to Northumberland Park.

On 6 March 2009 the 58 began its new contract at Lea Interchange, but its TNLs began giving way to new VNs (Volvo B9TLs this time). The 212 and 215 were taken over by CT Plus and East London respectively, and part of the gap in work was filled by moving the D6 from Dagenham to Lea Interchange, permitting the continued use of the depleting Trident stocks there. On the other side of town the 282 started another term with Greenford and the existing TNs.

Below: **On 19 March 2009 Northumberland Park's TNL 33098 (LN51 GOA) finds itself having to dodge roadworks at the southern end of Waterloo. This bus had come from an equally improbable garage for the TNL type, Westbourne Park, in June 2007.** *Author*

The good news for First was that the 23 and 295 were announced as retained in March, but there was bad news for their Tridents as the complement on all three would be replaced by new buses. The 341's TNs too would depart after that route was lost to Arriva London North. Of the myriad of school routes awarded in April, the 616, 692 and 699 were held but the 649 and 650 lost to Blue Triangle.

The large ongoing VN order included buses for TNL replacement from the 427 (including the Hayes share of the N207) to accompany its contract renewal on 10 April 2010, while the 607 gained two more years with its existing TNLs. On 1 May the U4 started a new contract and the U3 also at Uxbridge was allotted a single TN working at school times, for which Euro 3-spec TN 33178 was transferred from Westbourne Park; the U4's 03-reg batch (TN 33328-33342) were put through refurbishment, together with the 282's complement (TN 33277-33293) that had preceded them in delivery. Withdrawals were increasingly predicated on emissions certification, so the X-reg TNs from the 67 were earmarked for replacement with VNLs otherwise displaced from Northumberland Park's 259 and 476 by new VNs, and this took place in June. Even so, repaints to TNs and TNLs continued as better examples of each type were spared disposal.

When the 341 was taken over by Arriva London North on 16 October, the opportunity was taken to use its outgoing Euro 3 TNs from the 51-reg batch to upgrade the emissions spec on the 105 at Greenford, though it didn't help its tender bid, which was outbid by one from Metroline at year's end. The 30th saw the 295 renewed at Westbourne Park, though new buses were awaited to replace its TNs. The 23 began a new contract on 13 November with a similar promise of new buses to see off its TNAs that were still in the majority, and at Northumberland Park the 692 and 699 began new terms of their own with the existing TNLs. The transfer of the 92 from Alperton to Greenford permitted the first TN appearances with wanderers from the 105 and 282.

Tendering at the end of 2010 saw the D7 out and lost to Docklands Buses, but school routes 652, 656, 679 and 686 were retained and 608 added.

A new role for the TN and TNL classes in their dotage was refurbishment cover, with a pair of Uxbridge TNLs put into Greenford during March 2011 while the 92's VNZs were away, and similarly at Westbourne Park with nine TNs subbing for the VNWs on the 28, 31 and 328, which were about to begin renewed contracts with First but in reality had always seen regular TN, TNL and TNA visits.

On 2 July the 105 passed to Metroline and its TNs were withdrawn for disposal. The same month saw the announcement that the 357 had been retained by First with new double-deckers, thus setting the timer on what had become Northumberland Park's last solid Trident outpost. Time was running

Right: **All-over red was the order of the day by the time Greenford updated the 105's emissions profile with 51-reg TNs, though these were only six months newer than the original batch and the route was about to be lost on tender anyway. TN 33071 (LN51 GKA) is photographed setting off from Heathrow Airport on 24 May 2011, three months before its own withdrawal.**
Author

out for those not refurbished as well, as an order was placed during the month for the new Volvo B9TLs that would see off the 295's TNs, followed in August by one that would see to the entire 23 by the following April.

17 September saw the D7 leave for Docklands Buses, prompting the withdrawal of TNLs 33020-33028 and 33032-33035.

The need to clear space for Crossrail works, which would take most of the next decade, affected some of the land adjacent to Westbourne Park garage and thus a new site had to be found to put the overspill. On 1 October Atlas Road (AS) opened to take the 28, 31 and 328 and their VNWs and VNZs, and naturally a reserve of TNs, TNLs and TNAs joined them. These were rotated in and out of Westbourne Park at need and were present only until the Volvos' refurbishment programme was completed.

The 607 was announced in October as retained, though its 'existing buses' were unlikely to be the current TNLs. After the 207 ran the capital's last artics on 9 December, Uxbridge lost its allocation on the N207.

The entry into service of new VNs on the 23 during December began the moving on of its TNAs and residual TNLs; during the autumn a number of the longer Tridents had been gathered by First Games Transport, a subsidiary set up to serve the Olympic Games

site during its preparation and later staging. The 357 then received a batch of VNs of its own to dislodge Northumberland Park's last Tridents in association with that route's new contract commencing on 3 March 2012.

Despite an upturn in tendering fortunes for First London, the group as a whole was suffering financially and one option was to hive off bits to interested competitors. Accordingly, First sold the operations and buses of Northumberland Park to Go-Ahead, which would incorporate them into its London General brand. When this took place on 31 March and 130 buses left the fleet, six were Tridents (TNLs 33048, 33049, 33051 and 33231 plus TNLs 33075 and 33076).

In April the 607 was duly restocked, its TNLs coming off to be replaced by the VNWs lost from the 150 and joined in due course by DNs displaced from the 23 by that route's permanent allocation of DNHs. TNAs 33377-33382 were all that was left of that class by April, huddling on the 295 with what TNs were still going.

The staging of the Olympic games drew huge crowds, and extras were added to local services in and around the Olympic Park near Stratford. One such augmentation was to the 25, which drew VNs from the 58; taking their place were six 51-reg TNs reactivated from the withdrawal pool.

Above: **Similarly, the illuminated panels had more or less gone from the remaining TN and TNL fleet by the turn of the decade. On 10 July 2011 TNL 33093 (LN51 NRJ) is coming up to the Westfield shopping centre at White City; it had come to Uxbridge in July 2009 after becoming surplus at Northumberland Park, together with TNL 33098.**
Author

Above: **The sale of Northumberland Park's routes and buses to Go-Ahead on 31 March 2012 heralded the beginning of the end for First London. Lea Interchange soldiered on, putting out buses like TN 33045 (LN51 DVK), seen at Walthamstow Central on 11 August, but this bus had already gone by the time the rest of the First operation was sold on 22 June 2013.** *Author*

With its intended new buses diverted away, the 295 was earmarked to receive the rest of the VNs displaced from the 23 by the balance of the new DNs and DNHs, and when that was done TNAs 33377-33382 and TNs 33184, 33186-33192 and 33194-33196 were transferred to Dagenham, both to replace that garage's school-bus TNLs and to convert the 498 to 100% double-deck on 28 September; this route had already seen TNLs, especially on the journey that linked to the commercial 265 to Bulphan. Lea Interchange's last TNs came off at the same time.

With the completion of the 23 and 295's new or nearly-new allocations, just TNs 33197-33199 remained at Westbourne Park by October, and the recently-acquired TN fleet at Dagenham was gutted in December.

The sale of Northumberland Park had only helped FirstGroup's bottom line for a brief time and in April 2013 preparations were made to dispose of the rest of its London operations. They were to be divided, Lea Interchange and Westbourne Park (together wth Atlas Road) passing to the Transit Group of Australia, while Greenford, Hayes, Alperton, Willesden Junction and Uxbridge went to Metroline. All that would be left after that was Dagenham, whose fortunes had been beaten badly in a round of tendering that cost its entire double-deck roster.

At the close some interesting spots for Tridents presented themselves, notably the use of Dagenham's TNs and TNAs on the 368 on 1/2 June while that route's E20Ds were needed for a rail job. But on 22 June the grand transfer was executed. Of those Tridents to leave for Metroline at this time, TNs 33193 and 33328-33342 at Uxbridge went with the U4 and TNs 33277-33293 with the 282 at Greenford. To Tower Transit went just five, numbering for service Westbourne Park's TNs 33197-33199 and TNL 33036 plus long-time trainer TN 32822. Finally, the school routes were novated to Blue Triangle.

Dagenham's residual Trident fleet after 22 June 2013 consisted of TNs 32963, 33185, 33187, 33189 and 33191, TNLs 32900-32903 and 32929, TNAs 33377-33382 and trainers TN 32806 and 32807. The lowest-numbered four TNLs plus TN 32963 had come back from First Berkshire, though they were not used again and indeed two TNAs and the other four TNs quickly departed.

With the departure of the DN-operated contracts to Stagecoach East London, the remaining First Capital East operations, and Dagenham with them, closed down after service on 27 September 2013, bringing a close to fifteen years of First in London and ending a lineage that stretched back to 1986 and the first Ensignbus contracts for LRT.

Registrations

TN 801-853	T801-853 LLC
TN 854-887	T854 KLF, V855-863 HBY, T864-866 KLF, V867 HBY, T868 KLF, V869 HBY, T870, 871 KLF, V872 HBY, T873 KLF, V874 HBY, T875, 876 KLF, V877 HBY, T878-881 KLF, V882 HBY, T883-885 KLF, V886, 887 HBY
TNL 888-930	V988, 889-899, 990 HLH, W901-909, 895, 896, 912-919, 897, 921-924, 898, 926-939, 899 VLN
TAL 931-952	W931-939 ULL, W840 VLO, W941-949 ULL, W132 VLO, W953, 954 ULL
TN 954-983	X954, 611, 956-959, 612, 961-969, 613-975 HLT, Y223 NLF, X977, 978 HLT, Y224 NLF, X614, 981 HLT, Y346, 344 NLF
TN 984-1000	Y984-989, 932, 991-998, 933, 934 NLP
TNL 1001-1036	LK51 UZO/S/T/C-H/J/L-N, UYS-Z, UZA/B/F-H/JL-P/R/D/E
TN 1037-1071	LN51 DWA/C-G, DVG/H/K-M, GKD-G/J-L/O/P, GJJ/K/O/U, GKU/V/X-Z, GLF/J/K/V/Y, GLA
TNL 1072-1099	LN51 GOC/E/H/J/K, GNF/J/K/P/U/V/X, GME-G/O/U/V/X-Z, NRJ-L, GNY/Z, GOA, GLZ
TN 1113-1129	LT02 NVX/W/V/U/Z, NWA-D, NVL/K/M-P/R/S
TNL 1130-1140	LT02 ZCZ, ZBX-Z, ZCA/E/F/J-M
TN 1141-1199	LR02 LWW-Z, LXA-C/G/H/J-P/S-X/Z, LYA/C/D/F/G/J/K/O/P/S-Z, LZA-E, LT52 WVB-E, XAA-H/J/K
TN 1229-1248	LT52 WXG/H/J/K, WWV-Z, WVF-H/J-L, WUU-Y, WVA,
TN 1277-1293	LK03 NKC-G/P/R-U/W/X/Z, NLA/C/P/R
TN 1328-1342	LK03 UFD/E/G/J/L-N/P/R/S-X
TAL 1343-1386	LK53 EZV-X/Z, FCF/G/J/L/X-Z, FDA, EXT-X/Z, EYA-D/F-H/J/L/M/O/P/R/T-Z, EZA-F

Date	Deliveries	Licensed for Service
06.99	TN 801-822	TN 801-810, 812-814, 818-822 (**DM**), TN 811, 815-817 (**NP**)
07.99	TN 823-828, 830, 833-839, 841, 845-849, 852, 853	TN 823-828, 830, 833-839, 841, 845-849, 852, 853 (**X**)
08.99	TN 829, 831, 832, 840, 842-844, 850, 851, 854, 856, 857, 861, 864-866, 868-871, 873, 875-883, 885	TN 829, 831, 832, 840, 842-844, 850, 851 (**X**) TN 854, 856, 857, 864-866, 868-871, 873, 875, 876, 878-881, 883, 885 (**DM**)
09.99	TN 855, 858-860, 862, 863, 867, 872, 874, 884, 886	TN 855, 858-863, 867, 872, 874, 877, 882, 884, 886 (**DM**)
10.99	TN 887	TN 887 (**DM**)
02.00	TNL 888, 889, 891-897, 899, 900	TNL 888, 889, 891-897, 899, 900 (**UX**)
03.00	TNL 890, 898	TNL 890, 898 (**UX**)
04.00	TNL 909, 913	TNL 901-907, 909, 913 (**AT**)
	TAL 931-937, 940, 942, 944, 946, 948	TAL 931-934, 936, 942 (**DM**)
05.00	TNL 908, 910-912, 914-923, 925-928	TNL 908, 910-912, 914-920, 922, 923, 925, 927, 928 (**AT**)
	TAL 938, 941, 943, 945, 947	TAL 935, 937-941, 943-948 (**DM**)
06.00	TNL 924, 930	TNL 921, 924, 926, 929, 930 (**AT**)
	TAL 949-952	TAL 949-952 (**DM**)
02.01	TN 954-978, 980, 981	TN 954-973 (**X**), TN 974-978, 980, 981 (**ON**)
03.01	TN 979, 982, 983	TN 979, 982, 983 (**ON**)
06.01	TN 984-1000	TN 984-1000 (**G**)
09.01	TNL 1001-1016	TNL 1001, 1002, 1004, 1007, 1009 (**DM**), TNL 1013-1016 (**NP**)
10.01	TNL 1017-1021, 1023, 1025, 1027-1030, 1032	TNL 1003, 1005, 1006, 1008, 1011 (**DM**) TNL 1017-1021, 1023, 1025, 1027-1030, 1032 (**NP**)
11.01	TNL 1022, 1024, 1026, 1031, 1033-1036, TN 1047-1057	TNL 1022, 1024, 1026, 1031 (**H**), TNL 1033-1036 (**DM**), TN 1047-1057 (**ON**)
12.01	TN 1048-1061, TNL 1072-1083	TN 1048-1061, TNL 1072-1083 (**DM**)
01.02	TNL 1084-1090, 1092-1099	TNL 1084-1090, 1092-1099 (**DM**)
02.02	TNL 1091	TNL 1091 (**DM**)

Date	Deliveries	Licensed for Service
03.02	TN 1113-1121	
04.02	TN 1122-1129	TN 1113-1118 (**NP**), TN 1119-1129 (**UX**)
05.02	TNL 1130-1140, TN 1141-1154	TNL 1130-1140 (**UX**), TN 1141-1154 (**G**)
06.02	TN 1155-1165	TN 1155-1165 (**G**)
07.02	TN 1166-1177	TN 1166-1177 (**G**)
08.02	TN 1178-1190	TN 1178-1181 (**X**)
09.02	TN 1191-1199	TN 1182-1189 (**ON**), TN 1190-1199 (**X**)
11.02	TN 1229-1237	TN 1229-1234 (**X**)
12.02	TN 1238, 1244-1248	TN 1235-1248 (**X**)
04.03	TN 1277-1285	TN 1277-1285 (**G**)
05.03	TN 1286-1293, 1328-1342	TN 1286-1293 (**G**), TN 1328-1342 (**UX**)
11.03	TAL 1344-1347, 1350, 1352	TAL 1344-1347, 1350, 1352 (**X**)
12.03	TAL 1356, 1359-1361, 1363-1383	TAL 1356, 1359-1361, 1363-1383 (**X**)
01.04	TAL 1343, 1348, 1349, 1351, 1353-1355, 1357, 1358, 1362, 1384-1386	TAL 1343, 1348, 1349, 1351, 1353-1355, 1357, 1358, 1362, 1384-1386 (**X**)

Renumbered, 01.11.03

TN 801-887, 954-1000, 1037-1071, 1113-1129, 1141-1199, 1229-1248, 1277-1292, 1328-1342
 to TN 32801-32887, 32954-33000, 33037-33071, 33113-33129, 33141-33199, 33229-33248,
 33277-33292, 33328-33342
TNL 888-930, 1001-1036, 1072-1099, 1130-1140
 to TNL 32888-32930, 33001-33036, 33072-33099, 33130-33140
TAL 931-952, 1343-1386 to TNA 32931-32952, 33343-33386

Hired from East Thames Buses, 22.01.06-30.08.06
VP 3, 9, 12, 17, 19, 20 (X152, 161, 164, 169, 172, 173 FBB)

Disposals

05.05	TN 32827, 32834, 32836, 32837
06.05	TN 32823, 32825, 32828, 32830, 32832, 32833, 32835
07.05	TN 32820, 32824, 32826, 32829, 32831
09.05	TN 32821
12.05	TN 32811, 32848
01.06	TN 32802, 32803, 32808, 32812, 32817, 32819, 32846, 33808, 33241, 33243
	TNL 33130
	TNA 32932, 32933, 32938, 32943-32945
02.06	TN 32805
08.07	TNA 32931, 32934, 32941, 32947
09.07	TNA 32935, 32937, 32940, 32942, 32949, 32952
10.07	TNA 32936, 32946
11.07	TNA 32948, 32950
12.07	TNA 32939, 32951
02.08	TNL 33005
11.08	TN 32801, 32839, 32840, 32852-32854, 32872, 32873, 32879, 32882, 32883, 32886, 32887
12.08	TN 32809, 32841, 32843, 32845, 32847, 32849, 32857, 32875-32878, 32880
01.09	TN 32804, 32810, 32818, 32838, 32842, 32844, 32850, 32851, 32855, 32856, 32859-32862, 32864, 32874, 32881, 32885
02.09	TN 32863
	TNL 32900-32903
03.09	TN 32813-32816, 32865-32871, 33055-33058, 33060
04.09	TN 33113-33122
	TNL 32905
06.09	TN 32958-32962
07.09	TN 33141-33149, 33151-33155, 33159, 33165, 33166, 33168
08.09	TN 33150, 33157, 33158, 33161, 33163, 33164, 33167, 33169, 33170, 33172, 33174-33176
10.09	TN 33156, 33160, 33162, 33171, 33173, 33177
01.10	TN 32954, 33233-33240, 33242, 33244, 33247, 33248

Disposals

03.10	TN 33040, 33245, 33246
	TNL 33089
04.10	TNL 32888-32890, 32904, 32928
05.10	TNL 33008, 33009, 33012
06.10	TN 32965, 32966
	TNL 32898, 32910, 32913-32916, 33002, 33003, 33010, 33011, 33013-33016
07.10	TN 32964
	TNL 33001, 33004, 33006, 33007, 33017-33019
08.10	TNL 32891, 32892, 32917, 32919, 32921, 32924, 92930
09.10	TN 32969, 32974, 32980, 32983
10.10	TN 32970-32973, 32975-32977, 32979, 32981
	TNL 32897
01.11	TN 32986, 32987, 32992-32994, 33053, 33054
02.11	TN 32956, 32978, 32982, 32984, 32985, 32988, 32989, 32997, 32998, 33046
03.11	TN 32990, 32991, 32995, 32996, 33041
	TNL 33039, 33083, 33084
04.11	TN 32955, 32957, 32999, 33000, 33230
	TNL 33020, 33031, 33032, 33079, 33082, 33099
08.11	TN 33052, 33061-33064, 33066, 33069-33071, 33123-33125, 33127-33129
11.11	TN 33065, 33067, 33068, 33126
	TNL 33030-33023, 33025, 33027, 33028, 33034
12.11	TNL 33024, 33026, 33033, 33035
	TNA 33354, 33358
01.12	TNA 33348, 33350, 33352, 33353, 33355, 33357, 33359, 33360, 33365, 33367
02.12	TNA 33351, 33356, 33361, 33362, 33363, 33368, 33369
03.12	TN 32967, 32968, 33048, 33049, 33051, 33231
	TNL 32893, 32895, 32896, 32907, 33075, 33076
	TNA 33343-33347, 33349, 33364, 33366, 33370-33376, 33380-33386
05.12	TN 33050
	TNL 33072, 33073, 33090, 33093, 33132, 33134, 33136, 33137, 33139
06.12	TN 33059
	TNL 33074, 33080, 33081, 33095, 33098, 33131, 33133, 33135, 33138, 33140
07.12	TN 33037
10.12	TN 33049, 33043, 33044, 33232
	TNL 33086, 33087
11.12	TN 33045
	TNL 33077, 33078, 33088, 33091, 33092, 33097
12.12	TN 33042, 33047, 33178, 33184, 33186, 33188, 33190, 33192, 33194-33196, 33229
	TNL 33094, 33096
01.13	TN 33179-33183
05.13	*Re-acquired: TN 32963, TNL 32902*
06.13	TN 32822, 33193, 33197-33199, 33277-33293, 33328-33342
	TNL 33036
	Re-acquired: TNL 32900, 32901, 32903
08.13	TN 33185, 33187
	TNA 33377, 33382
09.13	TN 32806, 32807, 32963, 33189, 33191
	TNL 32900-32903
	TAL 33378-33381

London United

TA and TLA classes

Having acquired and assimilated the operations of Westlink shortly after its own privatisation, London United was thinking about low-floor double-deckers by the end of the 1990s. Early orders favoured the Volvo B7TL, but the win and retention of the 81 in March specified a double-deck proportion against five Dart SLFs, and this component was confirmed in May through an order for three Alexander ALX400-bodied Dennis Tridents, which would also serve as comparison with Hounslow's VAs and VPs then going into service.

The 81's new contract began on 22 July 2000 and its Lynxes were replaced by DPs made spare from the R70's loss on 19 August, while the double-deck component was supplied by Ms until the delivery of TA 201-203 in September. Service entry was on the 15th of

that month, with an immediate appearance on the Sunday 9. Of the three, TA 202 had the uprated 245bhp engine.

As the 81's TAs were under construction, the 131 and 267 were out for tender and both were retained, the 131 announced in April and the 267 in May. Only the latter was specified for new low-floor double-deckers, but it was later decided to add enough for the 131 so that its VAs could cascade Ms out, and when the order was made in May 2001 it was for 22 more TAs. To get Fulwell's drivers prepared as the new deliveries arrived, TA 203 moved there for training in September and the 131 began operating TAs on 30 November. The 267 followed from 5 December and the full batch of TA 204-225 was in service by the end of the year, with M support as necessary from the remaining members of that class.

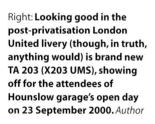

Right: **Looking good in the post-privatisation London United livery (though, in truth, anything would) is brand new TA 203 (X203 UMS), showing off for the attendees of Hounslow garage's open day on 23 September 2000.** *Author*

The future looked bright for the TA class when the 57, 71 and 281 were announced as retained by London United and the 65 was won back at the end of 2001. An order for 63 more TAs was placed, omitting the 281, which was scheduled to receive new buses in 2003. Until they arrived, the 71 was already host to Fulwell's new TAs on occasion, as were the 85, 281, 290 and 411, though more rarely. Plans to move TAs 201-203 to Fulwell to join the rest were shelved and these Tridents spent the rest of their lives at Hounslow. London United was still dual-sourcing with Volvo's B7TL, hence the gap in fleetnumbers caused by Wright-bodied VR 226-228 and indeed further VAs for new route 148 would follow.

Above: **The TAs for the 131 and 267 at Fulwell entered service during December 2001, and on 14 January 2002 we see TA 211 (SN51 SYO) emerging from Fairfield bus station in Kingston. The rules that accompanied the introduction of the new registration system mandated numberplate characters to 51mm width, but Alexander (which registered this batch with Edinburgh marks) still had a press with the older (and much more attractive) 57mm-wide letters and numbers.** *Author*

Left: **Working through Twickenham on 22 January 2002 is Fulwell's TA 225 (SN51 SZU), which has just ousted a Metrobus from the route that fielded that venerable type for the longest period.** *Author*

Right: **After only a few months in red and grey livery, TA 225 (SN51 SZU) was one of two London United Tridents to take on gold for the Queen's Golden Jubilee. It is displayed for all to see on a particularly sunny Brooklands runway on the 6 April 2002 iteration of Cobham bus rally.** *Author*

Right: **The rear view of TA 225 (SN51 SZU) is seen once the sun at Brooklands has come round to favour that end of the bus. All fifty Golden Jubilee buses had a sponsor, and this one's was Surf washing powder.** *Author*

Right: **And back into service, where the gold buses spread the message for six months. Seen at Kingston on 1 July 2002 is the other London United example, TA 224 (SN51 SZT), whose sponsor was Celebrations chocolates.** *Author*

Left: **London registrations appeared for the TA batch leased for the 65, 71 and 57, with numberplate characters now to the officially agreed width. Needing to see off elderly Metrobuses, the 71 was converted first and TA 235 (LG02 FAU) is in Eden Street in Kingston on 1 July 2002.** *Author*

2002 was the year of the Queen's Golden Jubilee, and two London United Tridents were selected to don gold livery. TAs 224 and 225 had subsidiary adverts for Celebrations Chocolates and Surf washing powder respectively and entered service in March, allocated to the 131 and 267 but wandering where they could. When the 281 had a Hounslow share due to being split in half for rugby fixtures at Twickenham, TAs were apt to turn out in strength.

TAs 229-292 (there now being 64 in the order) began arriving in April in time for the contract assumption of the 65 and retention of the 71 on 29 June. The first deliveries were put into service from 17 May to ease Metrobuses off the 71, and they also allowed the withdrawal of the 85's DNs until that route passed to London General on 29 June. On that date the 65 was assumed and all of TA 229-263 went into service. The last act here for the moment was the introduction

Left: **Fulwell's TAs had six months to visit the 85 before that route was lost to London General. Setting off from Putney Bridge Station on 23 June 2002 is TA 219 (SN51 SYY).** *Author*

of new night route N65 on 31 August, the same day as the commencement of the 57's new contract. Tolworth was thus last in line to receive its new Tridents (TA 264-292) and duly took the first ten of these to put into service from 26 July, but the moving up of the 148's introduction to 5 October caused the rest to be diverted to Shepherd's Bush to start the new route off (plus associated new night route N148) pending the arrival of its own VAs. Visits to the 220 ensued. TAs 279, 291 and 294 had a modified front fleetname incorporating a mention of parent company

Transdev. On the same day the 81 was reallocated from Hounslow to Hounslow Heath, but TAs 201-203 stayed behind, the latter using its own Metrobuses as double-deck supplements instead.

During November the 148's VAs were delivered and TAs 274-293 began being released to Tolworth to complete the 57. The two gold Tridents lost their Jubilee livery at the same time, and that finished off 2002. The 406, 418 and 467 at Tolworth were three new spots for TAs and the H22 was added to the tally of appearances at Hounslow.

It was now time to order the 281's new buses, and they were tacked onto a requirement for an upcount to the 111 to total 35 new TAs. They began arriving in March and TAs 312-317 were allocated to Hounslow for the 111's new contract beginning on 3 May. Then followed the 281's twenty-nine, which also converted school routes 671 and 681 and the similar augmentation of the 371.

With the ongoing OPO conversions of London's remaining Routemaster routes, London United's 94 at Shepherd's Bush now took its turn, being awarded to and retained by the company in April on the basis of new buses. They would thus have to be a bit more special than the usual, and in August 32 more Alexander-bodied Tridents were ordered, this time to 10.6m length. Pencilled in as TA

Right: **London United had two Routemaster routes and converted them to OPO at either end of 2004. For the 94, 32 10.5m Dennis Tridents with ALX400 bodywork were ordered and inaugurated a new TLA class. Moving past each other in Oxford Street on 28 January 2004, four days on from the conversion, are Shepherd's Bush's TLA 25 (SN53 KJA) and TLA 6 (SN53 EUM).** *Author*

347-378, they were reclassified TLA 347-378 and finally became TLA 1-32 upon delivery. The last ten had Voith gearboxes.

The 94's new contract took effect from 18 October but its OPO conversion was scheduled for 24 January 2004. The new TLAs, debuting a new interior with turquoise handrails and seat moquette of the same colour, were all delivered in advance of that date and indeed began taking over the 94 in crew mode from 13 January so that by the last day only five RMLs were left. Following the OPO conversion, Shepherd's Bush's TLAs were soon seen on the 148, Sunday 9 and even the 72 when restricted to the East Acton-Hammersmith section. After that, however, no more Tridents were ordered. Quiet thus settled over the TA and TLA fleet.

Right: **A new interior came with the TLAs, broadly turquoise-based; though not a particularly lovely colour, it had already gained a following from FirstGroup. This is inside TLA 14 (SN53 EUX) on 23 January, the last day of the 94 as a crew route.** *Author*

In March TLA 4 was given an advert for *Phantom of the Opera* scheme, in basic black. London's ultimately successful bid for the 2012 Olympic Games involved TfL wrapping buses in a blue livery, and in October TAs 345, 346 (the latter now fitted with a Caterpillar Euro 4 engine) and TLA 26 formed London United's Trident complement in this scheme. On 10 December TA 292 turned out on Christmas perennial K50, while another strange visitor restricted to the section away from Hammersmith Bridge was TA 252 on the 33 on 11 March 2005, going only as far as Barnes Common.

2005 began with the announcement of the retention of TA-operated routes 131 and 267, the latter with new buses. During the summer several Fulwell TAs were fitted with

Above: **Bought to add capacity to the 81 at school times, the three TAs lost that role when the 81 was reallocated to Hounslow Heath on 5 October 2001. They stayed at Hounslow and mixed with the VAs and VPs on the 111, 337 and H32. The H98 was DP-operated but still fielded more than a few double-deckers, like TA 201 (X201 UMS) at Hounslow on 20 March 2004.** *Author*

an air intake scoop on the front roof dome, plus twin extractors at the rear to take the air out again.

The Bid won, TLA 26 reverted to red in July and the two TAs followed in August. The inevitable downgrade of existing London United buses to red livery was well under way by now, though a grey skirt was still part of the effect by the time it came

for TAs to meet the spray booth, which in this class's case was as part of routine mid-career refurbishment for the 131, whose new contract commenced on 1 October.

On 12 November the TA class began moving again. The 267's conversion to SLE released enough TAs to Tolworth to convert the 406, while the 81's restoration to Hounslow meant its schoolday double-deckers becoming TAs

Right: **The 406, plying for decades between Kingston and Epsom down the main road, was an unlikely red bus route but settled in nicely as a cross-border link from regulated TfL territory to the wild lands beyond. It was converted to TA operation in November 2005 and here in Kingston on 18 February 2006 is Tolworth's TA 206 (SN51 SYE).** *Author*

again. The reallocation of part of the 391 from Stamford Brook to Fulwell permitted TAs to appear, but two TAs (214 and 215) were introduced to Shepherd's Bush as there weren't enough VAs to cover its four-bus PVR increase.

In March 2006 TAs 210 and 241 received all-over ads for Oyster, though this time the fronts remained in fleet livery (just a grey skirt in the former's case). Speaking of the fronts, Transdev now decreed that their name be emblazoned on vehicles rather than London United and Sovereign, and this was carried out by June with no changes to legal identities.

On 15 April a new route 691 was created out of the 671, and on 3 June a night service was added on the 281. School routes 697 and 698 were won from First and taken over on 2 September by Hounslow.

Despite winning new school route 696 and retaining the 671 and 691 in a tranche awarded in October 2006, London United lost the 406 to Epsom Buses. The two Oyster TAs lost their ads in December.

On 28 April 2007 the 406 was reallocated from Tolworth to Fulwell, taking six TAs with it, but then passed to Epsom Buses on 30 June, the same day as a night element was introduced to the 57. The 131 was boosted, double-deckers being supplied by converting the 671 and 691 to DPS operation. The 371 was now also at Fulwell, permitting increased TA visits.

iBus fitment was now due for London United, and between 6-22 August Hounslow and Fulwell loaned TAs to Shepherd's Bush so its own buses could go away. On 22 August nine First Tridents, TN 32958-32966, took their place and appeared on the 49, 94, 148 and 220. On 29 October they moved to Fulwell, visiting the 65, 71, 131, 267 and 281 and on 28 November began a spell at Tolworth on the 57 and 467 that lasted until 10 December when Hounslow took its place in line, TN visits being racked up on the 111, 120, 222, 697, 698 and H32. The TNs stayed put at Hounslow when iBus fitment moved on to Sovereign, VPs being loaned instead.

The loans didn't end with the return home of the roving six First TNs, as to furnish another increase to the 148, London United hired six TAs from Metroline on 1 February 2008 pending the delivery of additional Scania Omnicitys. TAs 81-84, 86 and 87 were replaced between 14-20 February by TAs 90 and 92 and TPLs 242-247, although TN 32966 lingered until 6 March and the last three Metroline Tridents were kept on until the end of June.

Above: **On 9 November 2007 at New Malden, loaned First London TN 32965 (X965 HLT) is taking the place of an indigenous Fulwell TA which has gone away to have iBus fitted. The normal-width blinds just about fit in the expanded aperture despite exposing the rollers underneath.**
Terry Wong Min

Right: **Metroline TAs and then TPLs followed the First TNs as unusual substitutes during the period of iBus cover, and here at Marble Arch on 16 February 2008 is TPL 245 (LN51 KXZ).**
Terry Wong Min

In February TLA 5 was treated to an advert for the DVD of *101 Dalmatians*, naturally in white with black spots, and it lasted a month. TLA 4 lost its own ad at the same time, after four years, though TLA 5 gained one for *Narnia* and soon traded that for *Quantum of Solace*. Otherwise, all-red was now the livery mandate with no skirts or stripes allowed at all, and TLA 4 and Tolworth's TA 271 were the first to receive it, the latter following repairs to fire damage suffered on 28 July 2006.

At the end of 2008 the 57, 65, 71 and 281 were all announced as retained on tender, the two extra years given London United for good performance now having expired. The 65 and 71 were awarded with new buses and the 57 and 71 with their existing TAs.

From 29 January 2009 TLAs 9 and 19 went on loan to Fulwell as refurbishment cover and TLA 4 did the same in May. Transdev were by now firmly wedded to the Polish-built Scania Omnicity and the resulting additions to the SP class took over the 71 between 29 June and contract commencement date (4 July, which also covered the 57, 65 and 281 plus the 371 with its school double-deckers). Unfortunately, the TAs that they were replacing were leased and thus disposed of rather than cascaded within the company, a modern and thoroughly wasteful practice. TA 258 was damaged by fire on 13 April and written off.

In June 2009 TLA 5 was given an advert for jewellery company TOUS.

Fulwell's Scania intake was broken by examples for Sovereign, but the balance for the 65 arrived in October and displaced more TAs, some of which gravitated to Tolworth but the rest joining those that Lombard Leasing was attempting to sell on.

As red repaints swept through the 03-reg variety of the TA class, 2009 ended with the retention of the 94 with its existing TLAs, while the similar future for the 111 did not imply the release of Hounslow's own TAs, which stayed put as support to yet more incoming SPs. Then, in January 2010, the 131 was announced as retained by London United with its incumbent TAs; the new contract on that route commenced on 2 October.

On 1 May 2010 the 697 and 698 were reallocated from Hounslow to Hounslow Heath.

Much of the TLA class was set to shift when twenty Green Bus-funded Enviro400 hybrids of ADH class were deployed to the 94 to fulfil increasingly stringent emissions requirements in central London. The 94's own contract applied from 16 October and the ADHs took over between 5-30 November; the TLAs stayed put in replacement of VAs from the 220, and in fact a refurbishment programme began on TLAs 1-14. Isolated TAs still hung on at Shepherd's Bush, transfers to and from each London United garage being commonplace. In spite of the upcoming loss of the 467 to Epsom Buses, it was converted to TA on 24 January 2011 using the last TAs leaving Shepherd's Bush, together with transfers from Fulwell made possible by the input of its first TLAs, theoretically for the 267.

The long-drawn-out merger of Transdev and Veolia produced one side-effect in which London United was sold to RATP, thus keeping the London bus company in French state ownership. The sale was effective from 3 March 2011 and saw Transdev vinyls removed in favour of new London United logos, albeit including RATP's River Seine-shaped device.

On 3 September 2011 the 467 was taken over by Epsom Buses, but the 697 started a new term; the TAs still available at Hounslow were newer examples following the withdrawal of TA 201-203 by May. Abellio's takeover of the 290 meant no further TA possibilities on that route.

Below: **TA 215 (SN51 SYU) is carrying the original design of air scoop when seen at Kingston on 6 April 2010, and it isn't half ugly. Surely the reinstitution of front upper-deck opening windows would have solved all these problems at one stroke, but that seemed beyond the wit of modern bus designers.** *Author*

Left: **Now in all red for a rare visit to the 290 at Staines on 14 February 2009 is TA 319 (SN03 DZV).** *Author*

Left: **At Kingston on 21 July 2010 school route 671 is in the hands of TA 334 (SN03 EBD).** *Author*

Left: **Displaced from the 94 by the arrival of new ADHs, TLA 28 (SN53 KJJ) was one of the longer Tridents redeployed to the 220 at Shepherd's Bush, and on 12 May 2012 it is seen at White City Central Line station, carrying the attractive and discreet new London United logo phased in by RATP.** *Author*

The 220's night service was converted from TLA to ADH operation on 17 March 2012, and the retention of the day route at this time spawned an order for 28 diesel-powered ADEs, thus setting the clock ticking on its TLAs. On 28 June the 81 began a new term with London United at Hounslow, theoretically discarding TA possibilities for new ADHs, but the 613 at Tolworth and the 671 and 691 began new terms with their existing buses, which could still include TAs.

In June Fulwell sent TLAs 9 and 19 back to Shepherd's Bush after a loan period of nearly three and a half years! The Olympics were now upon us, and between July and September TLAs 1, 2 and 16 carried all-over adverts for Visa.

The 220's new contract commenced on 20 October, and one of its side-effects was the reallocation of the daytime service from Shepherd's Bush to Park Royal, a garage inherited upon the takeover of NSL Services (previously known as NCP Challenger). Its concurrent conversion to ADE operation allowed TLA 1-4 to reintroduce the class at Fulwell, while TLA 5 struck up a new allocation at Tolworth and TLAs 6-8 went to Hounslow Heath for the 698 from 12 November. TLAs 1 and 2 were added on 14 December for the assumption of the 635 on 12 January 2013, with immediate wandering to the H91 and Christmas extras on the 27. But in January the TLAs went back to Shepherd's Bush and in came TAs 215-218.

Between November 2012 and March 2013 TLA 19 carried an ad for Thailand tourism. TLA 8 restored the class to Hounslow Heath in March and TLAs 17-30 (minus 31 and 32, which were returned off lease) went through refurbishment to replace the earlier ones, despite their own treatment fairly recently.

Of the three major TA-operating routes by mid-2013, one (the 281) went out for tender in June. On the first of that month Stamford Brook operated both TAs and TLAs for the first time each when examples were loaned to form extras on the 9 on the occasion of the closure of part of the District Line. Other TA firsts in 2013 were from Hounslow Heath (routes 116 and 285) and Fulwell (route 110), and finally a 65X with eight Fulwell TAs worked on 1 September for the London Mela held in Gunnersbury Park.

For the September school term Hounslow Heath swapped its TAs for TLAs, and TLA 18 gained an all-over advert for Nike, which it carried until the following January. Between October and February TLA 23 carried one for Malaysia, with a different design on each side.

2013 was the year the 'Borismaster' of LT class began entering squadron service, and the third such conversion, on 26 October, was of the 9 at Stamford Brook. Its VLEs were thus displaced to Tolworth to eject the 57's TAs, though this route had been granted two more years with London United. One last London United garage remained to see Tridents, and this was taken care of when TAs 231, 282 and 283 were put into Park Royal. Two more into Shepherd's Bush, TA 238 and 240, put an end to the VA class in November and further spare TAs transferred from Tolworth into Hounslow the following month ousted the last of the VPs.

2013 ended with the retention of the 281 but with the promise of SPs coming to replace its TAs once ousted from the 148 by additional Borismasters. It also finished off the London United red and grey livery, TAs 312, 317 and 318 being the last buses to carry it (or bits of it, as was the reality by then). On 6 January 2014 new school route 662, using a Tolworth TA from the small cohort remaining there, was created out of the 665.

15 February 2014 saw the 148 taken over by LTs, releasing the first SPs that the 281 needed in advance of its renewal on 5 July. More Scanias were released to Fulwell by the 10's conversion to LT on 26 April, and the 03-reg TAs now suffered the brunt of withdrawals. TA 314 had been deroofed on 23 December 2013 and now left the fleet.

On 31 May a sizeable reshuffle of capacity at London United saw the 131 and its TAs reallocated from Fulwell to Tolworth. The concurrent move of part of the 391 to Fulwell prompted TA appearances on this route.

On 14 July Putney Bridge was closed for extensive refurbishment that would take the whole summer, so routes approaching the bridge were turned short or diverted. Not needing as many buses with the curtailment of the 220 at Putney Bridge Station, Park Royal sent its four TAs to Fulwell.

One disadvantage of the Volvo B7TL over its Dennis Trident rival was excessive fan noise, and by July 2014 residents along the smarter portions of the recently VLE-converted 57 were beginning to complain,

Below: **Tolworth gained a second TA-operated main route on 31 May 2014 with the reallocation of the 131 from Fulwell. Carrying the correct TV garage code at Tooting Broadway on 23 February 2016 is TA 320 (SN03 DZW).** *Author*

Left: **On 25 April 2014 TA 248 (LG02 FBV) is operating the 49 out of Shepherd's Bush and is seen at the northern end of the Westfield complex at White City.** *Author*

Left: **Transferred from Tolworth to Hounslow, TA 281 (LG02 FDY) is at Uxbridge on 25 April 2012, in front of one of the ADE-class E40Ds that was more commonly on the 222.** *Author*

Left: **TA 249 (LG02 FBX) is seen on the 391 at Richmond on 3 June 2014, three days after the route transferred from Stamford Brook to Fulwell. Its normal Optare Solos migrated with it, but TAs now began to appear.** *Author*

Right: **Original Fulwell TA 216 (SN51 SYV) is turning out on the 110 on 10 June 2014, coming round the Hounslow one-way system.** *Author*

Right: **The TA class had numerous separate spells at Shepherd's Bush, examples leaving and then coming back when extras were needed. On 27 May 2015 TA 231 (LG02 FAJ) demonstrates at Piccadilly Circus.** *Author*

Right: **25 July 2014 was a sombre day for Londoners in that it was the final day of the 9H; while the army of photographers was getting ready to welcome RM 1627 through, local buses were fair game, like TA 240 (LG02 FBE) at the western edge of High Street Kensington.** *Author*

so it swapped buses with the 131, now also at Tolworth, so that the 57 reverted to TA operation.

Putney Bridge was duly repaired, and in September Park Royal got back three TAs; by October it was operating seven. September also saw TLA 23 receive two all-over ads in quick succession, first for Red Bull Culture Clash and then for Thailand, while stablemate TLA 24 was given one for the Burj Khalifa.

Just the 57 now remained with scheduled majority TA operation, together with the school routes at Tolworth, one of which, the 613, was back-projected from Worcester Park to start at Tolworth Station from 5 January 2015.

TA 283 was deroofed under Old Oak Common railway bridge on 10 November, putting it out of contention for survival. In January 2015 TLA 24 resumed red livery but TLA 21 gained an ad for Pepsi Max (which it carried until May). TLA 23 lost its Thailand ad in March.

During July and into August a handful of early SPs were introduced to Tolworth so that an equivalent number of TAs could be stood down from the 57 (and 131). The two years' extra on the 57 was about to expire and the route thus put out to tender, but the 131 was simultaneously awarded two years' more of its own for implementation from 3 October, so the TA class would cling on, albeit in ever smaller proportions. Not on the 57, though, which in October was announced as lost to London General.

2016 began with TAs 215 and 216 becoming trainers and six sold TAs returning for conversion to single-door private-hire specification for the United Motorcoaches division recently launched. The unit's new grey and red livery completed the look.

Part of an order for 56 Volvo B5LHs (VHs) placed at the end of 2015 depended on the likelihood of Hammersmith Bridge being strengthened sufficient to admit them on the 72, but this was a long shot and the gamble failed with the buses already bought. Instead it was decided to use the 72's contingent to replace the TLAs from the third of the 94 still fielding them, thus pacifying the emissions-obsessed within TfL for a little while. The first VHs were put into service at Shepherd's Bush on 10 March, allowing TLAs to stand down, though some of the outgoing Tridents popped up at Hounslow Heath as strike extras on the H91 on the 24th and three more were added to Tolworth. To fill in until all the VHs needed were in place, four TAs moved in to close out Trident operation at Shepherd's Bush.

At the death of Trident operation within London United, a renumbering exercise was executed that gave the buses five-figure fleetnumbers atop their existing class codes. The TAs had forty thousand added and the surviving TLAs were tacked on thereafter in the 40320s, though as with all these stunts, clashes were encountered (in this case with Scanias) so a rethink turned TAs 204 and 205 into TAs 40284 and 40285. It took about a year for buses to be physically renumbered, with new small white transfers.

Prior to further new VHs' takeover of the 85 on 2 July, the new Volvos were allocated to Tolworth from May and run in on the 131. 2 July was also the day the 57 left for London General, and the only TAs and TLAs now allocated were as spares spread around the garages. They still managed to take priority over the VLEs, which were withdrawn first. Underscoring their unlikely survival, three TAs were given all-over ads in July, TAs 40218 and 40237 for U-Switch (carrying them until the following April) and TA 40240 for Zoopla. While at Tolworth they operated on the 131

and 71, the latter having been transferred in on 2 July to replace the 85. The 371's pair of summer replacements while the second Petersham Hole was being filled in were known as 571 and 572, and they saw one TLA and one TA respectively. Fulwell, meanwhile, added the 216 to the list of Trident debuts, both TA and TLA classes featuring as part of a fully double-deck allocation until 21 December 2016 and sporadically thereafter. Hounslow's remnant could be found on the 110, 111 and 203, but Tolworth's 671 was withdrawn after the autumn term.

In December 2016 the 131 was announced as lost to London General, which would appear to herald the endgame for Tridents at

London United, but the type would endure even after the transfer, on 30 September 2017, reduced Tolworth from eighteen to six TAs. Hounslow, despite losing the 222 as a possibility on 16 September, could still field eleven TAs and one TLA, while Hounslow Heath had the other three TLAs and Fulwell two TAs. On 11 November Park Royal (PK) closed and London United moved into the former First garage at Atlas Road, renaming it Park Royal and instituting a new code, RP. TA 40223, the lone Trident assistance to the 220's ADEs, migrated with it.

The end of 2017 saw two TAs reactivated at Tolworth and two more plus a TLA at Hounslow. However, 13 January 2018 saw Hounslow Heath's three TLAs come off when the 635 was restarted with three new VHs.

TLA 40329 was now the last long example in service, at Hounslow. But still the surprises continued, when in February the new Park Royal doubled its TA allocation and TA 40221 reintroduced the class, yet again, at Shepherd's Bush. Even more improbably, TLA 40329 duly left Hounslow in March but found itself transferred to Park Royal with TA 40243, making four Tridents in total! The rationale was refurbishments of the 220's ADEs.

TA 40221 left Shepherd's Bush on 4 April, not waiting for big cuts about to be wrought upon the 94 in keeping with the sharp downturn in custom being suffered by all TfL services by this year.

In May 2018 London United made a concerted push against the remaining TAs.

Right: **The pitch of the last three London United Dennis Tridents was not one historically associated with the type, and nor was the 220's later operating garage, a new facility acquired from Tower Transit and renamed Park Royal to recall the previous bearer of that name just down the road. On 28 August 2018 in Putney Bridge Road TA 40247 (LG02 FBU) keeps the TA class alive for a little longer while its ADEs were undergoing contract refurbishment. One of the latter is seen receding into the background.** *Author*

Fulwell's TA 40229 did the morning school run on the 681 on the 14th and then retired, leaving just TA 40213 to finish on the 17th. 17 May also saw Tolworth's last knockings; of three operating that day on the 71, TAs 40238 and 40240 ran in after the evening peak and TA 40237 lasted until ten to one on the 18th.

Hounslow's still sizeable fleet came off next. TA 40246 last worked on 16 May, TA 40230 on the 21st, TAs 40234 and 40235 on the 23rd and the 24th saw two each on the H32 (TA 40232 and 40239) and H98 (TA 40242 and 40243); London Vehicle Finder records the last in as TA 40239 at 20:00 hours.

Registrations

TA 201-203	X201-203 UMS
TA 204-225	SN51 SYA/C/E-H/J/O/R-Z, SZC-E/T/U
TA 229-292	LG02 FAA/F/J/K/M/O/U, FBB-F/J-L/O/U/V/X-Z, FCA/C-F/J/L-P, FCU/X-Z, FDA/C/F/J-P/U/V/X-Z, FEF/H/J/K/M/O/P/T-V
TA 312-346	SN03 DZJ/K/M/P/R-T/V-X, EAA/C/E-G/J/M/P/W/X, EBA/C/D/F/G/J-M, LFL/M/P/R-T
TLA 1-32	SN53 EUF/H/J-M/O/P/R/T-Z, KHR/T-Z, KJA/E/F/J/K/O/U/V

Date	Deliveries	Licensed for Service
09.00	TA 201-203	TA 201-203 (**AV**)
10.01	TA 204, 205	
11.01	TA 206-214, 216	TA 206-214, 216 (**FW**)
12.01	TA 215, 217-225	TA 215, 217-225 (**FW**)
04.02	TA 229-237, 239-244	
05.02	TA 238, 245-263	TA 229-263 (**FW**)
07.02	TA 264-273	TA 264-273 (**TV**)
08.02	TA 274-292	
10.02		TA 274-292 (**S**)
03.03	TA 313-318	
04.03	TA 312, 321, 326-330, 332, 333, 336, 338	TA 312-317 (**AV**), TA 318-330, 332, 333, 336, 338 (**FW**)
05.03	TA 331, 334, 335, 337, 339-341	TA 331, 334, 335, 337, 339, 341 (**FW**)
06.03	TA 342-346	TA 342-346 (**FW**)
11.03	TLA 2, 3, 5, 8	
12.03	TLA 1, 4, 9-26, 29, 30	
01.04	TLA 27, 28, 31, 32	TLA 1-32 (**S**)

Inactive after 25 April, TLA 40329 was put back into service at Park Royal on 28 June but served only another week on the 220, finishing on 5 July. TA 40247 was the first TA on the 18 on 13 April.

The final trio of TA 40223, 40224 and 40247 fought on through the summer and into the autumn on the 220, even when the input of three VHs into Park Royal early in September threatened to take the Tridents off at last. TA 40224 nevertheless last operated on 5 September and TA 40223 on the 16th, leaving just TA 40247. Incredibly, TLA 40329 now found itself reactivated on 2 October to join it, and both the long and the short holdouts continued on into November. Even so, this month was where their stout resistance came to an end at last, TLA 40329 coming off after the 6th and TA 40247 at 20:15 on the 30th, after a full day on the 220. That finished off London United's Trident history after a period spanning just over eighteen years.

Renumbered, 04.16
TA 204, 205, 207-211 to TA 40284, 40285, 40207-40211
Survivors of TA 213-250 and TA 313-320 batches to TA 40213-40250, 40313-40320
TLA 1-8, 18 to TLA 40321-40329

Hired from First, 22.08.07-20.02.08
TN 32958-32966 (X958, 959, 612, 961-966 HLT)

Hired from Metroline, 01.02.08-06.08
TA 81-84, 86, 87, 92, 96 (T38 KLD, T182-184, 186, 187, 192, 196 CLO)
TPL 242-247 (LN51 KXV/W/Y/Z, KYA/B)

Disposals
07.09	TA 258
12.09	TA 251-257, 259-263
01.10	TA 264-270, 272-274, 276, 277, 279, 280, 291
02.10	TA 271, 275, 278, 287-290, 292
06.11	TA 201-203
12.12	TLA 31, 32
02.13	TLA 9-16
06.14	TA 314, 322, 336
07.14	TA 312, 319, 321, 324-329, 331, 333, 334, 337, 338, 340-342
08.14	TA 330
09.14	TA 323, 332, 335, 339, 344-346
10.14	TA 343
06.15	TA 281, 282, 284-286
08.15	TA 204-206, 207-212, 219, 283 (*TA 204, 205, 207-209 and 211 returned 02.16*)
09.16	TA 217
	TLA 17, 19-30
10.16	TA 236
12.16	TA 241
05.17	TA 40233
	TLA 40321, 40322
06.17	TA 40249
10.17	TA 40218, 40222, 40248, 40316, 40318, 40320
11.17	TA 40214, 40225, 40315
01.18	TA 40313
	TLA 40326-40328
02.18	TA 40250
03.18	TA 40220
04.18	TA 40231, 40245
	TLA 40323-40325
05.18	TA 40246
06.18	TA 40221, 40237, 40238, 40240
07.18	TA 40232, 40234, 40317
08.18	TA 40213, 40229, 40230, 40235, 40239, 40242, 40243
01.19	TA 40207-40209, 40211, 40223, 40224, 40244, 40284, 40285
08.19	TLA 40329
03.20	TA 40247

Metroline

TP, TPL, TA and TAL classes

For all the knockabout nature of MTL's short tenure in the capital, which saw the presentation of the MTL London fleet decline to truly dire levels, the group at least had foresight enough (and more importantly, the finance) to be on the ball when it came to placing debut orders for low-floor double-deckers in the capital. Against the tender retentions of important trunk routes 17, 43 and 134 (and their N-prefixed night counterparts), MTL ordered 65 Plaxton President-bodied Dennis Tridents in July 1998, but the same month saw the company's purchase by neighbouring Metroline and the order picked up by them.

At the same time Metroline proper had ordered sixteen Tridents of its own against the contract for the 260, but had plumped for the Alexander ALX400 body. All that could be done now was wait, but Metroline's forward planning was with a longer eye to the future than most companies, and in August an order was placed for 433 Dennis chassis on a rolling basis over the next four years, with Tridents as well as Dart SLFs. The existing orders found themselves included, and by February 1999 the first of the TP class was in build, to 9.9m length with central straight staircase and carrying 67 seated passengers (H45/22D). TP 1 was completed at Plaxton Wigan (the new name for the Northern Counties factory) and delivered to Dennis at Guildford, but as it turned out, this would not be the inaugural Metroline London Northern vehicle and a later build would assume its identity. TP 2 was delivered to Holloway in April for type training (including a disability awareness module), with the 43 chosen to be the first route to receive them. This route's roads had already been prepared with extra Red Route markings and stop relocations in the interest of a Community Partnership that LT Buses launched on 22 March. The buses themselves, cool-looking with their bonded glazing throughout, were marketed accordingly, with the word 'future...' carried in yellow under their Metroline fleetnames.

Service entry was on Monday 19 April 1999, four of the twelve TPs delivered by that time turning out on the 43. At the same time Metroline announced that the first Tridents of its rolling order would comprise 36 ALX400-bodied examples for the 140 and 182, the former being a particularly important tendering capture which secured Harrow Weald's future in the long term. The deployment of the original sixteen ALX400s

Below: **By March 1999, deliveries of the new TP class had commenced and examples like TP 2 (T102 KLD), seen in Islington on 22 March, were out and about training drivers.** *Author*

Left: **The 43 began its conversion from M to TP operation on 19 April 1999 and on 16 September of that year at Moorgate we see Holloway's TP 9 (T109 KLD), on a short-working that's about to return northward.** *Author*

(to follow on from the TP class as TA 66-81) was simultaneously changed from the 260 to the 16, in the first of a long series of decisions which would give central London routes priority for new vehicles (whether warranted or not!).

TA 66-81 began to arrive on 17 June, carrying a mess of registrations even more complicated than were on the TPs, and were put into service at Cricklewood beginning on 30 July. They displaced AVs from the 16 to Willesden's 260 and, like the ongoing conversion of the 43 to TP, displaced Metrobuses to sale. Further TAs from this batch trained Harrow Weald drivers in anticipation of their own forthcoming vehicles, at least some of which would be needed for 4 September, the date of the 140's assumption. Wanderings commenced straight away, to the 32 and 266, though Holloway hadn't seen fit to let its own TPs stray from the 43.

Left: **Interspersed with Holloway's TPs as 1999 drew on came the TA class with Alexander ALX400 bodywork. The first sixteen were put into Cricklewood to take over the 16 from AVs, though they had been ordered against the 260, which received the newish Olympians instead. TA 69 (T69 KLD) is seen on 31 July 1999, heading north through Kilburn.** *Author*

Above: **Harrow Weald was due 36 TAs for the regaining of the 140 and continuation of the 182, and until the former's takeover date the first TAs into the garage were put out on the 182. Here is TA 88 (T188 CLO) in central Harrow on 23 August 1999.** *Author*

The original TP 1 had been kept behind by Dennis to serve as a demonstrator, its duties taking it to Sweden during the summer of 1999, while TP 16 was despatched further afield to see if it could drum up custom for double-deckers in Canada, not hitherto a market for this mode. On 18 August Harrow

Weald put into service on the 182 all the TAs it had amassed so far, switching them on 4 September to the 140 and new school route 640, with appearances on the 186 (but not the 183, which was lost to Sovereign at the same time and thus was not carried on TAs' blinds).

Right: **The 186's LLWs at Harrow Weald were often supported by Metrobuses, and now the Ms' successors took on this role. Seen leaving Edgware bus station on 13 October 1999 is TA 91 (T191 CLO).** *Author*

During August the 134's batch (TP 32-48) began delivery, going into service on the 43 first; the first TP on the 134 was on 22 August and introduction followed tentatively thereafter, accompanied on 5 September by the conversion of the Sunday OPO roster on the 10. As the similar evening and Sunday working of the 13 was rostered off the 134, TPs began appearing here too. This batch had one-piece upper-deck front windscreens, balancing improved appearance against the likelihood of breakage and the cost of replacement (as to TPs 40 and 42 within six months of delivery). The inward-facing seat behind the staircase and a row upstairs was omitted, now rendering capacity H41/21D.

Right: **The 17 was the third Holloway route to convert from M to TP operation. Although all 65 TPs inevitably became mixed across the 43 and 134 as well, the 17 was started off with the highest-numbered units like TP 61 (V761 HBY), seen at London Bridge on 2 June 2000.** *Author*

Right: **Metroline had a rather sweet way of celebrating Christmas which persisted for some years, by which some of its buses had 'snow' applied to window corners for a suitably wintery look which, with global warming, was barely the case at all in London any more. TA 71 (T41 KLD) leaving Victoria on 16 January 2000 demonstrates the effort made allocating almost-matching registrations when so many had been taken out of circulation by the DVLA. T71 KLD was carried by TP 21 and that didn't match either!** *Author*

Harrow Weald's 140, 182 and 640 had their full complement of TAs by the end of September and the 17's TPs, including a second TP 1, were delivered to Holloway at the same time, converting the route between 5-9 October. Now that all sixty-five were in place, Holloway could now allow them to drift, all of the 4, 135 and W7 racking up TP appearances and the 271 and C2 completing the set by the New Year.

2000 began quietly but in March seventeen more ALX400-bodied Dennis Tridents were announced for September delivery; this time they would be to 10.5m length and classified TAL 118-134. Again the 16 took priority for these new buses, and would be cascading all but two of its TAs to the 32, still at Cricklewood, but the others would join Harrow Weald to replace the 186's double-deck element, operated by Ms.

Left: **Harrow Weald's TA 96 (T196 CLO) and TA 97 (T197 CLO) are seen together at Heathrow Airport Central on 28 July 2000, but not on consecutive running numbers; HD103 is behind them and is also a TA.** *Author*

Right: **The Sunday 13 was even shorter-lived with TPs than the 135, passing from Holloway to Edgware on 4 March 2000 and having to revert to M. On 12 December 1999 TP 39 (T139 CLO) is at Oxford Circus.** *Author*

On 4 March the 13's evening and Sunday Metroline portion was transferred from Holloway to Edgware, by necessity having to abandon TP operation for Ms again.

Despite the ongoing order for Dennis products, Metroline found itself tempted by Volvo's B7TL and in June 2000 ordered twenty-six of them for the 271 and W7, soon increasing the order to sixty to cover the 52 and an increase to the 134. Nevertheless, TAL

118-134 arrived in October and from the 23rd were put into service on the 16, allowing its TAs to move onto the 32, save TAs 73 and 80 which passed to Harrow Weald. By this time the latter's TAs were also visiting the H14, a Dart route. Cricklewood was simultaneously spreading its TAs (and now TALs too) to the 112, 189, 232, 266 and 316.

It wasn't just the 16 that hogged the new buses; a late change was made to the new

Right: **One of the setbacks of low-floor double-deck operation as the myriad types started to enter service was their extremely low seated capacity, and the only way to address this at the time was by specifying the longer chassis option on Dennis Tridents and Volvo B7TLs. Seventeen of the former constituted Metroline's new TAL class and took over the 16 in October 2000. Seen departing Victoria bus station on 7 February 2002 is Cricklewood's TAL 131 (X331 HLL).** *Author*

VPLs' deployment as soon as they arrived by which they would upgrade the 43 and allow its TPs to take over the 271 and W7. This took place from 17-31 January 2001, though the TPs were just as apt to turn out on anything else at Holloway, particularly the 4 and the 271 comparatively rarely.

On 19 July 2001 TP 15, running dead off the W7, overshot the roundabout at Crouch End and demolished the grocery on the corner.

After a year of VPL deliveries, Metroline was swayed back to the Trident, in October 2001 placing an order for 33 TPLs against the 263 (won on tender from First Capital) and C2 (to be double-decked). This order was increased to sixty when requirements for the 204 and 240 were taken into account, but, as with several earlier batches, minds were changed again and the new buses would appear on none of these routes! Indeed the

Right: **Another Holloway route to field TPs from time to time was the 4, otherwise relegated to the garage's flotsam that included ex-London Suburban Buses Volvo Olympians and the remaining Metrobuses, deteriorating sharply in appearance. On 19 May 2001 TP 29 (T129 KLD) is at the Angel.** *Author*

263 had a clearance issue at Barnet Hospital, so instead the 140 benefited from the TPLs' greater capacity and TPLs 237-254 were deployed to Harrow Weald when they arrived in January 2002, freeing TAs 100-117 to go to Potters Bar and start the 263 on 2 February. TPLs 255-274 were then deployed to Potters Bar from the 19th to effect a type change on the 82 from the recently-allocated VPLs and standardise the garage on Tridents. That displaced enough VPLs to Holloway to complete the 134 and thereby release enough early TPs for the C2. Potters Bar's new TA intake soon spread their net to the 82, 217, 231, 310A and 317 plus non-TfL 84 and 242, and the TPLs followed suit when they could.

Right: **Aside from low capacity and the risk of striking street furniture, the early low-floor buses were also felt too long and wide for the narrow streets served adequately by the compact Metrobus and Titan generation. The 263 had 10.5m TPLs ordered but wouldn't have been able to get them round the access roads at Barnet Hospital so had to cede them to the 140. Three design changes advanced by Plaxton since their 9.9m predecessors were gasket windows, forward staircases and blind boxes of equal depth so that the lower one could carry a destination in mixed upper- and lower-case destination. On 5 March 2002 TPL 250 (LN51 KYF) is seen at Harrow & Wealdstone station; the new registration system was a further progression.** *Author*

Above: **The 140's TAs were transferred to the 263 at Potters Bar and on 2 March 2002 we see TA 104 (T204 CLO) at North Finchley.** *Author*

December 2001 had seen the award to Metroline of a new route over the northern half of what was presently known as Stationlink. To be known as 205, the route had twenty TPs ordered for it. Then, in March, a comprehensive set of tender wins would massively increase this number, as well as that of the competing Volvo B7TL. The scoop of the 24 from Arriva London North was accompanied by the announcement at the same time of the retention of the 16 and 32, whose existing Tridents would be augmented by new buses, and finally the 139 and 189 would be getting new TPs with their welcome double-decking. The order, placed in July, comprised 81 TPs.

Left: **Further TPLs were allocated to Potters Bar for the busy trunk route 82, whose garage runs from North Finchley were almost as long as the route itself! At this point in time a temporary stand was in use at North Finchley, and on 2 June 2002 TPL 264 (LN51 KYP), which had replaced a VPL introduced earlier, is seen setting off from it.** *Author*

Right: **The C2 ran over busier roads than those who had introduced it with Volkswagen minibuses had realised, and after SRs and DNLs it was time to double-deck it, which was done with TPs displaced from the 134. On 30 March 2002 TP 52 (V752 HBY) is seen at Oxford Circus.** *Author*

Below: **The competing VPL and TPL classes would battle it out for dominance at Holloway over the next decade as Metroline shuffled its types again and again. On 4 July 2002 TPL 285 (LR02 BCF) is setting off from North Finchley on the 134.** *Author*

TPL 268 out of Potters Bar was one of Metroline's gold-vinylled contributions to the Golden Jubilee celebrations. It carried the colours, sponsored by Felix cat food, between May and December.

TPLs 275-296 were allocated to Holloway during May, releasing VPLs to Edgware to double-deck it in accordance with the terms of its contract applying from 27 April. The 240 was taken out of the VPL conversion

programme at this point, buying its by now extremely elderly Metrobuses a stay of execution that would take them into their third decade of operation!

TP 297-316 went seamlessly onto the 205 with its commencement out of Cricklewood on 31 August. It was originally planned to inaugurate the new Perivale garage, but this had to be postponed. TAs and Ms soon appeared. 12 October saw the 16, 32 and 189

Above left: **Potters Bar's TPL 268 (LN51 KZC) represented Metroline in gold for the Queen's Golden Jubilee; the treatment was predominantly vinyl with paint on the tricky bits. It is seen on 11 May 2002 at North Finchley.** *Author*

Above: **The 310A was one of the successful stabs at purely commercial operation by LBL, managing a decade and a half. All sorts of eclectic buses turned out on it over that time, but on 1 June 2002 the present Metrobuses found themselves joined by TPL 260 (LN51 KYU), seen in Ponders End.** *Author*

Left: **Allocated to Cricklewood to begin with, new route 205 was the northern half of the old Stationlink accessible service, and proved massively successful whereas the southern bore (latterly known as 705) withered and died. On 18 September 2002 new TP 305 (LT02 ZZK) is calling at Euston. This batch was leased, and would thus have a much curtailed career in London.** *Author*

renewed, the former pair having to furnish their increased PVRs with DLDs made spare from the 316's loss to Thorpes and the 189 awaiting its new TPs by year's end. The N16 also fell out of the reckoning for Tridents with its reallocation from Cricklewood to Edgware. New route N189 started and took its place, however.

On 9 November the 205 was reallocated to Perivale, taking TPs 297-316 with it (and allowing them to pop up on the 95 occasionally). Though the 24 was taken on by Holloway on this day, its allocation was VPs and Tridents rarely appeared after the first few days when TPs were drafted to cover the late delivery of half of the Volvos.

Right: **After working on the 16 during the day, Cricklewood's TALs would switch their blinds to N139 or N189 and keep going. Just such an adventure is captured after midnight on 13 July 2003 at Trafalgar Square, in the form of TAL 126 (X326 HLL).** *Author*

Left: **As low-floor double-deckers became the production norm, TfL's contractors ordered sufficient to replace Dart SLFs that had been all that was available when the accessibility imperative was getting under way. DLDs really did not belong on the 189, which had replaced M-operated 16A, and while its new TPs were awaited, TAs were often put out. At Oxford Circus on 1 October 2003 two have managed it, in the form of TAs 78 (T78 KLD) and 105 (T205 CLO).** *Author*

Left: **Another route where wheelchair accessibility trumped the needs of larger numbers of passengers expecting to sit down was the 232, set going again in 1999 with DLDs replacing its admittedly exhausted Metrobuses. However, the route suffered severe overcrowding as a lone conduit into Brent Cross from the north-east, and occasionally Cricklewood, one of a bewildering variety of garages to get handed the route at this point in time, would take pity and put out a TA, or even better a TAL. Passing Wood Green garage, now of Arriva London North, on 4 August 2003, is TA 101 (T201 CLO).** *Author*

Left: **Uniquely unchanged but curiously difficult to run truly efficiently, the 24 was won, lost and won back by Metroline. The company chose VPs for its 9 November 2002 start but often added TPs to the mix. The earlier breed was much less common, but here at Warren Street on 16 February 2003 is TP 4 (T104 KLD). A partial repaint has been accompanied by a new numberplate with the stingy 51mm-wide characters made standard upon the introduction of the new registration system.** *Author*

2002 ended with the award of the W8 from First Capital, who had taken it off MTL London in the first place. 2003 was to be a big year for Tridents, as this route was included in a repeat order for 37 TPs which would also double-deck the 217 and 231. Otherwise, the year's first change where Metroline was concerned came on 1 February with a change to the 10, whose contract was split and the western half of the route awarded to First London. Retaining the rest up to Archway was new route 390, keeping the Metroline RMs and RMLs plus TPs and TPLs on Sundays. What were by now routine PVR boosts encompassed the 4, 17 and 134 and TPs 348-362 were earmarked for this role. The 139 was renewed on the same date and TPs 363-402 began taking over, also furnishing the 189. Until the majority of the batch arrived, TAs were seconded from the 32, which filled in with DLDs. At Holloway a new N271 began over the daytime 271.

On 29 March the 390 and its RMLs were transferred from Holloway to the new King's Cross garage, but the Sunday OPO element remained with Holloway. TPs were loaned to the new base nonetheless and operated with conductors while the 390 was still crew. TP deliveries continued into April, the 139 and 189 having been completed in March. First up was the allocation of TP 419-428 to Holloway so that an equivalent number of VPLs could convert Edgware's 240 from M finally. TPs

429-445 duly took over the 217 and 231 from DML to accompany their contract renewal with Potters Bar at Metroline London Northern on 7 July. Potters Bar was due further TPs for the W8, but these were sent initially to Park Royal (ex-Harlesden) for its new route 460, which commenced on 28 June without its intended new VPs as yet. Until that route started, they worked on the 260 (from which the 460 would be derived) and 266.

Above: **Metroline continued to split its orders between Volvo and what was now Transbus, shifting the VP/ VPL and TP/TPL classes back and forth as required without ever really achieving 100% standardisation of one chassis or another. TP 427 (LK03 CGU), seen at King's Cross on Bank Holiday Monday 5 May 2003 when the 390 was OPO, was delivered to allow a VPL to head to Edgware, disregarding the resulting lower capacity.** *Author*

Left: **Potters Bar garage had, however, left its VPLs behind to standardise on Tridents and its TPLs for the 82 and TAs for the 263 were joined in 2003 by new TPs to take over the 217 and 231 from their DML-class Dart SLFs. On 15 June 2003 we see TP 429 (LK03 GFU) at Turnpike Lane.** *Author*

Right: **Park Royal garage was really in Harlesden and formerly known as such, but in order to attract drivers renamed itself. The 460 was intended for VPs, but the TPs intended for Potters Bar arrived first. TP 457 (LK03 GJG) is at Golders Green on 28 June 2003, the 460's first day.** *Author*

Below: **Holloway spent a short period on the 263, converting it from TA to TP upon its reallocation from Potters Bar. On 26 July 2003 TP 411 (LK03 CFE) is coming into Barnet.** *Author*

On 26 July the W8 was indeed taken over by Metroline London Northern, but a problem arose in that even though its intended new TPs replaced the similar First TNs, they rode slightly higher and thus fouled the bridge leading to Edmonton Green station. Until the road could be lowered by the same amount, Potters Bar borrowed DLDs from Perivale's 297, which took the TPs temporarily at Park Royal. This route had recently been put into Park Royal and had already tried out TPs wandering from the 205. To make room at Potters Bar, the 263 was reallocated to Holloway and converted from TA to TP, Holloway receiving newish TPs from Cricklewood and donating the TAs in exchange. Potters Bar managed to keep hold of three TAs and continued to mix them with its TPs and TPLs.

The 17 was renewed with Metroline London Northern on 26 July, with Holloway's existing TPs, and at night the N20 was added ex-First Capital, using Potters Bar TPs. On 30 August Potters Bar took over school route 626, using TPs.

Now that the 297 had tasted TP operation, which ended with the restoration of the temporary Tridents to the W8 on 2 September, it had seventeen of its own ordered for December delivery, but that was the last Trident order for the moment as Volvo was

the one to grab the seventy-strong order which would one-man the 6 and 98 in 2004, followed by the requirement for the 390 when it too lost its Routemasters. Further bad luck saw the 297's order for Tridents cancelled and sixteen more VPs substituted. But even then, a further twist ensued, as when these buses started arriving in December they were put into Holloway to ensure standardisation with existing based examples and TPs 412-426 were transferred to Perivale, converting the 297 after all!

Above: **Once the bridge at Edmonton Green had the roadway beneath it lowered, the W8's intended TPs entered service at Potters Bar after a temporary period at Perivale. On 17 October 2003 TP 451 (LK03 GHU) has just been under the offending bridge and is entering the bus station.** *Author*

Left: **On 22 May 2004 TP 420 (LK03 CFV) calls at Wembley, having formalised full-time double-deck operation on the 297 from Perivale.** *Author*

The 140, 182 and 640 were now approaching the statutory five years with their incumbent and were tendered again at the end of 2003, as were the 43 and 134. Harrow Weald kept hold of all three (the announcement coming in March with an accompanying order for 25 new VPs) and Holloway's two would similarly be retained. Then in March the 82 was put out to tender again and the C2 followed shortly after.

On 12 January 2004 new all-day school route 603 began with Potters Bar TPs; on 27 March it was reallocated to Holloway, which was much closer! This day also saw the 263 reallocated back to Potters Bar and the migration there of TPs 358, 361, 362, 398 and 404-411. During mid-March Metroline's remaining Metrobuses were withdrawn, save

for a handful at Potters Bar; the majority had been at Harrow Weald and were replaced by six TPLs transferred from Holloway.

A spate of renumberings of night routes that followed their day counterparts took the N off the N271 on 3 April and treated the N140 similarly on the 17th. Then, on the 24th, fell the N134, N139 and N189.

The 43 and 134 were announced as retained in May, adding three and four buses respectively to their existing PVRs.

In June 2004 Cricklewood's TAL 123 debuted a new Metroline livery whereby the blue skirt was much shorter, complying with a TfL edict to reduce still further the proportion of non-red. Repaints ensued, though some TPs had already had red painted around their headlight surrounds.

Right: **On 27 March 2004 Potters Bar gained back the 263 but kept TP operation, albeit with a slightly different blind set. On 26 September TP 433 (LK03 GFZ) heads south through Barnet.** *Author*

Right: **TPL 243 (LN51 KXW) was one of eleven TPLs transferred from Harrow Weald to Holloway in September 2004 when the 140 and 182 were refreshed with new VPs. It is seen on 15 October 2005 at Warren Street.** *Author*

With effect from the 4 September contract date changes, Harrow Weald was changed to become a Volvo B7TL garage; the new VPs ordered against the 140 and 182 indeed entered service there and TPLs left for Holloway, which sent them twenty-five further VPs, leaving just enough for the 24. Just the 640 was left with TAs (which could now wander to the H12 upon its takeup from Sovereign); the H14 going in the other direction had regularly seen TPLs but could no longer do so. This was also the 390's OPO conversion date, removing Routemasters from Metroline and also transferring Holloway's Sunday roster to King's Cross with the rest of the route.

London was by now bidding for the 2012 Olympics and TfL commissioned a series of all-over ads in blue; the first Metroline Trident to receive it was Cricklewood's TAL 126 in September. Stablemate TA 67 followed in October.

It looked clear by now that the Volvo B7TL had well and truly displaced the Dennis Trident in Metroline's affections, but a surprise order followed the announcement in September of the retention of the 266 and N266 on the basis of new vehicles. Even though no ALX400s had been ordered since TALs 118-134 as far back as 2000, there was

now no choice as what was now Alexander Dennis had deleted the President body from availability and closed down the factory at Wigan, Metroline indeed taking the last as VPLs 629-637. Thus were 22 TAs ordered to revive the class one last time before Alexander Dennis unveiled its all-new Enviro400. In the same tranches the 82 and C2 were retained by Metroline, and on 4 October the 143 added a double-deck school journey over part of its route. However, the 4, 271 and W7, all of which could field Tridents of one form or another despite the constant fluctuation of types at Holloway, were all put out to tender during the summer or autumn of 2004. Metroline retained all three.

During December the Metroline London Northern identity was formally deleted, Metroline absorbing its O-Licence through an increase to its own number of discs. On New Year's Day 2005 TfL followed suit by reassigning the routes to Metroline proper.

Changes to night routes on 5 February saw the N43 come off and a night service introduced on the 43, while the N20 gained a Holloway allocation and part of Cricklewood's N16 was transferred to Harrow Weald. On the weekends of 19/20, 26/27 February and 5/6 March, Holloway added double-deck extras to the 214, including TPLs and VPLs.

2 April saw the 82 begin a new contract with its existing Potters Bar TPLs, and on the 30th Holloway's C2 started its own new term with Metroline. The 266 was renewed on 21 May with a transfer from Park Royal to Cricklewood and conversion to Trident using new TA 638-659. At this point the opportunity was taken to close Park Royal and assimilate the Thorpes operations into Metroline, resulting in the redistribution of several routes; accordingly the 460 became a TP possibility with its move to Perivale and the 316 was added to TA or TAL capability at Cricklewood (the move of the 232 to North Wembley removing its own possibility to use Tridents). While able to field TPs at Holloway, the 4 was converted from V to AV operation until step-entrance buses were formally banned from TfL operations by the end of 2005.

That was the last of the new Tridents with Metroline, TA 648 coming late due to the fitment of a Euro 4 engine. Metroline was the launch customer for the Trident's successor,

the integral Enviro400 (though still based on the nominal 'Trident II' chassis referred to on the manufacturer's plate), and in theory they were for AV and LLW replacement.

The 205 was affected particularly badly by the terrorist bombings of 7 July 2005, adding ad-hoc augmentations by First and Blue Triangle on top of its regular Perivale TPs and Vs made spare from the 4. On the 25th a vandalism incident at Perivale prompted the loan of two Harrow Weald TAs, which worked on the 460 and 205.

On 20 August the W7 started a new Metroline contract with its existing TPs and whatever else Holloway saw fit to throw at it. Repaints to the early TPs were almost complete by now, the shallow blue skirt distinguishing these as well as the early batch of TAs and TALs. A white roof was also specified as part of routine repaints, in a rather desperate attempt to mitigate the extreme heat problems caused by the gradual deletion from new buses' spec of front upper-deck opening windows.

Notting Hill Carnival always threw up some regular unusual workings, the most relevant of which for this book's purposes being the use of double-deckers on the 316 (borrowed from the 266's TA allocation).

The Bid won, the Back the Bid buses were restored to their respective fleet liveries, TAL 126 losing its blue in August and TA 67 regaining red in September.

With the Routemaster about to bow out, TfL had simultaneously ordered the standing down of all step-entrance buses by the end of 2005, but the 4 remained AV-operated with none of the expected new Enviro400s that would indirectly replace them yet on the horizon; therefore Metroline hired six TNs made spare at First and put them into action at Holloway from 21 November. They were first used on the 214 as Dart replacements and then moved en bloc to the 4, on which they were joined in December by ten more. They were similar enough to existing TPs to fit in well and soon wandered to the 17 and 271.

Left: **Turn ninety degrees to the left from the previous photo on the same day and one could see the 4 as it debouched from Dartmouth Park Hill. This was also turned over to hired First TNs so that its AVs could be withdrawn and thus render all contractors 100% low-floor by the end of 2005. Holloway's regular set of KM/NN blinds don't sit all too well in the wider apertures of TN 32806 (T806 LLC), however.** *Author*

At the end of 2005, as repaints concluded to the TA 66-81 batch and the balance of the early TPs, livery experiments were conducted in order to determine the best new scheme for the incoming TE class and emblazon ComfortDelgro's brand better than some subsidiary stickers had been doing recently. The main effect was to lighten the blue skirt to a remarkably sickly shade and add an orange line above it (TA 105), while TA 96 added the orange line to the existing shade of blue.

2006 began with the transfer of the 643 from Perivale to Cricklewood on 21 January. As the new TEs arrived, they allowed the 24's existing VPs to ease out the hired First TNs, with two returned on 23 January, ten in February and two in March, but two then came back! TNs 32958 and 32964 were sent

back to First on 20 May, leaving TNs 32959 and 32960 to linger as long as 25 August.

After six months of repaints and the delivery of the latest TEs and DLDs in the light-skirted livery, a halt was called and subsequent repaints brought back the darker colour; TAs 104 (skirt only) and 114 had been the only Metroline Tridents to receive it, aside from the prototypes, TAs 92, 96 and 105, which were restored to original condition. At the same time, the TA 66-81 batch had their upper-deck bench seats replaced with Fainsa Cosmic individual seating. Frivolous lawsuits relating to people catching themselves in the tip-up seats were warded off by effectively punishing everybody else through the locking out of use of these seats from late 2006 onwards, reducing capacity by one downstairs (two on the early TPs).

Right: **Compare the skirt colours on TA 204 (T204 CLO) and TPL 276 (LR02 BBJ) at Brent Cross on 8 May 2007; where the President's is the elegant shade of dark blue introduced by Metroline a decade previously to cement its post-privatisation image, the putative replacement is just sickly, and, as it turned out, wouldn't last.** *Author*

Right: **The full pastel horror on Cricklewood's TA 114 (V314 GLB), reposing at the first Waterloo stand of the 139 on 3 December 2005. The route was later pushed down the Waterloo Road to turn opposite the Old Vic.** *Author*

2006 had proven quiet, with no further new Tridents and all transfers now based on existing vehicles. The next twelve TEs were allocated to Holloway, which in turn sent ten TPLs to Potters Bar, which released eight of its own TPLs and two TPs to Cricklewood for a huge boost to the 16's PVR on 2 December. These transfers united at Cricklewood buses fitted with Metroline's iRIS control system, which was about to be superseded across this and every other London fleet by TfL's own iBus.

Having put an end to the Metroline London Northern identity via the increase in Metroline discs, the company treated its Thorpes and Armchair brands similarly, adding 205 more discs on 20 October and having the contracts ressigned formally on 6 January 2007. Where Armchair was concerned, its twenty-one ALX400-bodied Tridents on the 237 were brought into the overall fleet, though they retained their DT class codes even as preparations were made to repaint them out of their red, orange and

black into Metroline livery (the blue skirts going on first). Like the 16, the 237 required its own PVR increase, so TAs 81, 83 and 84 were sent from Harrow Weald to Brentford. As well as the 237, the DTs at Metroline had a school journey on the E8 added for them from 6 January.

The fitting of iBus gear sparked a long-running series of inter-company transfers which would provide much more variety

hitherto. Metroline started the ball rolling wth the acquisition of six ex-Metrobus Tridents recently displaced from the 261 by new Scanias, and after repainting them, numbered them ET 765-770 for a short-term sojourn at Harrow Weald on the 140, 182 and H12 beginning on 30 January 2007. By 3 February the TAs at Brentford returned to Harrow Weald, replaced there by four 05-registered examples from Cricklewood, while the

rotation of iRIS-fitted TPLs into Cricklewood via Potters Bar continued. After that the 460 (and 611) at Perivale was converted from VP to TP during April to standardise that garage on Tridents; the VPs left for Holloway, leaving just TP 1-65 at the latter. Holloway's TPLs similarly departed, being replaced by VPLs from Edgware (which had converted their 204 to new TEs) and allowing all the iRIS-fitted TPLs to concentrate at Cricklewood.

Perivale occasionally fielded TPs on the 90 and was gearing up to make them available when the 7 came in from First on 23 June. Routine loans to and from Metroline garages paid no attention to standardisation, with TA 641 and TAL 129 working out of Harrow Weald on 12 April.

On 14 April the C2 added a night service, obliging the weeknight Holloway allocation on the N5 to be transferred to Edgware.

Right: Scania's N94UD and later N230UD progression formed a measure of competition to Dennis and Volvo, or would have done if they hadn't been so heavy and late in delivery. Metroline tried some out as the SEL class when it needed some particularly high-end vehicles with which to take over the 7 on 23 June 2007, but until they were altered to bring their weight down, had to make do with TPLs transferred into Perivale. One such was TPL 242 (LN51 KXV), sent by Holloway and still carrying that garage's code when seen at Marble Arch on the first day of operations. *Author*

Right: To free existing Perivale TPs to join the acquired TPLs on the 7, Metroline hired eighteen Tridents from neighbouring First London. TNA 32952 (W952 ULL), its DDA-spec blinds ill-fitting in its wider blind boxes when seen at Wembley on 23 June 2007, was one of the ones that had operated the 7 anyway upon its OPO conversion. *Author*

Right: First London had also taken Plaxton President bodies on the 10.5m version of the Dennis Trident, but knew them as TNs and TNLs. On attachment to Perivale when seen on 23 June 2007, TNL 32905 (W905 VLN) is seen heading the other way at Wembley and its blind boxes do fit the borrowed blinds. *Author*

Mindful that the 7's new Scanias were not going to be in place by the takeover date due to the need for tilt test-related modifications to their East Lancs bodywork, Metroline despatched Holloway's eleven remaining TPLs to Perivale on 15 June; these were intended to serve as refurbishment cover but started off the 7 and N7 on the 23rd as well as appearing on the 297, 460 and 611. On 30 June eighteen long-wheelbase Tridents were hired from First (twelve TNAs and six TNLs) to put onto the 297 and thereby ensure that Metroline-liveried buses stuck to the 7, 205 and N7. The new SELs eventually began arriving and the first entered service on 31 July. The TPLs stayed put for the moment, covering the 205's PVR increase that had accompanied its extension to Mile End on 28 April. Seven further SELs were on order for this task. The First hires departed during August and September, TNAs 32936, 32946 and 32948-32950 being the last to go on 18 September. However TNLs 32900-32905 were hired again to keep the temporary TPLs company pending the delivery of the seven new SELs.

TA 67 had already worn one ad when a Back the Bid bus; between August 2007 and March 2008 it received a scheme for Venezuela tourism in combination with the promotion of reduced fares for Income Support recipients. Routine repaints now swept through Brentford's DTs, and paint quality as a whole was stepped up after having been found to be sub-standard when the red colour faded quickly to pink! The similarly unattractive light blue skirt colour was consigned to memory at the same time.

The introduction of new Cricklewood-operated route 332 on 13 October was part of a plan to alter routes along the Edgware Road corridor, and it commenced with another batch of new TEs, but TAs and TPs appeared from the first day. On 27 October JFS school routes 628 and 688 had two Holloway TPs added, unusually as augmentations to existing Arriva London North contracts.

The loss of the 24 to London General on 10 November precluded any further Holloway Trident appearances, rare as they had been. The 316 was also capable of Trident visits since its return from Thorpes and was double-deck again during 2007's incarnation of Carnival. The E8 gained another school DT. However, another round of musical buses was in the offing at Metroline, designed to upgrade Holloway's 134's age profile with the TEs spare from the 24; as part of this exercise Harrow Weald lost its remaining TAs to become 100% VP, barring the six ETs which were to be kept around a little longer. Perivale's hired TNLs hung on in decreasing numbers until 21 December, DLDs having to stand in on the 297 until SELs 803-809 began arriving at the end of the month.

On 22 December school route 634, run hitherto by Potters Bar TPs, was taken over by Arriva London North. That garage's 231 was announced as lost to First Capital at the same time and routes 263, 297 and 460 were put out to tender. Rounding off 2007 was the loan of five ex-Harrow Weald TAs to Travel London for standby cover on that company's East London Line rail replacement route ELC,

though a much greater cause was identified for these buses, which began receiving repaints in preparation. This was Perivale West's 210, extremely busy but never trusted to permanent double-deckers until formal conversion from its former Thorpes Dart SLFs between 15-20 February 2008. Prior to that, the assistance was taken off the ELC so that the TAs could be loaned to London United for an augmentation to the 148 and then replaced by spare TPLs until June.

During March, further necessity for modifications to the first batch of SELs led to the loan of TP 61-65 to Perivale to cover their absence; they were kept to the 297. The Perivales were apt to loan to one another, with West's TA 86 sighted on the 297 on 30 March.

Of the TP-operated routes out to tender, the 297 and 460 were announced as retained by Metroline, plus the existing 626, N5 and N20, though the 460 was awarded on the basis of new buses. The 297's award, also with new buses, included a night service, which was introduced on 7 June. Fate would see neither the 297 nor 460 take the new buses promised them. During the period of loan of TPLs to

Below: **Even at half the length of its historical extent, the 210 had always been busy enough for double-deckers, had successive authorities now baulked at risking getting them through the extremely narrow North End Road between Golders Green and Hampstead. The gamble to convert it paid off, however, and on 25 July 2008 Perivale West's TA 84 (T184 CLO) is seen at Golders Green. Two-line blinds into a three-line blind box had produced a distinct waste of blank Tyvek.** *Author*

London United, Metroline also loaned two pairs to Travel London in May and June to address a shortage at that company. A third company to use Metroline TPLs was Go-Ahead's Docklands Buses, whose new route 425 beginning on 5 July had been let down by late Scania deliveries. The six in question spent the month before that filling in for iBus cover at Stockwell (London General). Potters Bar's own TPLs began going through refurbishment during the summer, at the same time as Metroline experienced iBus fitment without the need to take in any loans of its own; indeed members of the early TP batch served from Potters Bar and both Perivales in this role. Holloway even got TPLs back for a bit under this programme (including TPL 255, whose repair after a fire on 6 September 2006 had taken nearly two years!).

On 7 June the 231 was taken over by First Capital, freeing five Potters Bar TPs for transfer to Perivale. The 28th saw the 460 renewed with Enviro400s expected, plus the 143's school TP element and 643. Then came the start of new contracts for the N5 and N20 from 26 July. The 16, 32, 139, 189, 205 and 640 all found themselves put out to tender during this portion of the year and the 263, after a long delay, was announced as retained in June, again with new double-deckers (and this time it would actually receive them!).

Once again the 16 hogged the new buses, the 460's batch of TEs being diverted here when they arrived in July and August 2008, and it was decided that the 297's batch would also go to Cricklewood. As iBus fitment approached completion, TPs from either end of the age spectrum were moved into Brentford and converted the E8 temporarily to double-deck, with associated appearances on the 190 as well as the 237, which would expect them. The E8 was already out to tender at this juncture, and indeed it was planned to use additional TPs from Cricklewood's 52-reg stock to ease out the DTs, which were leased. The early TPs (48-51) assisting at Brentford were then loaned to Docklands Buses to replace that company's hired TPLs during August. TPLs 237 and 238 went on to CT Plus, but the longer-term nature of their loan resulted in their becoming known as

HTP 1 and 2 while there. On 17 August TPs appeared at Harrow Weald as iBus cover, but it was three days later that the five ETs were withdrawn, replaced by VPs ex-Holloway On 30 August Metroline came off the 628, 683 and 688.

Despite having been edged off the 16, Cricklewood's TALs stayed put and were repainted, with the 32's batch of T-reg TAs put into store and TPs transferred to Brentford, where they finished off the DT class by 9 October. That also allowed the six 05-reg TAs to come back. Before leaving the company outright, some of the DTs were loaned to Travel London (the next incarnation of which, Abellio London, would become home to many of them). In October eleven TAs and the five ETs were loaned to the East London Bus Group (formerly Stagecoach), which was now undergoing its own iBus programme. Together with four TPs, they were divided between East London (Rainham garage) and Selkent (Plumstead garage).

With so many of its most important routes up for grabs as 2008 came to an end (now including the 237, which was extended on 29 November to the new Westfield shopping centre at White City), Metroline suffered a blow in November with the award of the 205 to East London. Less of a loss was the 640, which would be taken up the following autumn by Arriva the Shires.

Left: **Three years into the delivery of new TE-class Enviro400s, enough TPs were now available to replace the DTs at the former Armchair's Brentford garage. TP 377 (LR52 KWV) was one such transfer and on 27 September 2009 is caught making its way round the perimeter road leading from the White City stand to the extensive new bus station constructed at the shopping centre's Shepherd's Bush exit.** *Author*

Holloway had not generally been associated with TPLs since its examples departed earlier in their careers, but the necessity to provide VPLs for Edgware's double-decking of the 107 brought back several of the type in December and January. At this point Perivale West was letting its TAs wander from the 210 to the 143, a new venture for them.

On 7 February 2009, the morning after the N20 gained back its weeknight Holloway share, the 263 was renewed with Metroline, its TPs being replaced by new TEs into Potters Bar. The displaced Tridents moved into Cricklewood to release some of the recently-allocated TEs to head to Perivale West in time for its assumption from Perivale proper on 7 March. This was part of a tidying-up exercise whereby the 210 was reallocated with its TA fleet from Perivale West to Cricklewood. The outgoing Perivale TAs from the 297 were stood down following that route's move to the other Perivale, despite being only seven years old; fourteen of these had been part of the 205's original batch spanning TP 297-316.

Left: **It's curious how schoolchildren were not even trusted with being able to understand via points on their school routes, leading to the unattractive solution seen on TPL 240 (LN51 KXT) at Brent Cross on 21 October 2009. The 611 was a section of the 112 that was slightly too busy for the main route's single-deckers but not busy enough to merit full conversion of the whole routes.** *Author*

Above: **Twice had the E2 been converted to single-deck and twice it was restored to double-deck, the first time with DMSs replacing SMSs and in 2009 with TPs replacing Dart SLFs. TP 378 (LR52 KWW) is almost at the end of its journey to Ealing Broadway on 27 September 2009.** *Author*

In March good news brought the retention by Metroline of the 16, 32, 139 and 189, all with new buses, while the 217 and W8 found themselves tendered. All the TAs and TPs loaned to East London came back in March and April, the TAs being revived at Cricklewood so as to allow TPs to leave for Brentwood to convert the E2 to double-deck on 30 May, prior to the delivery of its own new TEs.

After thirteen years of Metroline red and blue (including the abortive light-blue skirt aberration!) all-red repaints were ordered by TfL and the first such was TAL 123 in June. It would take six years to treat the whole fleet, and many of the repaints at first were just partial to go over the skirts.

27 June 2009 saw the C2 extended from Oxford Circus to Victoria; Holloway added four TPLs to release existing TPs.

Right: **When Holloway gained back TPLs it was for keeps; although the class constituted only sixty vehicles, they did some concerted moving between four garages in their fourteen-year careers. This is TPL 244 (LN51 KXY), seen diverted away from the 134's usual New Oxford Street direction to stand while the Tottenham Court Road area was undergoing revamping in concert with Crossrail construction.** *Author*

Left: **One of the expansion routes, the 205 was a roaring success but Metroline was a little too far away to run it successfully enough to be awarded another contract. Nor was East London, come to think of it, whose Bow wasn't particularly closer to line of route than Perivale had been, or at least not until the route's extension to Mile End. On 19 June 2009 TP 409 (LK03 CFA) is leaving Liverpool Street station, on a section that was later cut out to make overall progress quicker.** *Author*

On 29 August the 205 duly departed for East London; some of its TPs were transferred to Brentford (its 237 now awarded and expecting its own new Volvo B9TLs) so that earlier TPs could be returned off lease to Dawson Rentals. This new method of ownership had increasingly seen buses leaving London after just the five to seven years of their contract terms rather than replacing earlier examples in the traditional manner, leading to a surfeit of older buses operated until they fell apart, more or less (and with the lower longevity of low-floor buses by comparison with their predecessors, after what seemed like a wastefully short career overall!). The balance of the SEL fleet at Perivale moved over to the 460.

During October the E2 was converted from TP to TE and large numbers of 52-reg TPs were decommissioned, going into

Left: **The 217 and 231 had operated as a pair for many years due to their common section down the Great Cambridge Road, and under Potters Bar the first time had even run on a combined schedule. Although the routes returned to that garage under contract from Metroline, the next round of tenders severed them when the 231 was awarded to First Capital. For the moment we see TPs 433 (LK03 GFZ) and 449 (LK03 GHJ) laying over at Turnpike Lane on 20 July 2010.** *Author*

storage at the now closed North Wembley garage, though some escaped to Potters Bar. Tendering progress as 2009 wound down was that the 17, 217 and W8 were kept, though new buses were intended for the 217 once the recession of the moment had been powered through, and the 210 was offered out. On 9 January 2010 the 237 began its new contract and the 30th saw the 139 follow suit, on the heels of the 32 and 189 since 10 October; the 16 could also still field Tridents alongside its scheduled TEs and now hybrid TEHs.

TPLs 237 and 238 came back from CT Plus in February 2010 and were put into action at Perivale. From 27 March the 237 began to operate its new VW-class Volvo B9TLs, the TPs released going to Holloway (either direct or displacing others from Cricklewood) to cascade VPs to Willesden to double-deck the 302. This was when the first TPs began departing off lease, receiving a repaint to as-new condition before they left.

Contract renewals with existing TPs (plans to upgrade them having fallen victim to the straitened economic times) were Potters Bar's 217 on 5 June and the 17 (Holloway) and W8 (Potters Bar) on 24 July. The 210 was also due a new contract to start on 25 September, but a raft of new Enviro400s began arriving for this and a proportion of the 139 and 189 under their own contracts. Some of these were TEHs, paid for by the Green Bus Fund. In any case the T-reg TAs were now in their second decade and fair game for disposal, which occurred by the autumn, aided at Cricklewood by ex-Brentford TEs displaced by further new VWs.

With daytime running lights now becoming fashionable as a perceived safety aid, TP 454 returned from accident repair to Potters Bar in June with a pair of LED banks under the headlights. The overstrained turbocharged engines in Tridents had begun to earn the type an unhappy reputation for going up in flames, and TP 445 was thus consumed on the W8 at Winchmore Hill on 21 August. TP 433 followed suit on 29 November in Barnet High Street!

On 11 December the 460 was reallocated from Perivale to Willesden and lost its TPL contingent for VPs; the 611 was thus converted to SEL as its cross-link now derived from the 7. The TPLs lingered at Perivale until January 2011 and then left.

Below: **Blink and you'd miss 'em; the 02-reg contingent of TPs departed after just seven years; even most DMSs managed that much. Although undoubtedly good for the bottom line, it seemed a wasteful practice to lease buses just for their contracts and then take them away rather than use them to replace older buses in the time-honoured manner. On 18 October 2010 TP 303 (LT02 ZZH) is at the Angel under Holloway stewardship and has acquired an upper-case ultimate, though strangely deprived of the word 'Station', misleading passengers; the 43 didn't terminate on the bridge, after all. This bus left the fleet the following March.** *Author*

All of TA 66-117 were now earmarked for sale to Ensignbus, but three were used by them on the 25 on 29 November when the tube was on strike. Heavy TA withdrawals took place in December and into January 2011 as TEHs arrived at Cricklewood (with 26 more now ordered to finish off the 139), while the TPL class returned to Harrow Weald for a few months when three were allocated there as VP refurbishment cover, the Volvos being the existing buses for retained Metroline contracts on the 140, 182 and H12. Five TPs joined them in January. Otherwise, all of the TP 348-402 batch was withdrawn by March and disposed of by May. A handful of early TAs still held out at Cricklewood, but an order for Volvo B9TLs was now placed which, in Metroline's typical convoluted style, would cascade other vehicles to let them leave the company.

Left: **The early TAs had now come to the end of the road, departing in 2011 after ten and a bit years. On 18 October 2010 Cricklewood's TA 107 (T207 CLO), with three months left to go, is making the right-hand turn from Oxford Street into Regent Street, but across a much-recast Oxford Circus junction in which a Japanese-style diagonal crossing has been added to the other four. Most helpful for crossing pedestrians, but a nightmare for photography!** *Author*

During the first half of 2011, the 82, C2 and W7 were put out to tender in that order, and the first announcement, in August, was of the loss of the C2 to Abellio. The 4, 43, 134 and 271, all capable of TP or TPL operation when Holloway saw fit, were also under offer at this time. All were retained with new buses, barring the 271 which was to keep existing vehicles, but with the likelihood of Enviro400 cascades to form this component, the clock was set ticking on the early TPs. One loss with Tridents in mind, however, was Cricklewood's 266, which was announced in August as going to First in May 2012.

Although fire-damaged TPs 433 and 445 were repaired and returned to service during 2011, TP 448 was another casualty on 21 May and TPL 296 was destroyed outright on 15 October.

In October new TEHs entered service on the 139 and 189, with TPLs now leaving to strengthen numbers at Holloway and Potters Bar. This got in the way of the planned cull of the early TAs, which nonetheless commenced by introducing new VWs on Perivale West's 297 and sending its TEs to Cricklewood to displace TPs. Seven of the early TPs at Holloway were withdrawn at this point and two were sold.

At the end of 2011 orders were placed for buses, variously VWs and TEs, which would eject Trident varieties from the 32 and W7, plus any lingering at Holloway. Before the C2 went, a TPL took the opportunity to appear on it, as did Potters Bar's TPLs on the W8.

After a break in TEH deliveries, the purge of Cricklewood's TAs resumed in December, three more being withdrawn that month and the rest lasting on the 32 until 27 January 2012. The TPs and TPLs working at Harrow Weald had spent a year there but most now left, coming to Holloway. In advance of their removal from the 266 and repurposing for Olympics use, the TA 638-659 batch now began refurbishment by Hants & Dorset Trim, but that obliged twelve of the withdrawn TAs to be reactivated at Cricklewood.

On 24 February TP 420 caught fire on its way back from MoT work to Holloway and was destroyed.

In order to free DE-class Enviro200s to displace DLDs for Olympics-related refurbishment, Brentford converted the 190 to double-deck from 10 March, taking three 03-reg TPs from Holloway plus the only three still working out of Harrow Weald.

New Metroline contracts commenced on the 43 and 134 (4 February) and 31 March

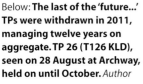

Below: **The last of the 'future...' TPs were withdrawn in 2011, managing twelve years on aggregate. TP 26 (T126 KLD), seen on 28 August at Archway, held on until October.** *Author*

(82), but on 28 April the C2 left for Abellio, this latter change and the entry into service of large numbers of VWs on the two Holloway services (and by association night routes N5 and N20 and the 143 school journey) causing the withdrawal of two-thirds of the early TPs by May. Then fell the 266, taken over by First on 19 May and releasing the 05-reg TAs, which completed their refurbishment programme and then went into store ready for the Olympics. All this finished off the T-reg variant of the TA class that had fought

to the last on the 32. The opportunity was also taken to replace Cricklewood's TALs with TPLs leaving Holloway, three of the ALX400s (TALs 121-123) lasting until 7 June.

On 30 June the N16 was reallocated from Edgware to Cricklewood, permitting Tridents again. The surviving original TPs had their execution stayed to provide extras on the 17 during the Olympics, and they had already pretty much left the W7 before its contract renewal on 18 August. TAs 638-659 were twenty-two of ninety Metroline vehicles

allotted to Olympics duty and indeed stayed for the smaller-scale Paralympics before returning to Cricklewood where they were spread around the 32, 139, 189, 210 and 332 with the TEs (the newest eleven of which were being used on Olympics duty before taking over the 32) and TEHs. Other buses used thus were the last nine VPLs and six VWs, which together with TEs displaced from Cricklewood by the (slowly) returning TAs were put into Holloway. Although that put an end to the career of the original TPs by October, the later variants and their extended TPL counterparts (withdrawals of this type now beginning by year's end) would hold out there for another three years, nominally on the 4 (renewed on 29 September with the 271) and 43. Similarly the TPs put temporarily into Brentford managed to stay put, as adjuncts to the VWs and mostly on the E8 rather than the 190. TAs 651 and 652, the last to come back from Olympics duty and subsequent storage in December, were allocated to Holloway, adding a variant there.

At the end of 2012 twenty-eight TEs were ordered for the 82, and on 12 January 2013 Brentford's school route 635 was taken over by London United. On 28 February the 82's conversion from TPL to TE began and was broadly complete by mid-April, though Potters Bar was to keep hold of TPLs 273 and 274 for use on the 84, long since departed from 'London Transport' but still the same route and never having had its number re-used. In August TPLs 241 and 249 were pulled out of

sales stock for the same sort of augmentation to the 242, another historic route abandoned in 1986 but still extant.

Despite the dwindling to penny numbers of the TP class, thirty-four more broadly identical President-bodied 9.9m Tridents came into stock when the purchase by ComfortDelgro of half First London's operations on 22 June 2013 created Metroline West. TPs 1508-1524 (formerly TNs 33277-33293) were allocated to Greenford for the 282 and TNs 1525-1539 (ex-TNs 33328-33342) were Uxbridge's for the U4; TP 1507 was an earlier example with bonded windows which, as TN 33193, had found its way to Greenford as a backup. Three existing TPs immediately headed over to Uxbridge to assist, lasting a year there.

With the conversion of the 82 to TE operation, its fellow Potters Bar services 217 and W8 with their fleet of TPs were now the last routes at Metroline proper wholly scheduled for Tridents; Holloway's TPs and dwindling number of TPLs were second-string vehicles helping out on the less important contracts, principally the 4 (which would have its new vehicles repeatedly diverted seemingly for ever after!), while after the withdrawal of TP 430 after 22 October, Cricklewood could field just TA 638-659, predominantly on the 32 and 210. Still, on 31 August school route 634 was taken over by Metroline, replacing the 626 which was lost to Sullivan Buses on the same day (and which had purchased two of the former Metroline TALs).

Left: **Potters Bar's TPL 283 (LR02 BBZ) swings towards the home stretch into Victoria on 17 June 2012. This was its last year in service, withdrawal coming the following March.** *Author*

Left: **Two batches of TPs were created out of the members of the TN class inherited from First on 22 June 2013, and those at Uxbridge for the U4 are exemplified by TP 1532 (LK03 UFP), coming into the bus station on 14 July. It was formerly TN 33335 and new as TN 1335.** *Author*

Left: **Greenford's contingent for the 282 was replaced quickly; TP 1520 (LK03 NKZ) lasted a little longer. Seen at Greenford on 3 June 2014, it was new as TN 1289 before becoming TN 33289 in the First London renumbering of 2003.** *Author*

The 'Borismaster' of Wrightbus NBfL type and LT class was now a reality, and the third conversion to these sort-of-crew-operated was to Holloway's 390 on 7 December. Its VPLs stayed in place, instead releasing TEs to Potters Bar to replace that garage's TPs from the 217, beginning on 10 January 2014. The TPs not selected for withdrawal at this time were transferred to Holloway with the intention of seeing off its last TPLs, but the long Tridents proved more stubborn than realised. Three of the sold TPs were bought by Galleon Travel and popped up on the 8 during another Underground strike day, 29/30 April 2014. Three more left Potters Bar for Uxbridge for the duration and served on the 607 (TP 434 once and TP 449 twice) and U4 (TP 453 for three days), after which TP 449 was sent on to Brentford and the other two to Holloway.

July saw the beginnings of moves against Metroline West's TPs, with the 282 gradually taken over by TEs displaced from the E1 and E3 in keeping with its upcoming contract renewal. A couple were spared through being moved over to Uxbridge to stiffen the U4's allocation.

On 2 August the 112 was taken over by Metroline with operation from Cricklewood. While its new DEL-class E20Ds were awaited,

TEs and TAs deputised, but predominantly the latter due to the TUPE'd Abellio staff being familiar with similar vehicles.

TPL 249 at Potters Bar was repainted yellow with a blue front in August, not just to distinguish it as a non-TfL bus but so that an advert for the Busnet pass could be emblazoned on the sides. The 84 was given a frequency increase on 27 September and TPs 437 and 441 were added to its complement.

The 112 was converted to DEL between 23 October and 6 November and the TAs resumed regular service on the 32 so that TEs could leave for Potters Bar and start off the 34 and 125 upon their takeover from Arriva London North on the 8th.

From January 2015 further TEs from the ex-First fleet were put through refurbishment and moved to Uxbridge to start the process of converting the U4 from TP. Five TPs left Potters Bar in February and in March Greenford's sole TP 1508 was withdrawn. The process of withdrawing TPs from Uxbridge, Brentford, Holloway, Potters Bar and Cricklewood dragged out over the rest of the year as various schemes that would be expected to release the buses needed to replace them were either inadequate in scope (the 332's conversion to MMC-style TEH) or postponed by other requirements for the Tridents. One such was the 558, a route mounted between 8-30 August to cover the eastern end of the Victoria Line and offering an unexpectedly popular round-the-corner link not already provided by the 158 on which it was based. New VWHs into Willesden

for the 6 and 98 displaced VPs to Uxbridge in July but failed to finish the TP class there either; as well as the U4, they popped up on the A10 and U3 from time to time. Nine of the U4's withdrawn TPs nonetheless gathered at Cricklewood, which was given the responsibility for the 558. There they were joined by five from Holloway, five from Brentford and four from Potters Bar. Even after this work was done, the TPs returned to service, the ex-Uxbridge examples bringing this variety to the 32 briefly.

Between 25-30 September Cricklewood's 16 was converted from TE to LT and the 168 followed on 10 December, between them releasing enough TEs to make a serious go of replacing the Dennis Trident within Metroline. Four garages' remaining TP stocks were withdrawn over the Christmas week, Uxbridge last operating TP 1531 on the U4 on 24 December, Potters Bar running TP 457 on the W8 on the 27th, Brentford running TPs 411 (route E8), 413 (E2) and 415 (E8) on the 30th and finally Cricklewood, which operated TPs 446 and 455 for the last time on New Year's Eve, both on the 210.

Below: **Holloway's TPL 267 (LN51 KZB) looks sharp in all-red as it crosses the Nag's Head on 6 August 2015, and has even managed to keep hold of a full blind set. The class's time was coming to an end, however, and TPL 267 would survive into 2016 to become the last in service at Metroline.** *Author*

Left: **The last week of 2015 saw withdrawals scythe through the Tridents at every Metroline garage save Holloway. On 8 April Uxbridge's TP 1525 (LK03 UFD) calls at Hayes & Harlington station.** *Author*

Left: **Potters Bar's TP fleet also fell at the end of 2015, the W8 managing to hold on to examples like TP 459 (LK03 GJV), which is coming round the roundabout at Edmonton Green on 2 September 2014. It was sold in March 2016.** *Author*

Left: **Brentford had also retained a number of TPs despite otherwise being colonised by VW-class Volvo B9TLs; seen at Ealing Broadway on 16 October 2014 is TP 453 (LK03 GHX), but this bus would be withdrawn before 2015 finished and ultimately disposed of in January 2017.** *Author*

Right: **TP 410 (LK03 CFD) was the last in service at Holloway, on 29 February 2016, and finished off the Trident at Metroline as a whole, other than the TA 638-659 batch. On 5 May 2015 it is heading across Waterloo Bridge and is carrying a KM blind that almost, but not quite, fits in the narrower aperture.** *Author*

Below: **Four TPLs lingered as driver trainers, and on 9 December 2015, when photographers' attention was otherwise concentrated on the running day commemorating ten years since the withdrawal of the Routemaster from all-day service, TPL 287 (LR02 BCO) is caught in Whitehall, training a future Perivale driver (though none of that garage's routes went anywhere near Whitehall!). It was withdrawn in July 2017.** *Author*

Aside from Cricklewood's TA 638-659, three TPLs turned into trainers and of the commercially-operated examples at Potters Bar, just six TPs (405, 410, 417, 419, 421 and 458) and five TPLs (263, 265, 267, 270 and 271) at Holloway remained with Metroline as 2015 segued into 2016. Upon Holloway's final runs on 29 February, when TP 410 operated on the 17 and TPL 267 on the 43, Metroline's 'future', as shown off so proudly by the first TPs nearly seventeen years earlier, was now part of its past.

Another route selected for LT conversion was the 189, and its fairly drawn-out treatment between 30 June and October released TEs for replacement of the majority of the 05-reg TAs. However, seven of them survived and continued to operate into 2017 and onward (albeit sans TA 659 after 17 November). During that year two joined forces with the Hertfordshire TPs and TPLs, one of them even returning to Cricklewood when the latter came off in March 2018. To all intents and purposes they been forgotten

Above: **North of the border, there wasn't such a mania to replace buses still with plenty of life left in them, and Potters Bar eventually amassed half a dozen Tridents to man the 84 and its later offshoot 84A on a commercial basis. On 8 September 2016 TPL 273 (LR02 BAV) is still in Metroline's blue-skirted livery some time after it had vanished from TfL-contracted routes, and is heading downhill through Barnet. Sale came in May 2018.** *Author*

Left: **And then there were just the 05-reg TAs at Cricklewood, which kept going and going. TA 659 (LK05 GHH) is visiting the 189 at Oxford Circus on 13 February 2015, but Borismasters would eventually take over this central London route.** *Author*

about, continuing blithely on the 210 and any other Cricklewood route that had need of them. To round up these last Metroline Tridents' extraordinary fortitude, TA 645 last ran on 29 October 2018 but TAs 641-643, 648 and 657 comprised the remaining quintet still in service. A low-emission corridor established along the Edgware Road prohibited them from the 32, but that didn't stop them from concentrating on the 210 with school trips on the 643, and continuing to do so well into 2019, although TA 657 fell out after 6 March. Two more lasted only till the end of April, TA 645's last day being the 23rd and TA 643 coming home for the last time in the wee small hours of the 27th.

The endgame was now beginning. London's bus operators between them had taken delivery of over 2,200 Tridents (be they Dennis, Transbus or Alexander Dennis) between 1999 and 2006, but the withdrawal of Stagecoach East London's 17811 after service on 19 August rendered TAs 642 and 648 not just Metroline's last Tridents, but the last ones in service of all. TA 642 was inactive after 13 August but reappeared on the 210 on the 31st to double the remaining tally. TA 648, meanwhile, had strayed off the 210 to the 643 just eight times in 2019, and that was just what it did on what turned out to be its last day in service, Monday 18 November.

It all had to end sometime, and when it did, it was quiet. With TA 648 off at ten past eight in the morning, TA 642 completed one last full day on the 210 as W255 and reached Brent Cross for the last time at 01:18 on the morning of Tuesday 19 November.

Top: **Still going on 11 August 2016 is TA 657 (LK05 GHF), passing Golders Green bus station, which had been omitted from the 210's path in the interests of speeding up the service.** *Author*

Above: **Metroline's last Tridents defied withdrawal, their numbers reducing gradually but working on long past the finish of their fellows. Coming through the post-gyratory arrangements at Archway on 26 May 2019 is TA 648 (LK05 GGP), one of just two left in service by then.** *Author*

Right: **TA 642 (LK05 GFX) was the other survivor at Cricklewood, and on 26 May it is seen at the foot of Highgate Hill. It battled its fellow to be London's last Trident, and ultimately won.** *Author*

Registrations

TP 1-65 T101-110, 81, 112-120, 71, 122, 73, 124-129, 97, 98 KLD, T132-146 CLO,
V747 GBY, T148 CLO, V749-765 HBY

TA 66-81 T61, 67-69, 37, 41, 72, 43, 74-76, 87, 78, 79, 89, 38 KLD

TA 82-117 T182-199, 218, 201, 202 CLO, V303 GLB, T204-207 CLO, V308-317 GLB

TAL 118-134 X341, 319, 336, 337, 322, 343, 324, 335, 326-329, 342, 331, 332, 339, 334 HLL

TPL 237-296 LN51 KXP/R-W/Y/Z, KYA-C/E-H/J/K/O/P/R-Z, KZA-D,
LR02 BAA/O/U/V, BBE/F/J/K/N/O/U/V/X/Z, BCE/F/K/O/U/V/X-Z,
BDE/F/O/U

TP 297-316 LR02 BFF/J, LT02 ZZD-H/J/P/R/S/U-X

TP 348-465 LR52 KVM/O/P/S-Z, KWA-H/J-P/S-Z, KXA-H/J-P/S-X,
LK03 CEJ/N/U/V/X/Y, CFA/D-G/J/L-N/P/U/V/X-Z, CGE-G/U/V,
GFU/V/X-Z, GGA/F/J/P/U/V/X-Z, GHA/B/D/F-H/J/N/U/V/X-Z,
GJF/G/U/V/X-Z, GKA/C/D

TA 638-659 LK05 GFO/V/X-Z, GGA/E/F/J/O/P/U/V/X-Z, GHA/B/D/F-H

Date	Deliveries	Licensed for Service
03.99	TP 2, 4-6	
04.99	TP 3, 7-10, 12, 13, 15	TP 2-10, 12, 13, 15 (**HT**)
05.99	TP 11, 14, 18, 19, 25, 26, 29	TP 11, 14, 18, 19, 25, 26, 29 (**HT**)
06.99	TP 20-24, 27, 28, 30, 31	TP 20-24, 27, 28, 30, 31 (**HT**)
	TA 66-71	
07.99	TP 17	TP 17 (**HT**)
	TA 72-81	TA 66-81 (**W**)
08.99	TA 81-102	TA 82-97 (**HD**)
	TP 16, 32-38, 40, 42, 44-46, 48	TP 16, 33-38, 40, 42, 44-46, 48 (**HT**)
09.99	TA 103-116	TA 98-114 (**HD**)
	TP 1, 39, 41, 43, 47, 49-65	TP 1, 39, 41, 43, 47 (**HT**)
10.99	TA 117	TP 32, 49-65 (**HT**)
		TA 115-117 (**HD**)
10.00	TAL 118-130	TAL 118-122 (**W**)
11.00	TAL 131-134	TAL 123-134 (**W**)
01.02	TPL 237-244	TPL 237-242 (**HD**)
02.02	TPL 245-265, 267	TPL 243-254 (**HD**), TPL 255-265, 267 (**PB**)
03.02	TPL 266, 268, 269	TPL 266, 268, 269 (**PB**)
04.02	TPL 270-274	TPL 270-274 (**PB**)
05.02	TPL 275-296	TPL 275-296 (**HT**)
08.02	TP 297-316	TP 297-316 (**W**)
01.03	TP 348-368	TP 348-362 (**HT**)
02.03	TP 369-402	TP 363-402 (**W**)
03.03	TP 403-415, 417, 418, 422	TP 403-415, 417, 418 (**W**), TP 422 (**HT**)
04.03	TP 416, 419-421, 423-428	TP 416 (**W**), TP 419-421, 423-428 (**HT**)
06.03	TP 429-455, 457-460, 463	TP 429-455, 459, 460, 463 (**PB**),
		TP 446-455, 457, 458 (**PR**)
07.03	TP 456, 461, 462, 464, 465	TP 456, 461, 462, 464, 465 (**PB**)
04.05	TA 638-644	
05.05	TA 645-647, 649-659	TA 638-647, 649-659 (**W**)
06.05	TA 648	TA 648 (**W**)

Re-registrations
12.03   TP 2 from T102 KLD to WLT 826
05.12   TP 2 from WLT 826 to T102 KLD

Armchair Tridents brought into fleet, 06.01.07
DT 1-22 (KN52 NCD/E, NDC-G/J-L/O/U/V/X-Z, NEF/J/O/U/Y, NFA)

Acquired from Metrobus, 01.07
ET 765-770 (LV51 YCC/E-G/J/K)

Acquired from First London, 22.06.13
TN 1508-1539 (LT52 XAD, LK03 NKC-G/P/R-U/W/X/Z, NLA/C/R,
UFD/E/G/J/L/M/N/P/R-X)

Hired from Metroline, 19.11.05-25.08.06
TN 32806, 32958-32960, 32964, 32967-32970, 32974, 32975, 32978-32981, 32983
(T806 LLC, X958, 959, 612, 967-969, 613, 974, 975, 978, 979, 614, 981, 983 HLT)

Hired from First, 30.06.07-18.09.07
TAL 32936, 32937, 32939, 32940-32942, 32946, 32948-32952 (W936, 937, 939 ULL, W840 VLO,
W941, 942, 946, 948, 949 ULL, W132 VLO, W951, 952 ULL)

Hired from First, 30.06.07-17.08.07 and 18.09.07-21.12.07
TNL 32900-32905 (V990 HLH, W901-905 VLN)

Disposals
10.08	ET 765-770
12.08	DT 11, 18
01.09	DT 7, 9, 10, 12, 15, 20
02.09	DT 1-4, 8, 13, 16, 17, 21, 22
03.09	DT 5, 6, 14, 19
04.10	TP 297, 298, 300
05.10	TP 301, 302, 306, 309, 357
06.10	TP 310, 312, 348, 358, 361, 362, 364
07.10	TP 299, 316, 354, 363, 365
08.10	TP 313, 353, 371, 374
09.10	TP 304, 352, 367, 382
10.10	TP 311, 315, 349, 351, 355, 356, 359, 368, 369, 370, 388
11.10	TP 366, 373, 381
	TA 75, 97, 103, 110, 111
12.10	TP 360, 372, 375, 378, 386, 389
	TA 66, 80, 89, 94, 106, 109, 112
01.11	TA 77, 81, 83, 84, 86-88, 90, 96, 101, 104, 107, 116
02.11	TP 305, 350, 377, 379, 383, 384, 387
	TA 85, 95, 98, 113, 115, 117
03.11	TP 303, 314, 392-394, 396, 399, 402
04.11	TP 397, 401
05.11	TP 376, 380, 385, 390, 391, 395, 398, 400
09.11	TA 70, 91-93, 102, 105, 108, 114
	TP 24, 29
10.11	TP 21, 26, 47
	TPL 296 (scrapped 09.12)
11.11	TP 23, 25
12.11	TP 32, 45
01.12	TP 22, 49, 51, 53
02.12	TP 420
05.12	TP 2, 13, 28, 30, 31, 33, 39, 41-43, 52, 55-57, 62
06.12	TP 8, 10, 11, 17, 18, 20, 36, 37, 40, 44, 48, 50, 54, 58-61, 63, 64
	TA 67-69, 71-74, 76, 78, 79, 82, 99, 100
	TAL 123, 132
07.12	TP 16
	TAL 118-122, 124-132, 134
09.12	TP 1, 3-6, 12, 14, 15, 19, 38, 46, 65
10.12	TP 7, 9
12.12	TP 27, 34, 35, 47
01.13	TPL 237, 240, 262, 272, 275
02.13	TPL 238, 242
03.13	TPL 239, 243, 245, 252, 256, 271, 283
04.13	TPL 248, 250, 251, 254, 255, 257-260, 276, 279, 281, 285, 288, 290, 294, 295

Disposals

05.13	TPL 293
07.13	TPL 277, 289, 292
02.14	TP 430
03.14	TP 425, 426, 428, 431, 438, 439, 447, 448, 461, 462
05.14	TP 436, 442, 443, 464
06.14	TP 412, 416, 429, 463
08.14	TP 406, 427, 432
10.14	TP 1523
03.15	TP 445, 450, 456
04.15	TP 1511, 1513, 1516, 1519, 1527, 1528, 1533, 1538
05.15	TP 423, 452, 1508, 1509
	TPL 246, 286
06.15	TAL 133
07.15	TP 1507, 1512, 1515, 1517, 1520, 1521, 1522, 1537
09.15	TPL 261, 278
12.15	TP 414, 434, 449, 1529
	TPL 268
01.16	TP 403, 405, 407, 421, 422, 451, 458
02.16	TP 404, 417, 457
	TPL 263
03.16	TP 410, 419, 437, 459, 1518, 1530
	TPL 270
04.16	TP 408, 409, 413, 415, 433, 446, 455, 460, 1535
	TPL 265
05.16	TP 1510, 1531
07.16	TP 1514, 1525, 1532, 1536
	TPL 253, 269, 280, 291
08.16	TP 411, 1526
10.16	TA 639, 640, 644, 646, 647, 655
11.16	TA 650-652, 658
12.16	TP 418, 424, 1524, 1539
01.17	TP 444, 453
	TA 638
06.17	TA 654, 656
07.17	TPL 241
11.17	TPL 266
05.18	TPL 247, 273
06.18	TPL 249, 274
10.18	TA 659
	TPL 267
03.19	TA 641
06.19	TA 643, 645
11.19	TA 648
12.19	TA 642
06.20	TPL 264

Connex / Travel London / Abellio London

TA class (9701-9720, 9722-9843)

Operators of the South East and South Central rail franchises, Connex chose next to expand into bus operations and in June 1999 founded Connex Bus UK to bid for London bus services.

They couldn't have got off to a better start, winning from London Central the important trunk route 3 and its night accompaniment N3 for implementation in 2000, and while an order for 29 Alexander ALX-bodied Dennis Tridents was placed a garage was readied at Coomber Way, Beddington Cross.

Operations commenced on 5 February 2000, the new 9.9m Tridents (TA 1-20, 22-30 without a TA 21) coming in red with a shallow dark blue skirt topped by a yellow band. With a capacity of H45/20D, they had central staircases and, for the hills in the southern part of the 3, the 245hp version of Cummins's engine.

2000 proceeded smoothly, with little to trouble the 3's TAs, which eked out their downtime on rail replacement work, but in October Connex picked up a second double-deck route with the award of the 196 from London General. Eight more TAs were ordered, and even before they had arrived the 60 was awarded. After a turbulent 1999 where the failings of Capital Logistics and Driver Express were brutally exposed, the route had been reassigned back to Arriva London South and then tendered again.

Right: **With a clean and straightforward look to its Connex livery, TA 7 (V307 KGW) lays over at the 3's Oxford Circus stand on 2 April 2000. Unique among ALX400 customers, Connex specified foglights.** *Author*

Left: **By the time it came to order Tridents for Connex's second double-deck route in 2001, much had changed with the advent of the DDA; staircases were now in the forward position, the foglights were gone and even the blind boxes were different now that destinations had to be in mixed upper- and lower-case, supposedly for easier readability. TA 32 (Y32 HWB) demonstrates at Brixton on 5 May 2001, the first day of the 196's new Connex contract.** *Author*

On 5 May 2001 the 196 was commenced with TA 31-38, which differed from their predecessors through having forward staircases and DDA-tolerated blind boxes. As they arrived, seventeen further TAs were ordered for the 60.

Connex's other tendering victories had comprised minibus routes for which Dart SLFs were taken but one capable of using TAs and beginning to do so this year was the 405 to the south of Croydon.

Expansion beckoned when Connex purchased Limebourne and Travel London on 7 July; probably most important in the long run was the base at Battersea that came with the companies. And still there was more to come, with the 157 awarded from London General in June.

Left: **By the turn of the century it was realised that there was big money to be made renting out bus rears to advertisers. Making the right turn from Oxford Street to Regent Street on 25 June 2001 is TA 6 (V306 KGW), hawking Gillette's Venus razors.** *Author*

Right: **A blip to the orderly deliveries of TAs in time to take up the 60 on 1 September 2001 necessitated the hire of several broadly identical ALX400-bodied Tridents already built for Stagecoach East London. TAS 449 (Y449 NHK), seen in south Croydon on the 60's first day with Connex, was one of those taken on hire, all that was needed to distinguish it as a Connex bus being a pair of company vinyls over the not dissimilar Stagecoach 'beach ball' livery. By then the logo itself was a new one.** *Author*

It wasn't all plain sailing; not all the 60's intended new Tridents (TA 39-55) had made it to Beddington Cross in time for the 1 September start date, so Connex hired six Stagecoach East London TASs of similar design that were about to go into service at North Street. All the 60's TAs were in place by the end of September and it was now time to await the 157's seventeen, most of which entered service with the route's takeup on 1 December. Again help had to be sought from Alexander, which sent six more TASs from a batch going into service at Catford, plus another one coming from Catford itself.

Below: **Existing Beddington Cross TA 12 (V312 KGW) is also seen operating the 60 on 1 September 2001, halted just before the Croydon flyover.** *Author*

Right and below right: **All-over adverts revolutionised the field when permitted to return to London, and soon the streets were awash with them. Particularly noteworthy were the fifty Golden Jubilee buses in 2002, three of which were Connex Tridents. On 23 April of that year TA 5 (V305 KGW) is rounding Trafalgar Square, in the last summer before its pedestrianisation.** *Both: Author*

In April 2002 the 156, one of the routes inherited from Limebourne, was retained by Connex Bus on tender but with a promotion to double-deck after eleven years. Along the same corridor the 344 was similarly felt too busy for its current Dart SLFs and a plan to double-deck that was announced as well. TA 71 was demonstrated on the 344 on 30 April with the Mayor and the press in attendance, and to complete this set of welcome double-deckings, the 211 (inherited from Travel London with dual-doored Optare Excels) was added to the list. 56 more TAs were thus ordered.

Fifty London buses were earmarked for treatment to gold vinyl (with painted ends and fiddly bits) for the Queen's Golden Jubilee in 2002, and Connex's two were TAs 5 and 38, done in April. TA 38 was a route 196 motor despite the intention for two from the 3 to be done.

On 6 June the 344 commenced its conversion from DCL to TA, followed on 3 July by the 156; a restriction in Chelsea held the new Tridents back from the 211 for the moment, though a couple attempted it.

Left: **The 157 was Connex's fourth double-deck route, taken over on 1 December 2001 with yet more TAs. Deliveries now featured the new registration number format, drawing greater attention to the fact that buses like TA 71 (YN51 KWF), seen at West Croydon on 26 May 2003, had been registered in Sheffield.** *Author*

Three separate strike days that summer and autumn saw TAs turn out on the C1, and the new buses also found themselves wandering to the C3. Although all three conversions were of Battersea routes, the new buses were loaned to Beddington Cross as fit.

The collapse of London Easylink on 21 August prompted help to be sent by Connex, which put three new TAs into action on the 185 that afternoon and the day after. These were further deployed to the 53's reactivated peak-hour extras on 2 September but for that day only.

The 156's new contract commenced on 14 September, including an extension from Clapham Junction to Vauxhall. The need to get the TAs already delivered onto the 211 forced its eastbound rerouteing via

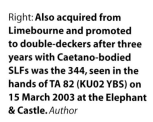

Edith Grove rather than Beaufort Street on 23 November, but it was a success and the Tridents completed the replacement of all remaining Connex DCLs and XLs.

As it turned out, Connex Bus's rise was deceptive; the company's league table position was never particularly great and its financial state even less so, so offering the company for sale began to be thought about. TA 3 was deroofed in Millbank on 3 December 2002 and TA 38 was returned to red in February 2003. In March TA 5 lost its Celebrations adverts that had come with its gold livery and the rest lasted all the way to June.

Connex had by now lost both their rail franchises, so it was deemed not worth holding onto the struggling bus arm. On 7

Right: **2003 heralded an explosion in all-over advert buses, and the 3 was the ideal pitch for them, with eyes on the route's buses from the politicians of Whitehall and Millbank to the high-end shoppers of Regent Street. Even fashionistas perhaps to be found further south were catered to, with the treatment of TA 1 (V301 KGW) to a Vivienne Westwood design. On 9 April 2004 it is seen coming up to the 3's terminus at Crystal Palace.** *Author*

Right: **Then came the schemes for the West End musicals; having come to the end of this particular route 3 journey on 19 May 2004,** *Les Miserables*-**liveried TA 5 (V305 KGW) is in the bus station with its ultimates (DDA-spec, incidentally) already turned for the journey back.** *Author*

Right: **TA 10 (V310 KGW) advertised** *Chitty Chitty Bang Bang* **between February 2004 and July 2005. On 25 June 2004 it is at the Oxford Circus end of the 3.** *Author*

February 2004 National Express bought the bus operations, bringing the Travel London identity back not only to the city but most of the routes it had lost in the first place! Prior to that a new Connex logo had found its way into buses, but it didn't last long and on 26 February the formal transfer took place. The first award to the revived Travel London was of the 381, while the 344 was retained with its existing TAs. But, since National Express West Midlands preferred Volvo B7TLs, no further Tridents would be ordered.

Four Beddington Cross TAs were given all-over ads at the end of February, TA 1 for Vivienne Westwood was joined by TA 5 for *Les Miserables*, TA 9 for *The Woman in White* and TA 10 for *Chitty Chitty Bang Bang*. In June TA 1 exchanged its ad for one extolling the live-action *Thunderbirds* movie. Then came a rash of fashion-themed wraps in September with TA 7 in white for Julien McDonald, TA 100 in white for Tristan Webber and TA 101 in black for Alice Temperley. This trio were further treated to blue 'Back the Bid' adverts for London's bid for the 2012 Olympic Games. TA 1 kept its *Thunderbirds* ad until February 2005, making much more of an impression than did the bomb of a film!

Travel London ended 2004 with the retention of the 211, offered out that June. This company, like a few others on TfL contracts, had now specified all-over red as their livery and some of the existing TAs began to lose their skirts as 2005 progressed.

On 30 April the 196 was extended from Brixton to Elephant & Castle over a section vacated simultaneously by once-fellow Travel London route 322.

Aggressive expansion brought in the 188 and 343 during 2005 and saw the operations of Telling-Golden Miller and Wing's Buses incorporated into the fleet as a whole, while the existing 211 began another term on 2 July. That was when a bus numbered TA 21 entered the fleet, but for some bizarre reason this was not a Trident at all but one of the 60's old DAFs!

Its bid for the Games successful, TA 7 reverted to red in April and TA 10 lost its own ad in July. TA 100 continued to back the bid until October and TA 101 until November.

In August the 196 was lost back to London General and when it was transferred, on 6 May 2006, the TAs displaced were transferred over the next two weeks to the C3; not bad for a route begun with one blue Sherpa! The C3 had been tendered and retained and was now one of the routes earmarked for expansion in connection with the Western Extension of the Congestion Charge zone. The 60 was announced in February as lost to Arriva London South, but the 157 was held on to. In March the 3 was put out, and this had to be held at any price! Thankfully for Travel London, it was, together with another CC-related expansion route which was to be known as 452.

22 April saw the 152 taken over from Centra, and for now it was operated with a mix that included TAs. On 3 June the 344 had four buses added to its PVR, using up the rest of the former route 196 TAs that hadn't already been transferred to Battersea for the C3. 11 July, however, saw the loss of TA 45 to fire at Old Coulsdon while on the 60. TA 58 was damaged in an accident on the N3.

When the 60 was handed over to Arriva London South on 2 September, its TAs, though intended to start the 452 off pending its own allocation of new Enviro400s, eased some of the V-reg examples off the 3. Four began work temporarily on the Kingston University contract operated out of Fulwell. In October TA 5's *Les Miserables* advert was updated to a new design and TA 14 received one for *Casino Royale*.

Below: **After ads and bids it was back to mundane operations, and mundane it was with the phasing in by Travel London of an all-red livery. On 21 May 2005 TA 51 (YN51 KVM) is seen pulling up to the old Streatham Garage stand of the 60.** *Author*

On 11 November a night service was added to the 344. 2 December saw the 157's new contract start and the 152 formalised permanently with the double-deck element coming off other than as guests. The 452 duly began between Kensal Rise and Wandsworth Road and was Battersea-operated with TAs.

2007 began with the delivery of the first Enviro400s, classified ED, and their gradual takeover of the 452. Then followed the renewal of the 3 and N3 on 10 February, though V-class Volvo B7TLs were now supporting the regular TAs. Battersea gained an allocation on the N3 on Friday and Saturday nights.

Unfortunately for traditionalists, Travel West Midlands did not support class codes and renumbered Travel London's fleet into their own sequence from 10 March, rendering the TA class 9701-9720 and 9722-9829.

Above: **Travel West Midlands's Birmingham heritage cared little for the traditions of its sister city, so from 10 March 2007 Travel London's class codes were deleted. TA 92 thus became 9792 (KV02 USH) and is seen at the Elephant on 25 May 2009.** *Author*

Right: **Subtle changes to the 3's Trident fleet as it rolled into another contract are evident in this 31 March 2007 shot of TA 13 (V313 KGW) rounding Trafalgar Square. First of all, there is the change of name from Connex Bus to Travel London, which identity would itself eventually be superseded; then, a repaint to all-red has erased Connex's blue skirt. Travel West Midlands-style fleetnumber characters have appeared on the front to contrast with traditional Johnston, but before long these too would be replaced by an alphanumeric fleetnumber that would turn this particular bus into 9713. Finally, the blind boxes have been altered to allow the fitment of a new set to only two-line depth, to make room for a mixed-case ultimate to fulfil the perception that this format was easier to read. This bus dodged withdrawals of most of its batch at this time and survived until 2012.** *Author*

The entry into sevice of the 'EDs' (now 9401 up) permitted the Kingston University services to revert to 'TA' after a spell with Dart SLFs (now numbered in the eight thousands), while Tridents began to drift back to the 152 and completed the upgrading of the 3's age profile so that early members could depart for West Midlands. 9705 took its

Les Miserables ad with it and 9714 reverted to red. 9718 was recalled, however, to cover for 9786, which suffered fire damage on 20 May.

What was now Travel London was already well established on rail replacements, but two fixed services commissioned to cover the upcoming transformation of the humble East London Line into part of the city-spanning

Left: **With memories fresh of the orange-liveried ELX and ELT, which were so successful as replacements for the East London line that they nearly became permanent services, TfL recommissioned versions for the two years that the construction of the Overground was expected to take. They weren't as busy this time, however, as evinced by this 23 December 2007 shot at Canada Water of a lightly-loaded 9730 (V330 KGW).** *Terry Wong Min*

Overground were awarded in June 2007; these were the ELC and ELP, both specified for double-deckers. To furnish these, the disposals of 'TAs' to West Midlands were cancelled and the eleven already despatched were reclaimed.

A hefty increase to the 156 from 1 September required four more 'TAs' into Battersea, which were returned early examples, while the Kingston University routes were cemented with the repaint of 9706, 9707, 9715, 9723 and 9725 into white livery to release 9726-9729 back to normal service. Otherwise, routine repaints to Tridents over the second half of 2007 were fast eliminating the red and blue Connex livery.

Routes ELC and ELP began on 23 December with thirteen 'TAs' from Walworth (including formerly white 9707 now surplus from Kingston University); they were refurbished and repainted for this task. The ELC was boosted on 2 January 2008, but 'TA' availability was now at capacity so five Metroline Tridents (also TAs but retaining that identity) were borrowed between 31 December and 25 January to free existing examples; the fifth, TA 99, lasted a little longer, leaving on 21 March. Passenger numbers were not as high as anticipated; indeed, they preferred to use normal routes like the 188, which had four ELC/ELP-allocated 'TAs' added on 19 January to cover the closure of the Jubilee Line on that day only.

Tendering over the cusp of 2007/08 put out the C3 in October; Travel London retained it with its existing buses.

The one-bus ELP was withdrawn on 24 February 2008 and two buses were taken off the ELC so they could all be added to the 381 instead as peak-hour Canada Water-London Bridge shorts. This was tidied up via a few transfers so that the 381 could remain all-Volvo B7TL ('V'), but it failed to address a general shortage, so two Battersea 'TAs' were sent temporarily to the 381 at Walworth and two more Metroline Tridents were taken on loan. This time they were Plaxton President-bodied TPLs 244 and 245, which joined Walworth's fleet between 2-31 May. When they went back, TPLs 259 and 260 were hired from 7 June till the end of the month.

Below: **It was all about replacements in one form or another in 2008 and 2009; when the innovative and eventually enormously successful iBus technology was being installed into every TfL-contracted bus, a group of roving double-deckers filled in at company after company while buses were sent out to either Clapton or Norwood garages, where the equipment was fitted. In May Travel London was allotted two Tridents normally belonging to Metroline, and in Rotherhithe on 8 May 2009 is TPL 244 (LN51 KXY).** *Terry Wong Min*

Even though the East London Line reconstruction was ongoing and additions to the 188 had to be made on several weekends this summer to cover similar closures of the Jubilee Line, the ELC was halved on 19 July.

Routine tendering during 2008 put up the 156 and 344 in May, the first mentioned being announced as retained in August. The 156's future was set with the order of Enviro400s to replace its Tridents. On 4 October the C3 began its new term with Travel London.

Yet more oddments appeared in September in a year that had been full of them. This time it was for iBus fitment cover, and once again Travel London looked to Metroline to help out. DTs 1-6, which had started out on the 237 as Armchair vehicles, were borrowed, joining the four 'TAs' displaced from the cut to the ELC. Between 22 September and mid-November they appeared on the 3, 157 and N3 out of Beddington Cross and then moved to Walworth eight days later when that garage's buses began leaving for iBus conversion. There they operated on the 381 before moving on to Battersea and the 156, after which they lingered so as to serve the World Travel Market at the ExCel between 10-13 November. When Fulwell took its turn during December, Beddington Cross's 152 proved the buffer shed by sending its Darts to cover and letting Tridents stand in.

The four 'TAs' on the Kingston University services had red skirts added to the white livery, breaking the uniformity a little. On 13 January 2009 9711 became the 400's dedicated bus at Byfleet.

The 344 had had to wait for its tender announcement, but in January 2009 Travel London proved successful again and more Enviro400s were ordered.

Although Travel London had turned around its London bus operations since the days of Connex mismanagement, National Express as a whole was not doing so well and needed cash, so on 21 May sold Travel London to NedRailways, the Dutch state operator. After a lull following the completion of the sale on 9 June, it was decided that a thrusting new name was needed, and in September a belter was picked out of the bin of computer-generated Euro-names designed to be offensive to nobody speaking a myriad of different languages. Therefore, from 31 October Travel London was rebranded as Abellio London.

Tellings-Golden Miller (a second incarnation of that identity) took over the Kingston University contracts on 15 September, making the white 'TAs' redudundant. On the 25th the ELC was withdrawn, and with the renewal of the contracts on the 344 (22 August) and the

Right: **September 2008 saw six Metroline DTs new to Armchair come to Travel London for iBus cover. They spent their autumn at all three garages, personified on 22 September by DT 1 (KN52 NCD) operating Beddington Cross's 157 in Selhurst Road, but four years after they went home, fourteen of the class returned as full-time vehicles. DT 1, however, wasn't one of them.** *Bill Young*

156 (12 September) and their treatment to new Enviro400s, Tridents were now falling surplus. Refurbishment of the original route 196 and 60 batches was now complete, with work then begun on the newest units, but 9795-9811 were returned to Dawson Rentals.

On 31 October Abellio took over the 407, one of whose duties required a double-decker that invariably manifested itself in the form of a Beddington Cross Trident.

'TA' withdrawals were to drag out, as the company often needed to pull them out of mothballs at a moment's notice, for instance on the 152 again over most of 2010 for Dart refurbishment cover. Further Tridents drifted to Byfleet to work school routes for Surrey County Council, that garage amassing six until August while other examples still found renewed use as trainers that could be pressed back into service as required.

In July 2010 Abellio won the 172 from London Central, but after a continuous stream of new buses, this time the route was bid for with existing vehicles, only the company didn't have any to spare. Instead fourteen of the former Metroline and Armchair DT class Tridents would be acquired from Dawson Rentals and refurbished, taking the numbers 9830-9843.

In October the 3 was offered for tender again, with the Tridents likely to leave whoever won it.

2011 began with 9830-9843 taken into stock; these were former Metroline DT

2-4, 11, 7, 8, 15, 16 and 18-22 and some had already worked for the company. They were refurbished, an additional (or detrimental) feature being the conversion of the blind boxes to DDA standard with just one line of destination beside the number, but many took to the road with existing panels before being converted later. Already-owned 9829 was also done. They went into service with the takeover of the 172 on 19 March, though appearances to Walworth's other routes were widespread. The 188 had already seen plenty of 'TAs' to cover refurbishments now affecting the former V class, but the 343 was a new venture and the 40 very rare indeed.

Stability was ensured for Abellio with the award back of the 3 and 157 in March, though the TAs on both would be replaced by new Green Bus-funded hybrid E40Hs on the former and cascaded Volvo B7TLs on the latter. Six more E40Hs would come later to part-convert the 211.

Civil unrest across London led to the destruction by fire of 9755 on 8 August while on the 157 at Reeves Corner in Croydon; 9735 from the training fleet replaced it and this in turn was covered by 9736 from withdrawn stock that failed to sell at auction on 12 July. 9762 was also damaged by fire while at Crystal Palace on the 3 on 13 September, and 9733 and 9734 were reactivated to replace it. As these things invariably come in threes, 9758 was written off in December after an accident and left the fleet.

Right: **The final act in the seventeen-year history of Tridents at Connex/Travel London/Abellio was to secure fourteen second-hand ALX400s near-enough identical to existing stock and thus provision the 172 for the five years of its contract applying from 19 March 2011. Seen at Waterloo on 13 April, 9840 (KN52 NEO) was new as Armchair DT 19.** *Author*

3 December saw the 157's new contract commence, with Volvo B7TLs made spare from the E40H conversion of the 188 starting the replacement of Tridents, and on 11 February 2012, the 3 and N3 were simultaneously reallocated from Beddington Cross to Battersea to start off their own new terms in concert with conversion to E40H. Nine TAs made the move while the new buses were being delivered, but were then divided between those chosen to stay for Olympics augmentations and another contingent heading to Liverpool to cover a Merseyrail replacement contract awarded to Abellio.

In its old age (by modern standards), the Trident type seemed particularly susceptible to fires, and on 17 March 9831 was destroyed at Brockley while visiting the 343. 9828 stepped in to replace it.

Right: **By comparison with 9840 above, 9834 (KN52 NDO) has been fitted with a single-line blind box, as would all of these acquisitions. The effect is far from pretty, producing an aggressive and incomplete look at the same time as taking information away from the passenger on the ground. Seen at the Elephant & Castle on 13 November 2011, this bus was formerly Armchair and Metroline DT 11.** *Author*

On 31 March the 350 at Hayes was converted to double-deck operation, gradually gathering together 9763-9772, which were repainted for the purpose. Enough hybrids were now present for the Sunday spare to convert the C3 from Trident on 19 May. These were the 211's batch and eased out its TAs over June in time for the route's new contract beginning on the 30th. Of those displaced, 9773-9794 were repainted

white for Olympics duty under the auspices of LOCOG and 9733, 9734, 9736 and 9737 joined the 188's complement at Walworth.

9753, 9756 and 9757 served the Netherlands Olympic team and took them to the Holland Heineken House event at Alexandra Palace on 4-5 August.

After the Olympics five of the white Tridents were turned out on the 188 as Battersea-operated extras (without blinds

Above: **Hayes garage had come with the Wing's Buses operations and now proved useful for bids in the far west of London. The 350 was the descendant of Wings' old H50 and was double-decked on 31 March 2012 with ten 'TAs' like 9767 (YN51 KWB), seen at Hayes & Harlington Station on 9 June.** *Author*

Left: **Rail replacement and private hire had formed a major part of operations since Connex first appeared on the scene. On 11 August 2012 at Wood Green 9757 (YN51 KVP) is performing a service for the Dutch Olympic team between here and Alexandra Palace.** *Author*

Above: **Loosely affiliated with Abellio Surrey were the Green Bus school routes, and their cheery green and yellow livery was a breath of fresh air amid the monotonous red otherwise encountered when the TAs so painted were turned out on rail replacements. 9734 (Y134 HWB) is at Tower Hill on 10 October 2015.** *Author*

converted to single-door and donned this operation's colourful green and yellow livery once no longer needed at Walworth. Red ones stood in for them while repaints were progressing.

As 2013 commenced, the 350 was extended for two years, with Hayes sending its Tridents wandering to the 112 from time to time. With the retention on tender of the C3 in March and its planned upgrade to new buses, only the 172 would be left as a Trident route at Walworth, but there were multiple stragglers still around, including those otherwise occupied on training and another batch sent away for a second summer in Liverpool. White-on-black blinds began to appear during the spring, 9759 getting them first.

The C3 started its new contract on 5 October, but new E40Hs were ordered to cover this route as well as the 49 and E1. At Walworth the 172's fleet were apt to stray to the 35 now that this route was allocated there.

9740, 9742 and 9751 gathered at Beddington Cross to release four Dart SLFs during the spring. As soon as the E1 was taken over by Hayes on 31 May, Tridents appeared on it. The C3's new E40Hs arrived during June, but their spreading around Battersea allowed the 'TAs' to dodge withdrawal for the moment. Even so, the award and retention of both the 350 and 407 were with new buses, effectively dooming more of the type. One to see itself

or ticket machines) between 31 August and 6 September, after which some more visited London Central's 132 on the 7th and 8th before going off lease.

An unusual post-London deployment was to a set of Surrey school routes won by The Green Bus of Birmingham but operated by Abellio Surrey at Byfleet (already amassing white TAs for its own such routes for the council), and the eight selected were

Right: **The 381's usual complement was long-wheelbase Wrightbus Eclipse Gemini-bodied Volvo B7TLs formerly of V class, but Walworth's 'TAs' regularly turned out, as 9747 (YN51 KVD) is doing when espied at London Bridge on 8 March 2014.** *Author*

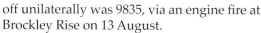

off unilaterally was 9835, via an engine fire at Brockley Rise on 13 August.

Not enough buses were available for the 201's assumption on 4 October, so Beddington Cross collected seven stray Tridents to use on the 152 and 407 and thus release the Dart SLFs needed. In the same month Walworth added seven Tridents spare from the C3's conversion at Battersea; two would be needed for a boost to the 172

applying from 10 January 2015 until the Old Kent Road extension of the 415 was put into play. Six more followed during that month, and they were needed, because yet another of the route 172 batch disgraced itself, going up in flames on 21 March at Honor Oak.

21 March also saw the 350's renewal with new E40H MMCs replacing its Tridents.

Despite the award of two more years to the 172's existing contract, 2016 saw the final push

Above left and above: **Two guest 'TAs' are 9763 (YN51 KVW) on the E1 at Ealing Broadway on 18 November 2014 and 9826 (LG52 XYL) on the 188 at Waterloo on 10 June 2015.** *Author*

Below: **9744 (YN51 KVA) with white-on-black blinds is on the 'V'-operated 157 at Wallington on 5 May 2016.** *Author*

against Abellio's other Tridents, commencing in February with the conversion of the 3 from E40H to Borismaster and the release of the E40Hs to cascade those 'TAs' still remaining on the 344, 381 and C3. The 211's intake of LTs in May completed that process, and twenty-six Tridents left the fleet.

The clock was now ticking; having bought itself two more years, the 172 was now out for tender. The 157 was lost to Arriva London South and departed on 3 December 2016, as

did the 152 to London General; two regular Trident pitches were now gone. In concert with E40Hs coming from Battersea, a handful of the 157's Volvo B7TLs transferred into Walworth to put an end to the ex-Armchair, ex-Metroline 'DTs' on the 172 for its last year with Abellio, just as it was announced as lost.

March 2017 thus knocked out the stragglers, 9822 being Walworth's last on the 381 on 8 March and Hayes's 9821 coming off the 350 after the 17th.

Registrations

TA 1-20, 22-30	V301-320, 322-330 KGW
TA 31-38	Y131, 32, 133, 134 HWB, Y235 HWF, Y36-38 HWB
TA 39-72	YN51 KUU-Y, KVA-H/J-M/O/P/R-X/Z, KWA-G
TA 73-111	KU02 YBH/J-P/R/S, KV02 URX-Z, USB-H/J/L-P/S-W, URL-O/R/P/S-U
TA 112-129	LG52 HWN, XZB, LB52 URZ, LG52 XWE, XYK/M/P/O/N/Y/Z, XZA/S/R, XYL, XZT, XYJ, XWD

Renumbered 9701-9720, 9722-9829 by Travel London, 10.03.07

Date	Deliveries	Licensed for Service
01.00	TA 1-20, 22-30	TA 1-20, 22-30 (**BC**)
04.00	TA 31-38	
05.00		TA 31-38 (**BC**)
08.01	TA 39-44, 46, 48, 50	
09.01	TA 45, 47, 51-55	TA 39-55 (**BC**)
11.01	TA 56-64	
12.01	TA 65-72	TA 56-72 (**BC**)
06.02	TA 73-82, 84, 86-96	TA 73-79, 81, 82, 84, 86-96 (**QB**), TA 80 (**BC**)
07.02	TA 83, 85, 97-99, 101-111	TA 97-99, 101-111 (**QB**), TA 83, 85 (**BC**)
08.02	TA 100	TA 100 (**QB**)
11.02	TA 113, 115-129	TA 113, 115-129 (**QB**)
12.02	TA 112, 114	TA 112, 114 (**QB**)

Acquired from Dawson Rentals, 02.11
9830-9843 (KN52 NCE, NDC-E, NDO, NDG/J/Y/Z, NEJ/O/U/Y, NFA)

Hired from Alexander, 01.09.01-30.09.01, due for Stagecoach East London
TAS 441, 442, 444, 449, 460, 472 (Y441, 442, 523, 449, 529, 472 NHK)
TAS 444 did not run for Connex and was re-registered LX51 FKO when passed to Stagecoach

Hired from Alexander, 28.11.01-14.12.01, due for Stagecoach Selkent
TAS 526-531 (LX51 FOJ/K/M/N/P/T)

Hired from Stagecoach Selkent, 28.11.01-12.01
TAS 524 (LX51 FOF)

Hired from Metroline, 31.12.07-25.02.08
TA 82-84, 86, 99 (T182-184, 186, 199 CLO)

Hired from Metroline, 02-31.05.08
TPL 244, 245 (LN51 KXY/Z)

Hired from Metroline, 07.06.08-late June
TPL 259, 260 (LN51 KYT/U)

Hired from Metroline, 22.09.08-mid November
DT 1-6 (KN52 NCD/E, NDC-F)

Disposals
07.06	TA 45
04.07	9705-9709, 9715-9718, 9722, 9723, 9725
	Reclaimed 06.07
09.09	9795-9811
04.10	9812
06.10	9703, 9736
08.11	9702, 9755
09.11	9707
12.11	9708, 9728, 9731, 9732, 9738, 9758, 9762
03.12	9831
09.12	9701, 9716, 9723, 9724, 9743, 9748, 9749, 9760
10.12	9704, 9710-9714, 9717, 9719, 9720, 9722, 9726, 9727, 9730, 9773-9794
01.13	9709
04.13	9705
08.13	9715, 9725
09.13	9746
03.15	9838
04.16	9740-9742, 9747, 9750-9753, 9761, 9763, 9766-9772, 9818-9820, 9823-9825, 9829
05.16	9754, 9764
06.16	9739
11.16	9757, 9765, 9815
12.16	9759, 9816, 9817
02.17	9830, 9833-9835, 9837, 9839-9843
03.17	9812, 9814
04.17	9836
08.17	9744, 9826, 9828
09.17	9737, 9756, 9813, 9821, 9822, 9827
10.17	9705, 9718, 9729, 9733-9736

Go-Ahead

PDL, TL and TPL classes

Of the London operators, only Arriva ignored the Trident completely, but Go-Ahead, surprisingly, wasn't far behind, taking only fifty and not particularly liking them.

London Central and London General had started off the low-floor double-deck era with extensive Volvo B7TL deliveries, so the addition at a late stage of an order for thirteen Plaxton President-bodied Dennis Tridents came as a surprise. These were ordered against the 88, already operating under a contract won at the same time as those applying to the 37 and 77A, which were re-equipping in the summer of 2000 with PVLs. It needed to be determined how many buses the 88 would need when it absorbed part of the 135 before the order was placed.

PDL 1-13 were delivered in October and were put into service from Stockwell beginning on the 7th; naturally appearances on the 37, 77A and weekend 11 followed.

When the 85 was won from London United in 2002, thirteen more PDLs were ordered against it, but in the event it was decided to allocate WVLs arriving at the same time to Putney instead and use the new Tridents at Stockwell with the rest. Thus did PDL 14-26 appear in June and July, with PDL 27 added. New routes for them to visit at Stockwell were the 188 and 345, and the 170 once the route was allocated there.

The WVL became as popular with Go-Ahead as the PVL had been (and was continuing to do so), but the Trident wasn't out of contention yet, as this summer the

Right: **On 23 April 2002 Stockwell's PDL 5 (X605 EGK) heads down Regent Street, but only as far as Stockwell. This particular batch of early Tridents were sluggish and noisy, especially if their exhaust pipes got crimped against street furniture.** *Author*

363 was awarded to London Central and sixteen more PDLs ordered. As construction commenced during the following March, this order was increased to 23, but once again their deployment was changed and all would enter service at Stockwell, making a total of fifty. When they arrived between March and April 2003, they displaced PVLs to cascade Olympians (NVs) to become trainers in place of the long-running but worn-out Ms and Ts. One design advance from this batch was plug exit doors.

28 June added another potential PDL route in the form of the N11, awarded from London United and allocated to Stockwell.

An untroubled career followed, broken on 3 June 2006 by the replacement of the 77A with new route 87 over the same roads; the

Left: **With the Trident you got a full-width rear window downstairs, even if it was higher and narrower to reflect the low floor. Normally Waterloo RML-operated route 11 was OPO with Stockwell vehicles (PVLs and PDLs) on Sundays, but uniquely on Saturdays too so that residents near the Red Arrow base could be spared vehicle noise. 9 November 2002 was a Saturday, and PDL 21 (PJ02 PZU) of the second batch is seen fighting its way out of Victoria bus station between Metroline London Northern TP 62 and PVL 161, a fellow Stockwell bus but a Volvo B7TL.** *Author*

196 also returned to Stockwell in 2006, with its allocated Es able to be subbed by PDLs if needed. Despite indifference to the Trident, Go-Ahead embraced its Enviro400 successor with gusto. Towards the end of the same year it was decided to convert PDL 1-13 to training work in replacement of NVs, and PDL 10 was the first one done, upon which it was allocated to Mandela Way. However,

it did not find favour in this role and was restored to passenger traffic in July 2007.

Trident numbers at Go-Ahead increased when Blue Triangle was taken over on 29 June 2007; included with routes 248 and 474 were East Lancs-bodied TL 901-915 and 916-923 plus Plaxton-bodied TPL 925-927. TPL 928, retained by the new London Bus Company, came on loan. However, TPL 927 suffered

arson damage at Romford Station on 23 August and the loss of TL 907 to an accident at East Ham on the 25th prompted the loan of PDLs 1 and 2 to Rainham, complete with Blue Triangle logos.

On 3 November Go-Ahead reorganised its east London holdings, which by now also included Docklands Buses, and the 474 (sprouting a night route at this point) was reallocated from Rainham (now coded BE) to Silvertown with TL 911-915, 917-923, TPL 926 and PDLs 1 and 2. The 248 (now fielding TLs 901-906, 908-910, TPL 925 and five SO-class Scanias plus LBC-owned TPL 924 and 928) was now under tender again and in March 2008 was announced as lost to East London. PDL 1 returned to Rainham in December, whilst TLs 907 and 910 and TPL 927 were

Right: **Attractive in their own right and appreciated by other companies, the Plaxton-bodied Dennis Trident failed to make a good impression on London General and the PDLs achieved less than a decade's service in the capital. The 88 remained their best-known pitch, and on 31 March 2007 PDL 16 (PJ02 PZO) is seen coming around what small proportion of Trafalgar Square was left to buses.** *Author*

Right: **On the same day in Whitehall, Stockwell's PDL 32 (PN03 ULR) is on its way to Wandsworth on the 87. This bus would outlast PDL 16 by four months, but still racked up just six years' London service.** *Author*

Right: **The year of iBus fitment threw up a host of unusual deployments as small knots of buses roved from firm to firm to release indigenous examples to the process. In July 2008 Silvertown took on loan six Metroline TPLs, which joined the originally Blue Triangle examples coincidentally carrying the same class code. As well as shoring up the 474, they also helped start up new route 425, on which TPL 927 (EY03 FNL) is seen at Clapton on 7 August.** *Ian Jordan*

Above: **After the Metroline TPLs and First TNs, London General dug into its own holdings and brought four Blue Triangle TLs to Stockwell during October 2008. Looking most out of place on the 345 at Stockwell on 8 October is TL 915 (PO51 UML).** *Ian Jordan*

all repaired and returned to service by mid-2008. Rainham and Silvertown were apt to swap their Tridents and Scanias around as required, and the three TPLs (soon down to just one with the return of TPLs 924 and 928) soon turned out on new route 425 introduced by Silvertown on 5 July, helped by hired Metroline TPLs 243-245, 261, 262 and 265 and PDLs 3-5 sent from Stockwell. PDL 2 joined its partner at Rainham in May.

iBus was the watchword for 2008, thousands of TfL-contracted buses being fitted with this innovative location and information system that was being refined constantly. To let the buses needed go away for the strictly scheduled fitment dates, a group of First TNs was set aside for cover, roving from company to company, and in September and early October TNs 32958-32963 and 33233 served at Stockwell on the 87, 88, 333 and 345. They weren't the only weird Tridents fulfilling this role.

East London duly took up the 248 on 27 September, in theory finishing off the TLs. Seventeen of them were sold, but four (TLs 912, 914, 915 and 917) gravitated to Stockwell at London General. They replaced the First TNs on iBus cover, turning out on the 87, 88 and 345 between 7-30 October, after which PDLs 1-5 returned home too. It was now decided to get rid of the PDL class as a whole, and the loss of London Central's 51 to Selkent on 6 December, together with PVLs displaced by simultaneous DOE deliveries to Sutton,

freed enough PVLs both to make a start on Stockwell's Trident holdings and replace Silvertown's remaining TLs and TPLs. These came off in February, replaced by PVLs (TL 922 being the last in service) and leaving just TPLs 925 in Go-Ahead stock. Twenty-one of the withdrawn PDLs were sent to Rainham temporarily for rail replacement work before sale, though PDLs 13, 19 and 23 were pressed into service at Silvertown.

On their way out, PDLs 16-18, 20, 21 and 25 saw use as iBus float cover with Arriva Kent Thameside's 428 at Dartford between 20 February and 11 March 2009, and in June PDLs 28-33 did the Wimbledon tennis service, three of them from Camberwell, who applied London Central logos. A further contingent then served the Hampton Court Flower Show, but on 24 July PDLs 47, 49 and 50 were the last to take fares at Stockwell.

Three ex-Blue Triangle TLs and two TPLs subsequently turned up with Sullivan Buses and two TLs found a home across town with Atbus. TPL 925, however, found itself transferred to Sutton to serve as a vehicle big enough for school route 669 from 25 September, and lasted there until May 2010. It was paced all the way to this date by PDL 13 at Silvertown, after which both were sold.

That would appear to have been the end, but on 31 March 2013 Go-Ahead purchased from FirstGroup the operations and buses of Northumberland Park garage, and with them came six Tridents that were otherwise

Right: **School route 670 drew its buses from two route 87 workings, and on 19 March 2009 PDL 30 (PN03 ULM) now has to get itself from Trafalgar Square to Clapham Junction as fast as it can to pick up the kids going back to Roehampton.** *Author*

Right: **Only able to furnish the bare minimum where blinds are concerned, PDN 6 (LT52 WXJ) is nonetheless a useful ad-hoc addition to the 425 at Stratford on 4 August 2012, as the Olympics were in full swing. It was formerly First TN 33231.** *Author*

functioning as spares to a modern fleet of Volvo B7TLs, B9TLs and Enviro400s. TNLs 33075, 33076 and TNs 33048, 33049, 33051 and 33231 were taken into stock as PDN 1-6 and remained in situ. Of these, PDN 6 was a guest on Silvertown's 425 in early August as part of local augmentations to routes serving the Olympic Park environs. They were nonetheless non-standard and when the 67 was lost to Arriva on 27 April 2013 six of its PVN-class Volvo B7TLs also acquired with the takeover of Northumberland Park were moved to replace them. PDN 1-6 were thus withdrawn on 20 May and sold to Nottingham City Transport.

Registrations

PDL 1-13   X601-609, 701, 611-613 EGK
PDL 14-27   PJ02 PZM-P/R-Z, RHF
PDL 28-50   PN03 ULK-M/P/R-Z, UMA-H/J/K

Date	Deliveries	Licensed for Service
10.00	PDL 1-13	PDL 1-13 (**SW**)
06.02	PDL 14, 16, 18-20, 22	PDL 14, 16, 18-20, 22 (**SW**)
07.02	PDL 17, 19, 23-27	PDL 17, 19, 23-27 (**SW**)
03.03	PDL 28-40	PDL 28-40 (**SW**)
04.03	PDL 41-50	PDL 41-50 (**SW**)

Acquired from Blue Triangle, 29.06.07
TL 901-915, 917-923 (V901-909 FEC, PO51 UMF-H/J-L/R-T/W-Y)
TPL 925-927 (V8 AEC, EY03 FNK/L)

Acquired from First London, 31.03.13
PDN 1-6 (LN51 GOJ/K, GKD/E/G, LT52 WXK)

Loaned from Blue Triangle, 29.06.07-07.07
TPL 924, 928 (VLT 110, PO51 UGF)

Hired from Metroline, 07.06.08-13.08.08
TPL 243-245, 261, 262, 265 (LN51 KXW-Z, KYV/W/Z)

Hired from First, 09.08-09.10.08
TN 32958-32963, 33233 (X958, 959, 612, 961-963 HLT, LT52 WWV)

Re-registrations
03.09   TPL 925 from V8 AEC to W81 TJU

Disposals
10.08	TL 901-909, 911, 913
11.08	TL 912, 914, 915, 917
01.09	PDL 4, 5
	TL 910, 923
02.09	TL 918-922
03.09	PDL 2, 7, 8
	TPL 926, 927
05.09	PDL 1, 6, 9-11, 21, 24
06.09	PDL 14-17, 25
07.09	PDL 22
10.09	PDL 18-20, 23, 26-50
01.10	PDL 12
03.10	PDL 3
05.10	PDL 13
	TPL 925
05.13	PDN 1-6

Metrobus

401-428

Already operators of route 161 since the ignominious faltering of its previous incumbent Kentish Bus, Metrobus solidified its hold on this route in March 1999 with an order for 15 East Lancs Lolyne-bodied Dennis Tridents to replace its all-Leyland Olympians.

Numbered 401-415 (though no physical numbers were actually carried on any Metrobus vehicles until the summer of 1999), the new buses arrived between July and September with a service debut of 7 August. The last four received V-registrations with the new 1 September introduction of a second year letter. No time was lost wandering to the 119, followed shortly by the 64, 261 and 320. Appearances on the original Metrobus routes were rarer, but the 353 and 354 were soon ticked off.

At the end of 2000 the planners determined that the 161 should have a frequency increase applying from 24 February 2001, and Metrobus ordered a sixteenth Trident, which was delivered on 1 June as 416.

Existing route 261 was awarded another term with Metrobus in July 2001, and twelve more Tridents were ordered. Contract assumption date was 1 December, shortly after which the resulting Nos 417-428 arrived, deliveries stretching out into January 2002 with first sightings on the 8th. Over the winter the 246 and 320 had been double-deck on Sundays and thus capable of Trident visits.

Right: **The first fifteen East Lancs-bodied Dennis Tridents taken by Metrobus for the 161 looked particularly smart in the company's blue and yellow, each shade of which had recently been lightened. Seen at Woolwich, General Gordon Place on 4 March 2000 is 409 (T409 SMV).** *Author*

Above: **When espied at Lewisham Bus Station on 15 January 2002, 417 (LV51 YCC) and 422 (LV51 YCH) had just gone into service on the 261. Both Tridents are displaying the white fleetnumbers introduced to Metrobus vehicles in the previous year.** *Author*

Left: **This North Greenwich shot taken in the sunshine following a fierce blizzard on 24 February 2001 allows comparison of East Lancs' rear treatment of the Metrobus batch of Tridents with what Alexander and Plaxton were doing at the same time; examples of the ALX400-bodied Trident for Stagecoach Selkent and the President-bodied Volvo B7TL for London General are visible alongside 402 (T402 SMV).** *Author*

Right: **Tridents from both the 161 and 261 batches at Orpington would frequently wander to the 64 and 119, operated by Volvo Olympians. Passing through Addington Village Interchange on 5 May 2003 is 402 (T402 SMV). Since going into service four years previously it has gained a numberplate with narrower characters, as per the regulations introduced with the new system on 1 September 2001.** *Author*

And that was it for new Tridents with Metrobus, as the company discovered the Scania N94UD series and fell in love, taking large numbers over the subsequent years of expansion, step-entrance replacement and consolidation under a red livery. None of the Tridents were repainted, and indeed Metrobus was kept separate from the fellow companies of Go-Ahead, which it had joined on 3 June 1999. Peace thus ensued, with no repaints and next to nothing to trouble the existence of 401-428 over the contract terms of the 161 and 261, both of which were kept hold of. Only at New Year did the Tridents get a day out, serving on special route A in town. The 233, whose side streets struggled to admit its own MPDs, managed to get 412 round on 29 September 2004.

Below: **On 14 June 2003 412 (V412 KMY) swings out of the Millennium Busway on the last lap of its journey to North Greenwich.** *Author*

Rebuilding work at Orpington over 2005 required the temporary transfer of several routes to Metrobus's Polhill facility, and one of these from 5 March was the 161, taking with it Tridents 408-423.

The clock was set ticking on the T- and V-registered Tridents in September 2005 with the placing of an order for 16 Scania Omnidekkas for the 161. These came in February 2006 and the 401-416 batch was stood down. In May twelve more Scanias were ordered to furnish another new term on the 261, and though these arrived in November as planned and entered service on 2 December, six were diverted to double-deck the 405 at Crawley. Before sale, 419 and 424 themselves visited the 405 between 4-8 December.

The stay of execution of the six remaining Tridents lasted well into 2007, though 427 and 428 were transferred to Crawley on 2 June. The 405's own new Scanias had now arrived, but their extra height and weight to meet Euro 4 standards caused them to fail the tilt test! 418, 422, 425 and 426 thus stayed on a little longer still. Finally, seats were removed from the new buses to further cut their heft and they duly cascaded the temporary Scanias to oust Metrobus's final TfL-service Tridents, which last operated on 7 August.

The 51-reg batch in its entirety (including 427 and 428, which lasted until July 2008 at Crawley) found its way to Big Bus after collection by lessors Wealden PSV, but not before interim adventures took six to Metroline as ET 765-770, after which these and a couple more went to East London and Selkent as iBus cover.

A coda to Trident operation occurred when Metrobus won routes 54 and 75 from Selkent from 25 April 2009 and 2 May 2009 respectively but could not field even one of their new complement of new Optare Olympus-bodied Scania N230UDs, so took the routes' outgoing Tridents on hire instead. The new buses proved excruciatingly slow to go into service, only taking over the 75 from 12 June and the 54 being done next, and the last hired 'TAS' did not leave Metrobus until October.

Registrations
401-428   T401-411 SMV, V412-415 KMY, Y416 HMY, LV51 YCC-H/J-O

Date	Deliveries	Licensed for Service
07.99	401-406	
08.99	407-411	401-411 (**MB**)
09.99	412-415	412-415 (**MB**)
06.01	416	416 (**MB**)
12.01	417-419	
01.02	420-428	417-428 (**MB**)

Disposals
Date	
03.06	409, 411, 415
04.06	402, 403, 414
05.06	401, 405-408, 410, 412, 413, 416
12.06	417, 419-421, 423, 424
09.07	418, 422, 425, 426
07.08	427, 428

Loaned from Selkent, 20.04.09-10.09
17480-17485, 17561, 17562, 17567-17569, 17571-17575, 17577-17579, 17581, 17582, 17584-17591
(LX51 FLV/W/Z, FMA/C/D, LV52 USF, HDO, HEJ, HFU/A, HFC-F/H/K-M/O/P/
S-V/X-Z, HGA)

Above: **The 54 and 75 were a huge coup for Metrobus, but things didn't get off to a good start when Optare failed to deliver any of the thirty Scanias needed in time for the two start dates, separated by a week. Accordingly, Metrobus hired the Selkent Tridents that had operated since the routes were converted, and here at Woolwich on 24 May 2009 is 17584 (LV52 HFS). With Selkent logos still in situ, all that distinguishes it as a Metrobus vehicle is one of the company's signature tall running-number cards mounted by the windscreen split. Their Scania replacements didn't finally start appearing until June 2009 and took four more months to all be in stock. As it turned out, both routes were lost back to their precedessors when tendered again five years later!** *Malc McDonald*

Armchair

By 2002 the long trunk route 237 was Armchair's bread and butter, but it was put out to tender that year. In May the welcome announcement of its retention was made, and 22 new Volvo B7TLs with Wrightbus Gemini bodywork were ordered. However this order was soon cancelled and replaced by one for an equivalent number of Alexander ALX400-bodied 9.9m Dennis Tridents.

In the interim since its last batch of new vehicles, Armchair had been compelled to adopt a predominantly red livery. The company had also adopted fleetnumbers with class codes, as relying on the registration numbers for one-look identification was impossible now that these were mostly made up of letters. Thus did the DT class make

its appearance in time for the 237's contract renewal on 11 January 2003, with the first appearance on the 8th and all in service within three days. All were in red with a black skirt and an orange band above it. As well as seeing off the company's existing all-Leyland Olympians and the newer six Northern Counties-bodied Volvo variants, the new Tridents were allocated to the double-deck school working of the 635, assumed on the same day with a single cross-working from the 237's PVR of 20.

Almost as soon as they entered service, the DTs wandered to the E8 and 190 and also inaugurated Armchair's participation on rail replacements.

On 3 April 2004 the schoolday 235 was renumbered 635.

Right: **Armchair changed its mind after ordering Wright-bodied Volvo B7TLs to replace the 237's Olympians and decided to go with Tridents. Buses like Brentford's DT 21 (KN52 NEY) were the result, seen at Hounslow on 19 April 2003, combining traditional Armchair orange with TfL's mandatory 80% red.** *Author*

Armchair remained a sleepy operation; so uneventful was its next year in fact that no further tenders were won and a buyout was beckoning if expansion was to be forthcoming. Thus did ComfortDelgro, Metroline's holding company, purchase Armchair's own holding company on 19 November 2004, but for the moment the company were kept separate, much as was Thorpes, acquired earlier in the year.

This couldn't last, of course. Having already subsumed Metroline London Northern, Metroline applied to increase its O-Licence by 205 discs to encompass both Thorpes and Armchair, and each disappeared with effect from 6 January 2007; the surprisingly varied subsequent fates of the DT class are now taken up in Metroline's chapter. DT 20 was the first into Metroline livery in December (albeit through a lower-deck repaint only whereby a blue skirt replaced the orange and black), even before the formal takeover.

At the very end of separate Armchair operation, Metroline sent TAs 81, 83 and 84 to Brentford, ready for the PVR increase on the 237 that would accompany the change.

Above: **On 3 June 2006 DT 21 (KN52 NEY) is seen again at Gunnersbury, showing how Brentford carried its running numbers on the nearside only. After its withdrawal by Metroline it was picked up by Abellio and, with a blind box conversion, went back into service on the 172.**_Author_

Registrations
DT 1-22   KN52 NCD/E, NDC-G/J-L/O/U/V/X-Z, NEF/J/O/U/Y, NFA

Date	Deliveries	Licensed for Service
12.02	DT 4, 5, 12	
01.03	DT 1-3, 6-11, 13-22	DT 1-22 (**AH**)

Company absorbed into Metroline on 06.01.07.

Blue Triangle

TL (DL) and TPL classes

Blue Triangle had existed on the fringes of east London for a decade, building up a fleet of classic London Transport buses and then venturing into rail replacement work, but it was not until the end of 1998 that the company started bidding for solid LBSL contracts. New route 474, which would unite the severed ends of the 69 and 101 in conjunction with the Jubilee Line Extension, was their first victory, and ten East Lancs Lolyne-bodied Volvo B7TLs were ordered.

The 474 began on 1 May 1999 with a collection of second-hand MCW Metrobuses, but Volvo's slow progress getting its new chassis to market caused the order for B7TLs

to be cancelled and replaced by one for nine Dennis Tridents with the same body. The resulting DL 901-909, to H45/21D capacity on the 9.9m body, arrived in October and the first was put into service on the 14th of that month.

Aside from the usual rail jobs, Blue Triangle proved their worth by assisting other operators when they fell behind; DL 901 assisted on Harris Bus's 150 in this manner on 14 April 2000. Another such spell of assistance was to newcomer London Easylink on the 185 for three weeks from 20 January 2001; DL 902 and two Metrobuses were fitted with blinds for it.

Right: **DL 905 (V905 FEC) pauses at the original Beckton bus station on 16 November 2000, eighteen months into the 474's tenure with Blue Triangle and a year since its conversion to Trident operation.** *Author*

Blue Triangle continued to grow, and so would the number of Tridents when the award of the 248 was made in February 2001, another fourteen were ordered. This tranche also scooped up school routes 649, 651 and 652, and indeed the 649 and 652 were taken up early, a sub-contract from Stagecoach East London applying from 1 September until the 29th when they were assumed in their own right together with the 248 and 651. The 656 was also worked in this way between 1-29 September but then passed to First Capital.

Until the new Tridents came, the 248 was commenced with Titans purchased from Stagecoach East London and existing Metrobuses. DL 910-923 differed through their forward staircases and DDA-compliant blind sets. The 368, a route already taken over on 24 March with Dart SLFs, began to see Trident appearances at this point, and indeed was frequently predominantly DL at weekends when the Darts were needed for rail replacement work.

All the stops were pulled out for New Year's Eve 2001/02, Blue Triangle manning a 23-bus route B between Aldwych and Victoria.

Arson damage caused to DL 905 in May 2002 necessitated the bus being sent for rebodying by East Lancs.

The collapse of London Easylink brought Blue Triangle back into action on the 185

Above: **The 185 stumbled at its birth with London Easylink, requiring help from Blue Triangle until the requisite paperwork came through. DL 902 (V902 FEC) was pressed into service during the three weeks this took, and on 20 January 2001, the first day, is seen at Forest Hill. Blue Triangle would be called into action again on the 185, this time when London Easylink fell to pieces for good.** *Author*

Left: **Blue Triangle put eight Caetano-bodied Dart SLFs into service on the 368 on 24 March 2001, but the use on this route of what had by now become TLs was frequent. At Barking station on 6 July 2003 TL 912 (PO51 UMH) demonstrates.** *Author*

Right: **Pete's Travel yellow still adorns TPL 924 (PO51 WNH) as it comes through Baker Street on 9 August 2003 on one of the year's many Underground replacement gigs.** *Author*

from 21 August 2002, and DL 902 took its already-fitted blinds back into service on that route, which was indeed entrusted to Blue Triangle for the next six months, although the company sub-contracted it to Arriva presenting London, which used its own Metrobuses.

At the end of 2002 two more Tridents were ordered for a pending boost to the 248, and in advance of their arrival came TPLs 924 and 925, two long-wheelbase Plaxton Presidents ex-Pete's Travel. TPL 924 had begun its career as a demonstrator in Dublin. In order to standardise their fleetnumbers,

Right: **By 14 February 2004 a re-registration had taken place using the mark from the drastically-lowered Routemaster RM 110. TPL 924 (VLT 110, ex-PO51 WNH) is seen on a Central Line job at White City.** *Author*

the DLs were reclassified TL and the new pair came as long-wheelbase TPL 926 and 927 with Plaxton President bodywork. When rebodied (with a forward-staircase body like the second batch), TL 905 came back on 20 February carrying the classification TL 905в, recalling the London Transport method of identifying rebodied vehicles.

The 185 was taken up permanently by East Thames Buses on 4 March 2003, while two new routes to be won were the 66 and 372, both of which would see subsequent TL and TPL appearances. In March the 474 was retendered; its retention was announced in October.

TPLs 926 and 927 arrived in April and were put to work on the 248 as planned, with the predictable forays to the 368. TPL 928 was a second-hand acquisition in July, from Liverpool Motor Services (also trading as Blue Triangle!).

Tridents visited the 108's southern section as extras following an event on 23-25 August.

TL 916 was another arson victim, this time on 11 December 2004, but was written off rather than being rebodied.

In June 2005 there was some chopping and changing to the school routes; Blue Triangle lost the 649 and 651 to First London. The terrorist attacks of 7 July prompted

Left: **Blue Triangle was used to blind boxes to various London Transport configurations, but the set that came with TPL 928 (PO51 UGF) was entirely provincial and stayed that way. On 18 December 2004 it has arrived at Lakeside on the 372, otherwise the province of 10.8m Dennis Dart SLFs.** *Author*

Left: **On 8 October 2005 TL 915 (PO51 UML) comes up to Romford Station on the 248. The route was now up for tender and Blue Triangle would lose it.** *Author*

Right: **The 66 was another Blue Triangle acquisition that liked to borrow the Tridents from the 248 and 474 from time to time. Seen setting off from the stand at Romford Station on 15 October 2005 is TPL 927 (EY03 FNL).** *Author*

replacement services, one of which added Blue Triangle Tridents to the 205.

On 17 December the 474 was extended from Beckton to Manor Park and five new Scanias joined forces with the existing TLs. The company's stalwart Titans and Metrobuses had now reached the end of the line, and on 4 January 2006 the 652, the only school route still run by that point, was formally converted to Trident operation. The route was awarded to First London in March, for September takeup. Then, the loss of the

368 to Docklands Buses on 25 March put an end to the regular Trident appearances.

As the new Scanias and Dart SLFs had come in all-over red, so did repaints to that sole colour begin to affect the existing TLs by the end of 2006.

On 29 June 2007 Go-Ahead bought the TfL operations and modern fleet of Blue Triangle, keeping hold of the name and thus obliging the classic fleet to become The London Bus Company Ltd. This account is thus continued under Go-Ahead's chapter (page 238).

Right: **On 3 June 2006 TL 904 (V904 FEC) comes into Canning Town bus station. The cream bumper is now red and the numberplate is one with post-2001 characters, but the look is still much the same as when this batch entered service.** *Author*

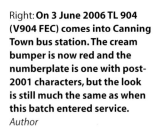

Above: **On 27 January 2007 TL 920 (PO51 UMV) stages through Romford, unaware as yet that even before the loss of the 248, its company will change hands five months from now and put an end to its London service career.** *Author*

Registrations
DL 901-909   V901-909 FEC
DL 910-923   PO51 UMF-H/J-M/R-T/V-Y
TPL 926, 927   EY03 FNK/L

Date	Deliveries	Licensed for Service
10.99	DL 901-904	DL 901-904 (**FL**)
11.99	DL 905-909	DL 905-909 (**FL**)
09.01	DL 912, 913, 914, 918	DL 912, 913, 914, 918 (**FL**)
10.01	DL 911, 916, 920, 923	DL 911, 916, 920, 923 (**FL**)
11.01	DL 910, 915, 917, 919, 921, 922	DL 910, 915, 917, 919, 921, 922 (**FL**)
04.03	TPL 926, 927	TPL 926, 927 (**FL**)

Renumbered TL 901-923, 01.03

Acquired from Pete's Travel, 12.02
TPL 924 (W81 TJU)
TPL 925 (PO51 WNH)
Swapped identities, 03.03

Acquired from LMS, 07.04
TPL 928 (PO51 UGF)

Re-registered
11.03   TPL 924 from PO51 WNH to VLT 110
10.03   TPL 925 from W81 TJU to V8 AEC, 10.03; named *Julia*

Disposals
06.07   TL 916 (written off)

Company sold to Go-Ahead, 29.06.07, with all Tridents except TPL 924 and 928

Tower Transit

TN, TNL and TAL classes

Convened on 22 June 2013 following the breakup of First London, Australian-owned Tower Transit inherited Atlas Road, Lea Interchange and Westbourne Park garages, plus their buses. However, by that time First had already disposed of most of the Trident fleet it had built up between 1999 and 2003, so Tower Transit came away with just five, numbering TNL 33036 at Lea Interchange and TNs 33197-33199 at Westbourne Park alongside VNWs on the 28, 31 and 328, plus trainer TN 32822.

When the final piece of First at Dagenham East was scattered to the four winds, TNs 33185 and 33187 were loaned to Westbourne Park on 29 August and taken on permanently six months later, at which point TNL 33085 was acquired.

In October 2014 Tower Transit's Trident fleet doubled at a stroke when six ex-Stagecoach 10.5m ALX400-bodied Tridents were hired from Ensign to bolster the 23 during its diversion away from Ludgate Hill. TAL 33200-33205 were formerly 18221, 18223,

Below: **Taken new for the 295 in August 2002, what became TN 33185 (LR02 LZE) was one of just five TNs inherited by Tower Transit. That said, it spent two more years in a tight-knit group of its own type, working out of Westbourne Park, as here at Golders Green on 28 August 2014.** *Author*

18225, 18230, 18231 and 18235 and from 18 November were put into service on the 23 out of Westbourne Park. TAL 33205 retained its all-over advert livery for the Lord Mayor's Appeal. Four more arrived in March 2015 by the same means; TALs 33206-33209 were ex-Stagecoach 17751, 17753, 17754 and 17752, but were renumbered shortly after into registration number order.

TAL 33205 lost its ad in September 2015 and returned to Ensign, followed on 31 October by the rest; the loss of the 295 to Metroline

Above: **TN 33198 (LT52 XAJ),** **one of the original TNs** **inherited upon the creation** **of Tower Transit on 22 June** **2013, is obliged to turn off line** **of route into the Harrow Road** **while Carnival was going on** **in the background; this was** **26 August 2013's iteration.** **This bus had been new as** **TN 1198 before thirty-two** **thousand was added to its** **stock number.** *Author*

Left: **TAL 33202 (LX04** **FXP) was one of five long-** **wheelbase Tridents hired from** **Ensign at the end of 2014; seen** **on 3 December of that year at** **Charing Cross, it had already** **spent ten years on the 8 as** **Stagecoach London 18223.** *Author*

Above: **TAL 33204 (LX04 FXW) looks smart as it rounds Marble Arch on 11 May 2015. It was previously Stagecoach London 18231 but was displaced from the 8 by a Borismaster.** *Author*

West had released the buses to replace them. The time left for the five TNs and two TNLs was set ticking, and indeed they were all withdrawn at the end of December 2015.

However, the story of the Trident at Tower Transit wasn't quite dead, as the assumption of the 69 from Stagecoach on 6 February 2016 had to be done by hiring the outgoing company's existing vehicles until its own DNs could be made spare when the VHs arrived for the 328. This happened between late March and 7 May, 18254 being the last.

Right: **TN 33187 (LT52 WVC) was a later acquisition along with TN 33185, and on 26 September 2015 is seen coming up to Marble Arch along the Edgware Road.** *Author*

Acquired from First Capital East, 22.06.03
TN 32822, 33197-33199 (T822 LLC, LT52 XAH/J/K)
TNL 33036 (LK51 UYE)

Acquired from First Capital East, 02.14
TN 33185, 33187 (LR02 LZE, LT52 WVC)
TNL 33085 (LN51 GMF)

Hired from Ensign, 10.14
TAL 33200-33205 (LX04 FXJ/L/P/V/W, FYB)

Hired from Ensign, 03.15
TAL 33206-33209 (LX03 BTF/V/Y/U)
TAL 33207-33209 renumbered TAL 33208, 33209, 33207 04.15

Hired from Stagecoach East London, 06.01.16-05.16
18237-18250, 18252-18256 (LX04 FYD-H/J-N/P/R-T/V/W/Y/Z, FZA)

Disposals
09.15   TAL 33205
11.15   TAL 33200-33204, 33206-33209
03.16   TN 33185, 33187, 33197-33199, TNL 33036, 33085
02.18   TN 32822

Above left: **Missing the 'TAL' part of its new identity since being repainted out of its old existence as Stagecoach London 17752, TAL 33209 (LX03 BTY) heads along the Strand on 15 May 2015.** *Author*

Above: **Having adopted ex-Stagecoach 'TAs' into their own fleet, Tower Transit now hired nineteen for the 69 pending the availability of its own vehicles from a roundabout source. Swinging into Walthamstow Central Station on 10 April 2016 is 18256 (LX04 FZA), with just the Stagecoach logos removed.** *Author*

CT Plus

HTL and HTP classes

Already operating the 153, not-for-profit Hackney Community Transport was awarded new route 388, one of the new services designed to complement the introduction of the Congestion Charge and exploit its hoped-for surge in bus ridership. Thirteen East Lancs Myllennium Loline-bodied Dennis Tridents were ordered to furnish a 25 January 2003 start date.

HTL 1-13 were in all red, receiving a huge letter 'C' device between decks and yellow fleetnumbers. When absolutely nothing else was available, they were known to turn out on the 153, albeit without blinds, but that was the extent of their wandering.

On 1 April 2004 CT Plus Ltd became the operating company, this being a subsidiary of Hackney Community Transport. On 25 September the 388 was extended from Mansion House to Blackfriars.

TfL's satisfaction with CT Plus's performance on the 388 was rewarded with a two-year extension, and there was more; the award of the W13 in August 2006 required one new double-decker at school times. The contract commenced on 10 March 2007 but construction of the new bus, Enviro400 EO 1, dragged out for over eighteen months due to problems at East Lancs' parent company Darwen and an HTL had to stand in. Finally it arrived in May 2008.

A further legal change at this point renamed the operating arm to CT Plus Community Interest Company Ltd.

Right: **On 13 March 2003 brand new HTL 4 (LR52 LTF) is seen in Threadneedle Street by Bank Station.** *Author*

On 16 August 2008 the 388 received another extension, this time to Temple via the long-unserved Embankment. Two more buses were needed, so CT Plus hired Metroline's TPL 237 and 238, two long-wheelbase Plaxton-bodied Tridents. Under CT Plus they became HTP 1 and 2. And another extension was in the offing, from Temple to Embankment Station from 1 November, even though this would only be until long-term work in the Blackfriars area was completed.

The 388 was retained upon tender with its existing vehicles, and a concurrent victory for CT Plus was the 212, won from First London for 6 March 2010 takeup with new Scanias. In January 2010 HTPs 1 and 2 were returned to Metroline and replaced by HTP 3 and 4, formerly London General PDL 42 and 50. To cover refurbishment of the 388's HTLs, HTP 5 was hired, better known as London General PDL 8. Paynes of Aylesford carried out the refurbishment, one unfortunate side effect

being the masking over of the bottom blind box so that the top one could carry both route and destination in an extremely unattractive fashion! The passengers suffered twofold with the simultaneous downseating of the HTLs from H45/23D to H45/17D, and in all cases the huge 'C' devices disappeared from bus sides in favour of unrelieved red.

In April CT Plus won school route 675 from Arriva London North and started it on 16 October with HTP 6, a leased Trident formerly known as London General PDL 39.

The HTL refurbishments were completed in May 2011 and the 675's HTP 6 was done too.

The 388 was withdrawn back to Blackfriars on 24 March 2012, but HTPs 3 and 4 were kept

hold of. Additionally, experimental E40H HEA 1 joined the 388's fleet on 25 February 2013. On 14 December the 388 was extended in the other direction this time, from Hackney Wick to Stratford International though the former Olympic Park. Three more buses were needed, two of which were HTPs 3 and 4 again, and a second HTP 5 was acquired; this was ex-Metroline TP 365.

CT Plus would have only five years with the 212, losing it to Tower Transit upon announcement of its tender tranche in June 2014, and a little later the 675 was lost to London General. The 388 was made safe for two more years, however.

With the departure of the 212 on 7 March 2015 HTPs 3-6 and HTL 13 were replaced by

Left: **Towards the end of their lives, someone must have kicked up a fuss about the legibility of the HTLs' blinds, and they were restored to their original configuration. A stroke of luck in this respect was the printing of white-lettered blinds with the full range of via points rather than the pitiful two otherwise allowed. HTL 9 (LR52 LWJ) is heading south past Liverpool Street on 19 December 2015.** *Author*

the half of the 212's Scanias that were kept. Just the original HTLs remained now, and their days were numbered when their own route came up for tender again, no matter who won. At least they had some measure of dignity restored for their last couple of years through the unmasking of their original blind boxes. As luck had it, CT Plus was successful again and an order was placed for sixteen ADL E40H MMC City double-deckers, following on from the batch that had assumed the 26 four months into its tenure that had started on 27 February 2016. These new buses visited the 388 frequently, but without reciprocation by the HTLs.

HTLs 2, 9, 11 and 12 were delicensed in December after varying periods of disuse and the rest followed in February 2017, spanning the commencement of the 388's new contract on 21 January. The last in service were HTLs 3 and 4, running to the close of operations on 20 February.

Registrations
HTL 1-13   LR52 LTO/N/J/F, LWE, LTK, LWF/H/J, PF52 TFX, TGZ, LR52 LYC/J

Date	Deliveries	Licensed for Service
01.03	HTL 1-11	HTL 1-11 (**HK**)
02.03	HTL 12, 13	HTL 12, 13 (**HK**)

Hired from Metroline, 16.08.08-02.10
HTP 1, 2 (LN51 KXP/R)

Acquired from London General, 01.10
HTP 3, 4 (PN03 UMB, UMK)

Hired from Ensign, 01.10-08.10
HTP 5 (X608 EGK)

Acquired, 10.10
HTP 6 (PN03 ULY)

Acquired from Dawson Rentals, 10.13
HTP 5(ii) (LR52 KWG)

Disposals
01.10	HTP 1, 2	03.17	HTL 1-6, 9
08.10	HTP 5(i)	04.17	HTL 7, 10-12
03.15	HTL 13, HTP 5(ii)	05.17	HTL 8
04.15	HTP 3, 4, 6		

Sullivan Buses

DEL class and various

On 15 November 2002 DEL 1 was delivered for prestige private-hire and rail replacement work. It was an East Lancs Myllennium Loline-bodied 10.5m Trident of DPH47/27F capacity. From time to time it would pop up on Potters Bar local 398, and when Southlands Travel was acquired in January 2005, spent time on that company's south-east London school contract.

Though Sullivan Buses ultimately preferred the Volvo B7TL for further orders, the Trident continued to figure and second-hand examples joined the fleet, beginning in January 2009 with TN 1-3, ex-Blue Triangle TL 912, 915 and 917 with East Lancs bodywork. On 18 March came TPL 926 and 927, long Presidents formerly with Blue Triangle.

From the autumn term of 2010 a contract was placed by the Nicholas Breakspear School in St Albans, and five ex-Stagecoach ALX400-bodied Tridents came into stock via Ensign. Numbered ALX 1-5, they were converted to single-door and fitted with seat belts. In the off hours they were turned out on new commercial route 330, introduced on 28 March 2011.

In February 2012 PDL 26 ex-London General was acquired; it was a Plaxton President-bodied Trident. It was followed in March by ALX400-bodied ALX 6, ex-Stagecoach 17548. June brought in TAL 123 and 132, long ALX400s ex-Metroline.

The award of TfL contract work for the 628, 653, 683 and 688, four school routes serving the JFS from 1 September 2012, required eleven buses, and TPLs 926 and 927 plus the two ex-Metroline TALs were earmarked as part of that eleven-strong fleet; to that end, the TPLs' yellow entrance doors were repainted red.

Right: **The busy routes serving the JFS were picked up by Sullivan Buses and employed, amongst others, ex-Blue Triangle TPL 926 (EY03 FNK) seen at Hampden Square on 10 March 2013.** *Ian Jordan*

TfL's satisfaction with Sullivan Buses' work on the JFS routes stood the company in good stead for the award of the 626 in December 2012, and although Volvo B7TLs were purchased for this, the mix of Tridents could regularly be seen after its introduction on 31 August 2013. TfL route 298, operated since 4 February 2012 with Enviro200 single-deckers, was a last resort for double-deckers. In February 2014 ALX 3 was sold.

A regular feature in the current decade has been Underground strike extras, and Sullivan Tridents made guest appearances on routes N15 and N55 on 14/15 June 2014.

In January 2015 the 692 and 699 were awarded, ex-London General, for 21 November takeup; although Scanias were the basis this time, Tridents were still possible. December saw the sale of ALX 5 and in February 2016 TN 3 was scrapped.

Yet more north London routes were won in the shape of the 617 and 629 (October 2016) and the 605 (January 2017), on top of the retention of the existing four, but with a Euro 5 and DDA emissions requirement, the existing Tridents would become surplus and indeed ALX 1, 2, 4 and TALs 123 and 132 were all withdrawn in April 2017. ALXs 2, 4 and 6 were sold to Ripley in June and ALX 1 was sold to Bryan Nash. TAL 132, however, was returned to service in June 2018, lasting until the end of the year when it too was sold for scrap.

Just TPLs 926 and 927 remained, and when the coronavirus lockdown hit in March 2020, there went their work. TPL 926 ran for the last time on 10 March, leaving TPL 927 to be the last Dennis Trident on any TfL service; it performed on the 626 until 08.30 on the 19th. Both remained licensed if needed again.

New, 15.11.02
DEL 1 (PJ52 BYP)

Acquired from Blue Triangle, 01.09
TN 1-3 (PO51 UMH/L/R)

Acquired from Blue Triangle, 03.09
TPL 926, 927 (EY03 FNK/L)

Acquired from Ensign, 07.10
ALX 1-5 (V116, 117, 139, 142 MEV)

Acquired from London General, 02.12
PDL 26 (PJ02 PZZ)

Acquired from Stagecoach London, 03.12
ALX 6 (LY02 OAX)

Acquired from Metroline, 06.12
TAL 123, 132 (X343, 332 HLL)

Disposals
12.15   ALX 5
02.16   TN 3
06.17   ALX 1, 2, 4
12.18   TAL 123, 132

Above: **On 9 August 2015 ALX 6 (LY02 OAX) is operating a Victoria Line replacement through Seven Sisters. As Stagecoach East London 17548, this bus would have passed through this junction regularly as a 67, and with Sullivan it remained cleared for TfL operation.** *Author*

Arriva the Shires

5421

Gradually encompassing the fleets of the former LDT the Shires (Arriva the Shires), County Bus (Arriva East Herts & Essex), Kentish Bus (Arriva Kent Thameside) and London & Country (Arriva Croydon & North Surrey), Arriva Southern Counties fielded only one batch of Tridents and few new double-deckers as a whole, but this batch operating on the fringes of London operations spread just one bus to TfL operations themselves. The source was a batch of thirty Alexander ALX400-bodied Dennis Tridents new to Arriva the Shires & Essex in 2000 and shared between Luton and Southend, far from London, but on 26 September 2005 the first of these, 5421, was loaned to Garston as an extra for the 142, which needed another schoolday bus and didn't have enough DAF DB250RS(LFs) to man it. It lasted here until March 2006, when a DLA was requisitioned from Norwood.

The Tridents from this batch spent the second half of their careers on the 310/311 pair out of Ware, though these had been withdrawn behind the London border at the end of 2005 and thus only figured obliquely.

Borrowed from non-TfL operation, 26.09.05-03.06
5421 (W421 XKX)

Below: **Seen in Edgware during November 2005 is Garston's 5421 (W421 XKX), bringing such oddities as three-track number blinds and Arriva corporate livery to an operation which had only recently shed those two provincial facets. After a spell displaying just 'School Bus', 5421 had a lazy blind made up for it with each terminus of the 142.** *Haydn Davies*

Arriva Kent Thameside

PDLs

Meanwhile, Arriva Kent Thameside ran no Tridents, its parent Arriva Southern Counties company in Maidstone preferring Volvo B7TLs, but between 20 February and 10 March 2009 its DAFs were being fitted with iBus equipment so needed cover. Thus borrowed from London General and run on the 428 so as to let its Dart SLFs cover other Dartford services were six Plaxton President-bodied Tridents no longer wanted and stored at Rainham, PDLs 16-18, 20, 21 and 25. Partial blinds were carried, with A4 sheets made up for the route numbers.

Below: **Six London General Dennis Tridents were borrowed from London General to furnish Dartford's 428 while its DAFs were away having iBus equipment installed. Seen on 10 March 2009 at Erith is PDL 21 (PJ02 PZU).** *Ian Jordan*

Hired from Go-Ahead, 20.02-10.03.09
PDL 16-18, 20, 21, 25 (PJ02 PZO / P / R / T / U / Y)

East Thames Buses

Not an operator of Dennis Tridents, LBL-owned East Thames Buses had ushered in the low-floor era with Volvo B7TLs to replace its Harris Bus-derived Volvo Olympians, but when iBus came along, a roving band of First London TNs were sent from operator to operator to allow their own vehicles to be fitted with complicated GPS-powered equipment. Unlike most operators, which sent their buses to either Clapton or Norwood, East Thames Buses' VWLs were treated by Siemens' mobile team.

Starting on 14 February 2009 East Thames borrowed TNs 32958-32961 and kept them to the 1, though the blinds didn't fit in the wide boxes First had specified. TNs 32958 and 32961 were returned late in March and the other two by 15 April.

Hired from First London, 24.02-15.04.09
TN 32958-32961 (X958, 959, 612, 961 HLT)

First Games Transport

Former **TNL** and **TNA** classes

In preparation for the 2012 London Olympic Games, FirstGroup established a subsidiary called First Games Support which amassed a whopping 250 buses to serve portions of the Games staged at remote locations where car use would be forbidden. As well as taking into stock 100 each of new Volvo B9TLs and Alexander Dennis E40Ds, First Games Transport (as the unit was shortly after renamed) was allotted fifty redundant First London Tridents, twelve of them TNLs and thirty-eight TNAs made spare following the conversion of the 23 to hybrid E40H operation. TNLs 33020-33028 and 33033-33035 and TNA 33343-33376 and 33383-33386 were converted to single-door and repainted into First's latest national livery.

During the Games the TNLs and TNAs were based at Hayes, from which they were put to work serving the aquatic events based on Eton Dorney. Similar but reduced work characterised the Paralympics held two weeks later, and after that they were all transferred to Glasgow.

Below: **TNA 33373 (LK53 EYR),** deposed from the 23 earlier in 2012, is seen at work on 31 July on one of the heavily-provisioned Olympic Games services based on Eton Dorney. *Terry Wong Min*

Ensignbus

Various

There is no modern London bus type that has not passed through the hands of Ensign on its way from the capital to pastures new, but from time to time the stage service-operating Ensignbus arm of the company picked out examples from the always extensive sales stock to add to its own fleet. After bedding in its Essex commercial routes with Metrobuses and then Volvo Olympians since coming back onto stage work, Ensignbus proceeded to repaint and put into renewed service low-floor buses from the first batches coming out of service. As well as ex-Reading Spectra 2s, odd Tridents were gathered up, starting in 2009 with 901 and 903 (V901, 903 FEC), former Blue Triangle TL 901 and 903 with East Lancs bodywork. In October 2009 came 101-106 (V147 MEV, V478, 479 KJN, V122, 115 MEV and V476 KJN); these were 10.5m ALX400s ex-Stagecoach and converted local route 22 to double-deck. 104 was soon re-registered 864 DYE.

March 2010 brought in 107 and 108 (X601, 602 EGK), Plaxton President-bodied short Tridents ex-London General (PDL 1 and 2). In August came 109 and 110 (X608, 613 EGK) from the same batch.

Right: **Sold by Stagecoach to Ensign in October 2011, 17153 (V153 MEV) was given a neat single-door conversion, and on 10 March 2012, awaiting further sale (ultimately to Weavaway), joined a DLR replacement bus service based on Beckton.**
Mark McWalter

While processing the TA 66-117 batch of ex-Metroline ALX400s from the end of 2010, Ensignbus took into stock 904-906 (T75 KLD, T197 CLO and V310 GLB) for strike cover on the 25. 901 and 903 departed in April 2011 after their conversion to open-top, and 904-906 left in June, but 908 (T87 KLD) and 109 (T38 KLD) entered stock at the same time. The next four of this batch were acquired in October as 191-194 (T191-194 CLO).

Ex-Stagecoach V149, 211 and 214 MEV and X385 NNO were borrowed from sales stock for rail replacement at the end of 2011, and in December East Lancs-bodied 195 (W5 ACL) was acquired from Aintree Coachline and became the latest Ensign bus to receive its cherished GVV 205 registration.

In May came 143 (X343 NNO), ex-Stagecoach 17343, while temporary rail job cover that month came in the form of 913, 928, 991 and 998 (T113, 128, 81, 98 KLD), ex-Metroline TPs. Next into sales stock and borrowed between June and October without Ensignbus fleetnumbers were TASs this time, formerly Stagecoach X232, X249, X258, X259, X353 and X354 NNO.

Acquired for the X80 in January 2013 came East Lancs-bodied 196 (PX55 AHG) ex-Stagecoach North West. In March of that year T103, 105, 106 KLD, X319 HLL and LX51 HJC were used on rail replacement.

The acquisition of five-year-old Volvo B9TLs in October 2013 prompted the sale of Tridents 101, 102, 104 and 106, followed by 191 in January 2014. In February 107 and 110 left and in May, 108 and 193. However, in July came 599 (T199 CLO), its place in a block reserved for hybrids occasioned by the fitting of a Vantage Power hybrid engine.

864 DYE, having left 104, migrated to 194 in October, and in December and January 156-159 (LX04 FXR-U), formerly Stagecoach East London 18226-18229, were taken into stock. To assist them on rail work came temporarily-numbered 909-912 (T748 JPO, Y848, 861 GCD and PK02 RDO).

Open-top 301 (LK03 GHY), acquired in May, was at one time Metroline TP 349; it was re-registered FFY 401 later. A raft of re-registrations cost 109 UJF 182 (which went onto 308, ex-T808 RFG), while 192 lost 392 MBF and 194 lost 864 DYE but gave 156 and 158 WLT 916 and 428. Then, in June, 105, 143, 192 and 194 were sold, followed by 308 in July and 109 in August.

In January 2016 Tridents 157 and 159 were re-registered WLT 307 and WJY 759. September saw 103 sold and 195 re-registered from GVV 205 to W56 PCC, after which it was sold. 599 was returned to Vantage Power at the end of 2016.

Trident 301 was sold in June 2017 and 156 in September. In October 157-159 regained their original registrations and 158 and 159 were sold. 157 followed in November. Finally for this account, 196 was sold in June 2018.

Below: **Formerly known as Stagecoach East London 18229, Trident 159 (WJY 759, ex-LX04 FXU) was pressed into service on the 86 on 12 September 2016, the occasion of a London Underground strike. Looking as splendid as everything does in Ensignbus's blue and silver, it is at Redbridge Central Library on the westbound bore of the Ilford one-way system.**
Mark McWalter

Big Bus

DA class

This elegantly-liveried open-top tour bus company had cut its teeth on first DMSs, then Titans, but by the mid-2000s it was time to progress further, to low-floor double-deckers. To that end, four East Lancs-bodied Dennis Tridents were purchased via Wealden PSV in December 2007. Formerly Metrobus 418, 426, 422 and 425, they became DA 1, 3, 6 and 9 (LV51 YCD/M/H/L), the first two commencing

Right: **Seen coming down Regent Street towards Piccadilly Circus on 29 June 2008 is DA 6 (LV51 YCH) in its first year of Big Bus ownership.** *Author*

Right: **On 28 August 2011 DA 1 (LV51 YCD) swings from London Bridge into Tooley Street.** *Author*

Left: **The new Big Bus livery of 2013 was a little lacklustre by comparison with the marvellous original, as shown on DA 2 (LV51 YCE) heading away from Victoria Coach Station on 6 March 2015.** *Author*

work in their natural state before joining the others as open-toppers. DA 3 was first into service on 23 December.

In March DA 4, 5, 7 and 10 (LV51 YCK/ J/O/F) were acquired, formerly Metrobus 424, 423, 428 and 420, and were all open-top from the start. Then came the other four from the original route 161 batch, now known as DA 2, 8, 11 and 12 (LV51 YCE/C/G/N) ex-Metrobus 419, 417, 421 and 427. Most of this batch had wandered before settling here serving as iBus fitment cover at Metroline

and/or Stagecoach, but a settled (if most premature) retirement beckoned.

In 2011 the DA 1-12 batch were upseated from PO45/23D to PO48/23D, and two years later a simplified livery began to appear. Between November 2014 and March 2015 DA 9 wore an all-over ad promoting tourism to Mexico.

After a decade in Big Bus ownership, the DAs have generally come off the front line and have been serving as information points at Charing Cross and Victoria stations.

Below: **Five years further on from the above picture, the livery was further modified to remove a bit more cream; DA 8 (LV51 YCC) demonstrates at Westminster on 1 July 2018.** *Author*

London City Tour

Despite the crowded nature of the open-top London tour bus market, Grupo Julia saw an opening and in 2015 introduced a large fleet of ex-Metroline Volvo B7TLs trading as London City Tour. When that supply ran dry Tridents were tried out, firstly from outgoing members of ALX400-bodied Abellio batches that had turned up at Dawson Rentals. In September 2016, KV02 URT, USN/T (formerly 9810, 9796 and 9800 and new as Connex Bus TA 110, 96 and 100) were the first acquisitions, as partial open-toppers.

Subsequent Tridents were from the batch leaving Abellio's 172, themselves having begun as Armchair buses. June 2017 brought in KN52 NCE, NDD/O (ex-Abellio 9830, 9832 and 9834, ex-Armchair DT 2, 4 and 11) as fully open-top. KN52 NEJ (ex-Abellio 9839, ex-Armchair DT 11) came in August and KN52 NDE (ex-Abellio 9833, ex-Armchair DT 5) in September, making eight and seeing off some of the ex-Willesden VPLs. After that, London City Tour bought ex-Metroline and London Central Volvo B9TLs until the company's closedown after service on 10 August 2018.

Below: **Seen on 24 September 2017 is KN52 NEJ, coming up Piccadilly to Hyde Park Corner. Formerly Abellio 9839, it was new as Armchair DT 11.** *Author*

Golden Tours

Various

Another tour firm to try its luck in London was Golden Tours, initially of Wandsworth Road but based at Hayes by the time its tour began on 18 June 2011. The early intake was entirely ex-Stagecoach 'TAs', within two years comprising nos 114, 138, 145, 148, 154-156, 158, 160, 163, 168, 188, 204, 327, 362, 366, 367, 373, 381 and 474 (V114, 138, 145, 148, 154-156, 158, 160, 163, 168, 188, 204 MEV, X327 NNO, Y362, 366, 367, 373, 381 NHK, V474 KJN). Put into service as part-open-toppers in a blue livery, the Tridents were progressively converted to single-door before several batches of new Volvos (B9TLs and then B5TLs) replaced them by 2016; two (138 and 156) had already fallen out through fire damage. Three returned for the 2018 summer season but all were withdrawn in 2019, no longer meeting emissions requirements applying in central London.

Below: **There wasn't actually any gold in Golden Tours' livery at all, as demonstrated by 381 (X381 NNO), formerly Stagecoach Selkent 17300 or TA 300), passing the Waterloo set of pedestrian underpasses on 25 November 2012.** *Author*

Totals

Company	Total	Fleetnumbers
Stagecoach	998	**TA** 1-73, 75-222, **TAS** 223-260, **TA** 261-401, 403-435, **TAS** 436-591, **TA** 592-614, 650-655, 17746-17853, 17854s, 17855-17975, 17976s-17999s, 18201-18277, 18451-18499
First	481	**TN** 801-887, **TNL** 888-930, **TAL** 931-952, **TN** 954-1000, **TNL** 1001-1036, **TN** 1037-1071, **TNL** 1072-1099, **TN** 1113-1129, **TNL** 1130-1140, **TN** 1141-1199, 1229-1248, 1277-1293, 1328-1342, **TAL** 33343-33386
London United	156	**TA** 201-225, 229-292, 312-346, **TLA** 1-32
Metroline	354	**TP** 1-65, **TA** 66-117, **TAL** 118-134, **TPL** 237-296, **TP** 297-316, 348-465, **TA** 638-659
Metrobus	28	401-428
Blue Triangle	25	**DL** 901-923, **TPL** 926, 927
Connex	128	**TA** 1-20, 22-129
Go-Ahead	50	**PDL** 1-50
Armchair	22	**DT** 1-22
CT Plus	13	**HTL** 1-13
TOTAL	2255	

Totals are for buses bought or leased new for LBSL/TfL services, 1999-2006.

Bibliography

Books
The London Enviro400, Matthew Wharmby, Pen and Sword 2016.
The London Volvo B9TL and B5LH, Matthew Wharmby, Pen and Sword 2019.

Magazines, Supplements, Articles and Periodicals
The London Bus (TLB), LOTS, monthly
London Bus Magazine (LBM), LOTS, quarterly
BUSES magazine, Ian Allan (to 2012), Key Publishing (2012-present), monthly
The Londoner, Visions, bi-monthly

Websites and Groups
London Bus Routes by Ian Armstrong (www.londonbuses.co.uk)
Bus Lists on the Web (www.buslistsontheweb.co.uk)
London Vehicle Finder (www.lvf.io)